The Railroad Jubilee.

AN

ACCOUNT OF THE CELEBRATION

COMMEMORATIVE OF THE OPENING

OF

RAILROAD COMMUNICATION

BETWEEN

BOSTON AND CANADA,

SEPTEMBER 17TH, 18TH, AND 19TH, 1851.

BOSTON:
1852.
J. H. EASTBURN, CITY PRINTER.

PREFACE.

The Editor of the following Report, who was requested to prepare it by the Committee of the City Council, to whom its preparation was in the first instance entrusted, deems it proper, for the purpose of obviating misapprehension, to make a remark or two in justice to the Committee. Had the work been executed by them, it would doubtless have been far better done; yet, from their relations to the City, and their official participation in the events described, they would have labored under some embarrassments which could not be felt by others not so situated.

The only directions which the Editor received from the Committee, were to make the Report as full and accurate as possible, and to use all despatch; in other respects he was left at liberty to adopt his own course and present it in such form as his judgment might approve. With these directions he has faithfully endeavored to comply, and has at the same time attempted, though, as he is fully aware, with very imperfect success, to give to the Celebration that character, which, after a careful consideration of all its relations, it seemed to him to be properly entitled.

Boston, February, 1852.

ERRATA.

Page 12, line 21, for " survives," read survive.
" 51, " 33, for " Twistdon," read Twistleton M. P.
" 60, " 31, for " Josiah P. Bradlee," read J. Putnam Bradlee.
" 80, " 30, for " Coombs," read Combs.
" 86, " 3rd and 4th, for " Surveyor of the Port," read Naval Officer of Port of Boston.
" 109, " for " A. Agassiz," read A. E. Agassiz.
" 125, " 19th and 22d, for " Stewart," read Stuart.
" 32, " 32, for " Stewart," read Stuart.

RAILROAD JUBILEE.

THE celebration commemorative of the completion of the great lines of railway connecting our City with the Canadas and the West, and the establishment by some of our citizens, of a line of Ocean steamships to facilitate and enlarge our commercial intercourse with the Old World, was an event which will long be remembered, and the history of which must form a prominent chapter in the social and commercial annals of Boston.

It was a celebration worthy of the occasion and of the character of the City by which it was instituted; a jubilee in commemoration of the peaceful and beneficent triumphs of science and skill, appointed by a City distinguished for the intelligent enterprise and resolute perseverance of its inhabitants, and for its faithful maintenance and promotion of all those great interests, Civil, Religious, Literary and Industrial, upon which the well being and progress of a community so essentially depend.

However extensive and brilliant may have been the public pageants on other occasions, no one, it is believed, has, on this Continent, surpassed, if any have equalled, that of the 17th, 18th, and 19th of September. And the magnitude of the enterprises which the varied ceremonies of those days were designed to celebrate, well entitled them to be thus distinguished, when they are considered in all their present and probable future bearings upon the interests, not of this City and State alone, but of all New England, the great West and the Canadas.

Other enterprises have been undertaken and successfully accomplished by our citizens, which were thought to be, and indeed were, worthy of especial commemoration. But these, however important to the interests of the City, were local in their design and influence. To increase the comfort, the conveniences and the general prosperity of the city or its immediate vicinity, was their primary object. How wise was the foresight which originated and conducted them, the present prosperity of Boston amply shows. But though each, in its design, looked only to the attainment of comparatively limited and specific results, yet its successful operation, by inspiring a spirit of confidence, by multiplying our resources, and extending our relations, served to prepare the way for others of greater magnitude.

Thus, step by step, each bolder and firmer than the preceding, has our City gone forward in her energetic career, until, from the construction of a bridge across Charles River in 1786, she has projected, and after many years' endeavor, has in a great measure brought to successful completion, a system of railroads whose united length exceeds a thousand miles. Of this great system Boston is the centre. Starting from within her limits, seven main lines extend in different directions through the State, and by their numerous connections and lateral branches, form, all over it, a network of iron. Animated by our example, encouraged by our success, and at times aided by our means, the people of the neighboring States have united their efforts with ours, and every obstacle to the easiest intercommunication has been overcome. Our borders have been crossed by railroads on every side that is not washed by the Ocean, great level highways have been extended through every State in New England, and we are connected by iron bands with the Canadas on the North, and the great Lakes and the Valley of the Mississippi on the west.

When we reflect that hardly twenty years have elapsed since the first shovelful of earth was moved on either of the public railroads now in operation in our State; that only so far back as the year 1834, a locomotive engine was for the first time introduced into New England; and that the earliest completed roads were not opened for travel through their whole length till the year 1835, [the Boston and Providence in June, and the Boston and Worcester in July ;] and then spread out before us a railway map of the New England States, and see what has been accomplished ;—that within the limits of our own small State upwards of a thousand miles of road have been opened for travel, and beyond our limits a thousand more in close connection with them, and tending to the same common centre, at an outlay (for the whole) of nearly a hundred millions of dollars, we can form some adequate conception of the mighty work that has been accomplished.

The Railroad Jubilee was designed, then, not only to express our joy at the final triumph of our efforts to accomplish enterprises of great moment, but to mark with distinctness, what, it is believed, will ever be considered a prominent era in the industrial and commercial annals of New England. And it is fitting that such events, as they occur, should be commemorated in a striking and public manner. They are points at which it is well to pause, and look back. Comforts, conveniences, blessings are showered on us in such profusion by the almost magic achievements of science and art, that unless reminded from time to time of their reality and value, we are in danger either of not thinking of them at all, or at least of estimating them at too low a rate. Such occasions naturally lead us to contrast the present with the past, and so to form a more vivid conception of the changes which a few generations or a few years have wrought, of the blessings which advancing civilization has conferred on us, and of the responsibility resting upon us to transmit, to our posterity, not diminished, but enlarged, the great inheritance which has descended to us.

And, in this view, it may not be inappropriate at this time to take a further retrospect. For, in estimating the character and meaning of this Celebration, it is important to take into consideration the qualities and condition of the community which originated it, and to glance at the nature and progress of the prominent events of its history prior to those immediately under consideration. Twenty years have sufficed to effect an immense change in the social relations, and the industrial interests of all New England. But the intelligence to guide, the wisdom and boldness to plan, the skill, energy and perseverance to execute, so essential to the working out of such a revolution, are not of the growth of twenty years; for them we are indebted in large measure to our fathers; and from the foundation of our City those qualities have constituted a portion of the legacy which each passing generation has handed down to its successor. And thus our triumphs of to-day were prepared for us in the past; and the event we have so recently honored, is but the last of a long series, whose united influence has wrought out results which can never be contemplated without admiration.

It is now little more than two hundred and twenty years since the settlement of Boston. Hardly seven generations of men have passed since the spot we now inhabit was a wilderness. "Accustomed as we are to the beauties of the place and its vicinity, and in the daily perception of the charms of its almost unrivalled scenery;—in the centre of a natural amphitheatre whose sloping descents the riches of a laborious and intellectual cultivation adorn,—where hill and vale, river and ocean, island and continent, simple nature and unobtrusive art, with contrasted and interchanging harmonies, form a rich and gorgeous landscape, we are little able to realize the almost repulsive aspect of its original state. To the eyes of the first emigrants, however, where now exists a dense and aggregated mass of living beings and material things, amid all the accommodations of life, the splendors of wealth, the delights of taste, and whatever can gratify the cultivated intellect, there were then only a few hills which, when the Ocean receded, were intersected by wide marshes, and when its tide returned, appeared a group of lofty islands rising from the surrounding waters. Thick forests concealed the neighboring hills, and the deep silence of nature was broken only by the voice of the wild beast or bird, and the warwhoop of the savage.

The advantages of the place were, however, clearly marked by the hand of nature; combining at once present convenience, future security, and an ample basis for permanent growth and prosperity. Towards the continent it possessed but a single avenue, and that easily fortified. Its hills then commanded not only its own waters, but the hills of the vicinity. At the bottom of a deep bay, its harbor was capable of containing the proudest navy of Europe; yet locked by islands and guarded by winding channels, it presented great difficulty of access to strangers, and to the inhabitants great facilities for protection against maritime invasion; while to those acquainted with its waters, it was both easy and accessible. To these advantages were added goodness and plenteousness of water, and the security afforded by that once commanding height, now, alas! obliterated and almost forgotten, since art and industry have levelled that predominating mountain of the place from whose lofty and imposing top, the beacon-fire was accustomed to rally the neighboring population on any threatened danger to the metropolis." *

Such was the spot to which our fathers came to establish for themselves a home; and such was the scene presented to their eyes. How wonderful the change, which, in the comparatively short period of two hundred years, has been effected! But the same bold spirit of enterprise that led them to encounter all the hazards and privations of founding a settlement in the unbroken wilderness; the same resolute perseverance, and unconquerable energy, that characterized their after career, have ever been prominent traits in the character of their descendants.

Civil and religious freedom were, indeed, the objects which rose high above all others in their view, yet the determined and self-relying spirit which actuated them in their struggle after these, gave life, vigor, and direction to all their acts, and soon, amid the shadows of the dark forest, the abode of the savage and the wild beast, were laid deep and secure the

* From an Address to the Citizens of Boston, delivered on the 17th September, 1830, at the close of the Second Century after the Settlement of the City, by the Hon. Josiah Quincy, L.L. D.

foundations of our city. Proud as we may be, in view of our achievements in the arts of peace; far-reaching and magnificent as may be our enterprises, yet nothing we can accomplish can ever surpass the real greatness of their exploits. To them, under Heaven, the prosperity, which this day crowns our City, is chiefly due. They lighted the torch to guide our steps. They left us the priceless legacy of their example, and the still more precious inheritance of their spirit. To fail to acknowledge, on such an occasion, our deep obligations to them, would be a wrong to ourselves. Our glory is, that we have not been unmindful of the lessons they taught, nor undervalued the legacies they left.

Familiar as we all are, or should be, with the history of our City, it may not be uninteresting or uninstructive to dwell for a few moments upon some of the points which place the past and the present in striking contrast, and briefly advert to a few of the events of by-gone years, which, though to us seemingly unimportant, were the prominent events of their day, and the germs of much of our present prosperity.

In the year 1630, a "single cottage from which ascended the smoke of the hospitable hearth of Blackstone, was the only mansion in the solitude," and an assessment of thirty pounds was sufficient for the purchase of all the local rights in the Peninsula which Blackstone possessed. Now, Boston and its vicinity, within a radius of five miles, contain at least 230,000 inhabitants.* The City itself has about 145,000, with an assessed valuation of one hundred and eighty-seven millions of dollars. In 1631, a small bark was built, at Mystick, by Gov. Winthrop. It was launched on the 4th of July of that year, and named the "Blessing of the Bay." "How strikingly in contrast the building of that little boat, the solitary instance of that year, with the annual productions that now come from the shipyards which line the banks of the Mystic—of the single voyage to Rhode Island, to trade for a hundred bushels of corn, with that commerce which now covers the wide waters from the Arctic to the

* Within a radius of sixty miles from the State House in Boston, there are one million of inhabitants, nearly all of whom are in convenient proximity to railways connected with the metropolis. The radius embraces parts of neighboring States.

Antarctic, and surrounds the globe with a constant procession of the white winged messengers of Peace and Plenty."

In April, 1635, the first "Free School" was established in Boston, twelve years prior to the law of the Commonwealth making the establishment of such institutions imperative. Not to be able "perfectly to read the English tongue," and to "know the general laws," our fathers denominated "barbarism;"—and from the day when they "entreated our brother Philemon Pormont to become schoolmaster, for the nurturing and teaching children with us," to this hour, when, what is equivalent to a capital of twelve hundred thousand dollars is invested in school houses, when two hundred schools are maintained, and nearly twenty-one thousand children educated, at an annual expense of three hundred and twenty-five thousand dollars, the people of Boston have never wavered for a moment in their attachment to the system of "free Schools," or in their generous support of it; and it is not too much to say, that in proportion to its means and population, no city in the world ever gave more uniform and unequivocal evidence of its earnest desire to diffuse intellectual power and moral culture through the whole mass of the community.

In 1679 the first fire engine was procured, and the first fire company organized.

In 1704 appeared "The Boston News-Letter," the first newspaper ever published in the British colonies in North America.

In 1710 a post-office was established, and mails were forwarded once a week to Plymouth and to Maine, and once a fortnight to New York.

After the conclusion of the war of the Revolution, the first great enterprise in which our citizens engaged was the construction of a bridge leading to Charlestown over Charles river. And it was an enterprise of no ordinary magnitude for those days,—and one respecting whose ultimate success there were many doubts. But the work was commenced, prosecuted with vigor, and opened for travel on the 17th of June, 1786. This occasion was celebrated with appropriate festivities. Salutes of thirteen guns were fired at sunrise from Bunker's and Copp's Hills; a long procession was formed which passed through the streets and over the bridge, and eight hundred persons sat down to a dinner provided for them on Breed's Hill. The number of spectators present on the occasion was estimated at more than twenty thousand. Now, besides the seven lines of railroad, five bridges, four broad avenues and two ferries are daily crowded with tens of thousands passing to or from the city.

These few reminiscenses and contrasts are, perhaps, as well calculated as any thing to show the steady yet rapid growth of the city; and to impress upon the mind the strong conviction, that not to superiority of natural advantages alone or chiefly must it be ascribed. In this connexion we quote from an address of Mr. Mayor Bigelow:—"So large an accumulation of people and wealth on a single spot, as is now found here, could hardly have been anticipated within a region of our country so little favored by nature. The sterile soil, the rugged surface, the stern climate, and the want of navigable streams in New England, would have seemed to render it improbable that it would ever be considerably peopled, or that any great commercial mart should arise within its borders. It would seem that such could only exist within the more central and southerly portions of the Union, under more genial skies, and in the vicinity of the great natural routes of inter-communication. But the resolution and intelligent industry of our fathers surmounted every obstacle. The region sneeringly stigmatized as having no natural productions for export but 'granite and ice,' now teems with three millions of the children of freedom, abounding in all the comforts of civilized life—and its metropolis ranks with the great cities of the globe.

"It is to be borne in mind, also, that that metropolis became an important city long before science and art had cut in sunder the hills, elevated the vales, and spanned the running waters, to unite her commerce in easy and rapid communication with more favored climes.

"If our people could achieve a position so prominent while

destitute of any of the facilities of intercourse with the interior, with which other cities were so abundantly blessed, what may we not expect of the future destiny of Boston now that her iron highways, extending in all directions, bring her into convenient proximity with every section of the land? Those who could effect so much under the most repelling circumstances, may be depended upon to avail themselves, to the full, of their new and ample advantages.

"The long winter of New England isolation is broken;—she now warms and flourishes in friendly and thrifty intercourse with the luxuriant West; and it is not too much to anticipate that the day will come, when there will be no greater or more prosperous city upon the American continent than the City of the Pilgrims." *

When we see a community steadily pursuing, through successive generations, the same onward and upward course, it can only be through the impulse of the same ever acting motives. A free school in the wilderness,—a house erected for the worship of God, within hearing of the war-cry of the savage, indicate clearly enough the principles which stimulated the energies of our fathers. In their vigorous pursuit of material advantages, they never lost sight of higher interests. If their harvests were abundant, if their trade was prosperous and their resources enlarged, the institutions of religion, of learning and of benevolence shared largely in the general prosperity. If they were successful in the accumulation of wealth, they were no less liberal in the distribution of it. To found a school or a college was as dear an object with them, as to add to their manufactures or extend their commerce; and the enterprise and thrift, which enabled them to foster and support their seminaries of learning, derived in return from them the intelligence which insured success. Thus in harmonious and happy union grew up together and in mutual dependence all the pursuits and institutions essential to the stability, progress and happiness

* "Inaugural Address to the City Council. By John Prescott Bigelow." Mayor. "Jan. 1, 1849."

of a people. And so now, and in this light, must be viewed the works of the present generation.

The forest of masts that almost encircles our city, the panting steamers and the fleets of freighted ships with outspread sails, which enliven our beautiful harbor; our crowded thoroughfares, ringing with the din of traffic and the noisy hum of industry; and our sometimes magnificent and always extensive and substantial railway stations, where no hour passes without the entrance or departure of some long train of cars, moved by its swift though ponderous engine, and filled with passengers or loaded with merchandize, furnish unequivocal evidences of the activity, energy and enterprise of our citizens. But when we see how liberally the wealth thus procured is devoted to unselfish purposes and noble ends; how the institutions founded by our ancestors for the maintenance of religion and the diffusion of intellectual and moral culture are upheld and extended; how all the "charities that soothe and heal and bless" are generously supported;—how much is the character of this activity and progress exalted, and what encouraging proofs are given that the spirit and the principles of our fathers "survives in the hearts and is exhibited in the lives of the citizens of Boston!"

It is one of the noblest features in the whole history of our city, that its industrial and commercial objects and successes have ever been made to subserve the highest interests of humanity; and to speak of them out of this connexion, and view them as merely mercenary in their aims and ends, would mar the truth, as much as it would deface the beauty, of that history. And now, while dwelling with, we trust not improper feelings of pride and satisfaction, on the successful results of our efforts to extend and enlarge our commercial relations, we may be pardoned if we do not forget, that while constructing a thousand miles of railroad, we have contributed millions for the general good.

But, leaving such considerations and looking at the event so recently celebrated only in its commercial character and its relations to the present, we shall still find that, viewed in any aspect, it was one of no ordinary importance; and we may see in it an illustration "how God draws the good of a higher sphere out of the benefits that lie in a lower order. The casual motive of the enterprise that has covered New England with nerves, of which our city is the brain, was not distinctly philanthropic. Perhaps it was chiefly selfish." * * * "But Providence had another and a higher use for those iron tracks and flying trains. After the mercantile heart had devised and secured them, God took them for his purposes, without paying any tax for the privilege, he uses them to quicken the activity of men; to send energy and vitality where before was silence and barrenness; to multiply cities and villages, studded with churches, dotted with schools, and filled with happy homes and budding souls; to increase wealth which shall partially be devoted to his service and kingdom, and all along their banks to make the wilderness blossom as the rose. Without any vote of permission from legislatures and officials, even while the cars are loaded with profitable freight and paying passengers, and the groaning engines are earning the necessary interest, Providence sends, without charge, its cargoes of good sentiment and brotherly feeling; disburses the culture of the city to the simplicity of the hamlet, and brings back the strength and virtue of the village and mountain to the wasting faculties of the metropolis; and fastens to every steam-shuttle that flies back and forth and hither and thither, an invisible thread of fraternal influence, which, entwining sea-shore and hill-country, mart and grain-field, forge and factory, wharf and mine, slowly prepares society to realize, one day, the Saviour's prayer, "that they all may be one." * * * * "It is good," then, "that mountains shall be graded, ledges blasted, fair roads built, deserts fertilized, swamps filled, marshes drained, and machinery invented; and just as fast as these objects are accomplished, better results than thrifty enterprise had in view supervene. There is more intelligence, more generosity, more enjoyment, more advantages for securing the great ends of human life."

* * * "The visit of our excellent Chief Magistrate and his Cabinet bore witness, by the speed with which they reached our city from the capital, to the effects of these material

benefits in making our countrymen acquainted with each other, and in cementing their fellowship. Those who indulge fears for the stability of our nation on account of the extent of its domain, and who justify those fears by the recorded fortunes of ancient empires that were broken by the weight of their territories, do not appreciate the difference between our condition and theirs, in a representative government and provincial independence. And yet, admirably devised as our scheme of government is to promise central vigor and permanence, and to avoid the perils that spring from breadth of territory, diversity of climate, variety in habits, prejudices, and the scale of culture, and the conflict of material and social interests, it is very doubtful whether its present extent would not prove too vast for the resources of our Constitution, if we had been left to the old means of communication and intercourse. The framers of our national charter would have considered the idea of bringing the shores of both oceans under its sway, and keeping their inhabitants in peaceful and fraternal communion, scarcely less than preposterous ; and, with mail-coaches for the only conveyance to Utah, and barks doubling Cape Horn as the swiftest mediators between Washington and San Francisco, the attempt would be almost useless. But when California may be brought within one week's distance, and the pioneers of Iowa and the planters by the banks of the Rio Grande may hear the debates that affect their interests in the capitol before the speakers reach their perorations, a new principle is introduced which must modify all calculations of national security drawn from the infirmity of Athens and the decline of Rome. Steam and the magnetic wires compel the correction of our political philosophy ; and, if there be a preeminent value in the structure of our civil constitution ; if it be a worthy subject for rejoicing that the breadth of a continent should be brought under its sway, and exhibit to the world the lasting triumph of the experiment of republican freedom, on a larger scale than any upon which imperial despotisms have yet displayed their transient strength, our gratitude is not more certainly due to Providence for the wisdom and patriotism of Washington, Franklin and Adams, than it is for the genius of Watt, the ingenuity of Fulton, and the mercantile energy which has threaded our forests with rail tracks and disturbed our waters with steamships that conquer tides and storms." *

Considered, therefore, either as one of a long series of events, which, dating from the early settlement of the city, and deriving their essential elements of success from the character and institutions of its people, have contributed to its growth and prosperity; or in its relation to the social and commercial interests, present and prospective, not of the city or the State alone, but of all New England; and, in view of the happy influence which it has already exerted, and is destined, in its fuller developments and still wider extension, yet more powerfully to exert, upon the political relations of the States of our Union, and upon our international connexions, the completion of the great system of railways which, starting from Boston, as a central point, and penetrating the neighboring States in all directions, have reached the Canadas and united the ocean to the proud rivers and the great inland seas of the West, was an event too important to be passed by unnoticed.

Whatever may have been the more immediate and apparent motives which originated and guided the enterprise,—allowing to selfishness, competition and rivalry their full influence,—to ascribe its successful execution to these alone would be to take but a superficial and imperfect view of it. It was sustained, encouraged, and consummated by the general, habitual and time-honored spirit of the community. It is the offspring, not more of commercial rivalry, than of wise foresight, enlightened patriotism, and disinterested devotion to the public weal.

Such being the character of the enterprise, and the nature of our relation to it as a community, it was natural, as the long anticipated day of its completion, to which we had been so largely instrumental, and in which our interests were so

* "The Railroad Jubilee. Two Discourses delivered in Hollis street Meeting-house. Sunday, Sept. 21, 1851. By Thomas Starr King."

deeply involved, was at hand, that the public attention should be turned to the subject, and that its importance should be more directly and fully realized.

Nor was it forgotten by the members of the government, in their consideration of the subject, that the proposed celebration would afford to the city a favorable opportunity to testify to the neighboring Provinces, and so to the whole of the British Empire, its respectful and friendly consideration. It seemed not improper that that Boston whose citizens played so prominent a part, for reasons satisfactory to themselves, in the revolution which separated the two nations, should now, for reasons equally satisfactory, be no less prompt, hearty and energetic in the work of their reconciliation. It seemed to them, that to improve this opportunity could not fail to be agreeable to the heart and attractive to the imagination of every one in the community. The City, too, is the metropolis of that Massachusetts whose citizens, as armed provincial or continental soldiers, had fought and lost and won many a fierce battle against the inhabitants of those provinces, but whose recollections of this border intercourse are associated with nothing worse than hard blows cordially given and gallantly returned,—not with instances of malignity, nor with any circumstances tending to impair their respect for the personal qualities of their former antagonists. As representing that community, therefore, it behoved Boston to avail herself of the chance so offered her to express to the people of the British Provinces her thorough appreciation of their character, and her desire to consider their present friendship as equally sincere and manly with their long-past hostility, and to say that while she remembers her competitors at those old Olympic Games with more affection than resentment, yet she is willing to propose to them that their mutual competition shall, in future, be of a different sort,—instead of testing each other's power of destruction, to vie with each other in mutual good offices, and in earnest efforts to advance the welfare and happiness of man.

Impressed with such views and feelings, and in the full confidence that their motives would be justly appreciated, and that their action would meet the hearty approval of their fellow-citizens, the Municipal Authorities of Boston adopted, at an early day, preparatory measures for the appropriate celebration of the crowning event which was deemed so auspicious to the social, political and commercial interests of the city. Encouraged by the many tokens of interest in the occasion, which were manifested both at home and abroad, and animated by the desire of rendering the celebration worthy of the character of the city over whose interests they presided, and in some measure commensurate with the magnitude of the work to be commemorated, they resolved to devote three days to this purpose, and accordingly designated the 17th, 18th and 19th of September to be observed as days of public rejoicing.

The occasion has passed; all the outward signs of rejoicing have disappeared; and the multitude, who had gathered to our City from far and near to witness our prosperity and happiness, to partake our hospitality, and share our joy, have long since left us. But the memory of those days still lives; the friendly and fraternal relations then formed, we trust, will never be destroyed,—and the happy influences which naturally emanate from such an occasion, will, as we hope, continue to exert a living power long after the name of the Railroad Jubilee shall have sunk into oblivion.

That Jubilee must, however, for a long time, be regarded as an interesting occurrence in the history of Boston. The magnitude of the enterprises whose accomplishment it was designed to celebrate, the number of distinguished persons from distant parts of our own country and from the neighboring Provinces of Great Britain, who honored it with their presence—the vast multitudes who gathered from all quarters to witness and share its festivities—the extent and variety of the preparations made to ensure its success, and the generous and hearty zeal for its promotion, manifested by every class of our citizens, all served to invest the occasion with more than ordinary interest. As a not unimportant event in our history, therefore, it is worthy of a permanent description; and, as furnishing a striking picture of the times, as expressing the sentiment and embodying some of the most important characteristics of the age, it will have a high value in the eyes of the future historian, and will be looked back upon by succeeding generations with the same interest, and let us hope, with something of the same pride and satisfaction, with which we now dwell upon the acts of those who have preceded us. But not for the future only should an account of this event be written. The interest in the occasion has not yet so died out in our own hearts, that we may not derive some satisfaction from a review of its pleasing features; and by the many sons of New England scattered all over our land and the world, it must be welcomed with some pleasure, if only as a voice from home, while, to those both at home and abroad, who are not familiar with our history, resources and institutions, it may serve to give more correct views of us as a community.

It is proposed, therefore, to give as accurate and circumstantial an account as is possible, of the three days' Jubilee, and every effort has been made to ensure its completeness, and also, to furnish in an Appendix such statistical and other matter as may have relation to the subject, or serve to illustrate the past or present character and condition of our City.

That there must be many imperfections in the manner in which this task has been executed, and doubtless some important omissions, every intelligent person will readily understand. It is hoped, however, that, as they are involuntary, if not unavoidable, they will be as readily forgiven.

THE JUBILEE.

On the 14th of July, the first public measure was adopted by the City Government for the institution of the celebration, by the passage of the following Preamble and Resolves :—

"*In Board of Mayor and Aldermen,*
July 14, 1851.

"The Mayor offered the following Preamble and Resolve :— Whereas it is understood that the line of Railways, uniting the Cities of Montreal and Boston, will be completed during the present month, and whereas it is desirable that an event so important should be appropriately celebrated—Therefore,

Resolved, That the whole Board of Mayor and Aldermen, with such as the Common Council may join, be a Committee with full powers to consider and report what action shall be taken by the City Government of Boston in the premises. Sent down for concurrence. Came up concurred, and

Francis Brinley, Esq., President of the Common Council,

Messrs. Charles H. Stearns,	of Ward	1,
James B. Allen,	"	2,
Hiram Bosworth,	"	3,
Henry J. Gardner,	"	4,
Benjamin Beal,	"	5,
John P. Putnam,	"	6,
James W. Sever,	"	7,
Daniel N. Haskell,	"	8,
Newell A. Thompson,	"	9,
Ezra Lincoln, (and by a subsequent vote, Otis Kimball,)	"	10,
Albert T. Minot,	"	11,
and Josiah Dunham, Jr.,	"	12,

were joined."

The following Preamble and Resolution, which is the one under which the Committee acted, was moved in the Common Council on the same evening, by Ezra Lincoln, Esq., as an original measure, and was adopted, sent up for concurrence, and concurred in: so that the two branches of the City Government equally and harmoniously commenced the movement.

"Whereas, it is understood that the line of railways uniting the Cities of Montreal and Boston, will be completed during the present month, and whereas it is deemed that an event so important should be appropriately celebrated, therefore,

Resolved, That a Committee of this Board, consisting of one from each Ward, to be joined by a Committee whom the Mayor and Aldermen shall appoint, be a Committee with full powers to consider and determine what action shall be taken by the City Government of Boston in the premises."

The same Committee was appointed under both resolutions.

At a meeting of this Committee on a subsequent day, the following Sub-Committees were formed, viz :—

On Circular. Alderman Rogers—Messrs. Sever and Putnam.

To arrange for a meeting of the Merchants. Alderman Holbrook—Messrs. Sever and Gardner.

On Invitation and Reception. The Mayor—the President of the Common Council, Aldermen Holbrook and Briggs—Messrs. Lincoln, Putnam, Haskell, Minot, Thompson, Sever, Kimball.

On Escort and Procession. Aldermen Kimball and Munroe—Messrs. Brinley, Dunham, Stearns, Beal, Allen, Haskell.

On a Public Dinner. The Mayor—Aldermen Smith and Munroe—Messrs. Thompson, Beal, Allen and Dunham.

On Railroad Maps. Alderman Kimball—Messrs. Lincoln and Minot.

On a Harbor Excursion. The Mayor—Alderman Grant—Messrs. Gardner, Kimball, Bosworth, Lincoln and Beal.

On Fire Works. Aldermen Briggs and Clark—Messrs. Haskell, Lincoln and Thompson.

On a Visit to Public Institutions. The whole Committee.

For the purpose of making the intentions of the City Government, as expressed by the above Preamble and Resolve, more generally known, of calling the attention of the citizens more particularly to the present and prospective magnitude of the interests involved in our railway enterprises, and of inviting their co-operation in the proposed celebration, the following Circular was issued :—

To the Citizens of Boston :

The City Government of Boston propose to celebrate, in an appropriate manner, the final completion of the great lines of railway uniting the tide water at Boston with the Canadas and the great West; and also the establishment of American lines of steamers between Boston and Liverpool. The importance of these events to the great social and commercial interests of our city can hardly be exaggerated. We are now about to realize, it is believed, the full benefit of those great enterprises, in the perfecting of which we have expended so much capital. There are now completed and in operation, in Massachusetts alone, about 1200 miles of railway; and in New England, about 2400 miles. Massachusetts has expended, in the completion of these roads, the enormous amount of $54,000,000 ; and it appears from the reports of the several railroad corporations in this State, made to the last Legislature, that there were transported over the Massachusetts roads alone, during the year 1850, 9,500,000 passengers, and 2,500,000 tons of freight. This statement, however, but imperfectly presents the advantages which we are to derive from these works. The railways of Massachusetts are but a small link in the great lines which connect us with remoter sections of our country.

The several lines connecting us with the Canadas, northern New York, the great lakes and the far West, are now completed, uniting us by railroad and steam navigation with thirteen States of the Union, comprising an area of 428,795 square miles ; the two Canadas, the lakes, with their 5000 miles of coast; and bringing within our commercial sphere a population of ten millions of inhabitants. The business of the lakes and the Canadas, and its rapid yearly increase, are worthy of especial consideration. It is estimated that the imports and exports of the Lake Harbors, exclusive of the Canadas, during the present year, will be $200,000,000. The annual increase of this business is found to be 17 1-2 per cent., thus doubling itself in less than six years. In addition to this, the imports and exports of the Canadas will amount during the present year to $50,000,000.

And now what are the advantages which Boston possesses, for doing this immense business? These are so manifest, that their importance will be readily appreciated. Her harbor is one of the finest in the world. Her wharves and storage accommodations are equal, if not superior, to those of any other city, and capable of indefinite extension. Her local position is unrivalled, and the enterprise and integrity of her merchants are well known. The lines of railway to which we have alluded, all centre in her and radiate from her. It is ascertained, from the actual results of this year's business, that under favorable circumstances, all kinds of provisions can be brought from the West, through these new lines of communication, to Boston, more speedily and at a less expense than to any other Atlantic port.

In this connection it may not be amiss to remark that the books of the Custom House show, that the merchandise transported to the Canadas from the district of Boston and Charlestown, for the six months ending June 30, 1851, was more than quadruple that of the six months next preceding January 1, 1851.

Merchandise can be landed at Ogdensburgh, on Lake Ontario, put on board the cars at that place, brought to Boston without trans-shipment, and from here exported to England by means of our steamships, in a much less time than it can be done by any other route. It seems to us, then, that Boston has every facility for becoming a great exporting as well as importing city. Cargoes from Liverpool in steamships, via Boston, may be delivered in Montreal in twelve days.

This fact, taken in connection with the fact that the St. Lawrence is closed by ice during five months of the year, and that the communication with Boston is uninterrupted during the whole year, must make Boston, as it seems to us, the port of entry for the Canadas, thus opening to us a business, the extent of which we have not begun to realize. The eligibility of our location as a shipping port for the Canadas, will be seen by the following statement of distances, as compared with New York.

	To Boston	To New York
From Liverpool, via Halifax	2876 miles.	3093 miles
" " direct - - - -	2856 "	3073 "
From Halifax - - - - - -	368 "	580 "
From Montreal - - - - -	344 "	398 "
The distance from Liverpool to Montreal via Boston is - -		3200 "
While via New York it is - - - - - - - - - -		3471 "

The difference between Liverpool and Montreal, in favor of Boston over New York, is 271 miles.

In view of the above facts, and in conformity with the expressed wishes of many of the citizens of Boston, the City Government propose to celebrate the completion of these lines of railways, by a festival in Faneuil Hall, and other appropriate ceremonies. It is proposed to invite to be present with us on that occasion, the Governor-General of Canada, his Staff and Cabinet, the leading members of the Canadian Parliament, the Corporation of Montreal, the leading merchants in all the Canadian cities and Ogdensburg, the President of the United States and his Cabinet, the Governors of the New England States, the Presidents of all the Railways in New England, the Mayors of the cities of New England, and others interested in railways and steam navigation.

We cordially invite the co-operation of our fellow citizens of Boston, in order that this celebration may be made in some degree commensurate with the great importance of the events to be celebrated.

For the Committee of Arrangements,

JOHN P. BIGELOW, *Mayor.*

City Hall, Boston, August 1, 1851.

The facts disclosed in this circular place in a strong light the importance of the growing trade of Canada and our relations to it; and as, on the completion of the lines of road leading northward and westward, we should be brought within twelve hours travel of Montreal, one of her principal cities, and thus the way be opened for an unbroken, rapid and mutually advantageous intercourse, it was peculiarly appropriate that our Canadian friends should be invited to be present at the celebration, and that we should give expression to our wish to be united to them by the golden chains of friendly and social regard, as well as by the iron bands of commercial interest.

To this end it was deemed advisable that a deputation from the General Committee should personally visit the Canadas. This was accordingly done, and the Sub-Committee, consisting of Mr. Francis Brinley, President of the Council, and Messrs. Lincoln, Putnam, Haskell, Thompson, Sever, Kimball and Gardner, proceeded upon their mission, charged with the following note of invitation from the Mayor to the Governor General:

"BOSTON, AUG. 8, 1851.

MY LORD,—

The City Government of Boston propose to celebrate, at an early day, with appropriate ceremonies, the completion of the great lines of railway uniting Boston with the Canadas and the Western States, and I am directed to invite you to honor us with your presence upon the occasion. The invitation I accordingly now most respectfully transmit, assuring you that your acceptance would gratify this community generally, and that you would be received by this City as a most welcome and honored guest.

A select Committee of our City Council are charged with the delivery of this note, and will solicit your compliance with the wishes of the Government and people whom they represent.

I have the honor to be, with great respect,
Your Lordship's obedient servant,
JOHN PRESCOTT BIGELOW,
Mayor of Boston.

To His Excellency the Earl of Elgin and Kincardine, Captain-General and Governor-in-Chief of the British Possessions in North America."

The Sub-Committee were, everywhere, received with the utmost cordiality, and entertained with that genuine English hospitality so familiar to our admiration, and all their bright anticipations were more than realized.

The following account of their visit, drawn up from a series of letters written, on the return of the delegation, by one of its members,* and published in one of the newspapers, (the Daily Atlas,) may be read with interest in this connexion. As the delegation represented the City of Boston, the courtesies and kindness extended to its members by the citizens of Canada require this public acknowledgement.

The Committee were furnished by the Presidents of the northern lines of railway with free passes over the various roads, and by our merchants and public men with letters of introduction to the Canadian merchants and authorities; and, animated with the desire to render the Railroad Jubilee of 1851 worthy of the character of the city whose representatives the were, they left Boston on Saturday, August 9th, and proceeded by the Boston and Maine Railroad to Lawrence, and

* Daniel N. Haskell, Esq.

thence by the Manchester and Lawrence, Concord, Northern, and Vermont Central Railroads to Northfield, Vermont. At Northfield they were most hospitably entertained, and had an interview with the Hon. Charles Paine, and his associates in the direction of the Vermont Central, and Vermont and Canada Roads, from whom, and from other gentlemen connected with the lines of road to Canada, they obtained much valuable information.

As it was the design and purpose of the City Authorities to make the celebration one of a general character, a portion of the Committee passed over from Northfield to Burlington to confer with the President and Officers of the Burlington and Rutland Railroad, and make arrangements with them respecting the passage over their road of such of our Canadian friends as might wish to travel by that route.

The Committee left Northfield at 5 o'clock, A. M., on Monday, August 11th, and arrived at West Alburgh, a distance of ninety miles, in three and a half hours running time, or four hours, including stops. They crossed Lake Champlain in the steamer Ethan Allen, and found that arrangements had been made for their accommodation by the agents and officers of the Ogdensburg, or "Northern" Road, as it is called in the region through which it passes.

In crossing Lake Champlain, the steamer's course was parallel with the extensive structure, built under authority of an act of the New York Legislature, passed at its last session, by means of which the trains will pass across an opening between two piers, upon a long floating barge, propelled by steam, and arranged to float into square sections at each end of the piers. This work is so nearly completed that only a short time will be required to enable a train to cross this open space. The roads which terminate at this point have a large area secured for their accommodation.

The cars of the Ogdensburg Road were here taken. The train consisted of five well-filled passenger cars, and the smoothness with which it passed at a high rate of speed over the rails, was the subject of general remark. The road passes through a level region, and although the soil does not appear to be in a very high state of cultivation, yet, at some points of the line, there is sufficient evidence that it is capable of producing heavy crops. When settled upon and improved, this country will doubtless be one of the finest agricultural regions in the northern part of the United States.

New buildings are already springing up along the entire course of the road, and at each stopping place there were unmistakable evidences that the increased facilities for business, which the road furnishes, were exerting a most beneficial influence upon the trade and growth of the small towns through which it passes.

At the town of Malone, about sixty miles from Rouse's Point, the Committee met T. P. Chandler, Esq., President of the Ogdensburg Road, Col. C. L. Schlatter, its superintendent, and Mr. Hoyle and Mr. Horton, two of the directors.

These three gentlemen accompanied the Delegation over the road, and Col. Schlatter kindly offered to go to Toronto with them. The offer was accepted, and as this gentleman was well known throughout the route, his assistance was of great service. The officers of the railroad, and all persons interested in the various lines communicating with it, expressed deep interest in the objects of the Committee, and most kindly offered them their aid.

The train, after leaving Rouse's Point, reached Ogdensburg in five and a half hours. This place is four hundred miles from Boston. The average speed at which the entire journey had been accomplished was twenty-two miles an hour, including stops.

The lands owned by the railway company at Ogdensburg are very extensive. The buildings are very large, and make a fine appearance from the water. A short examination showed that the most ample arrangements had been made for the accommodation of all kinds of freight, and for the safety and convenience of vessels engaged in its transportation.

The deputation took passage, at Ogdensburg, in the steamer Niagara, for Lewiston, and as the boat passed out into the middle of the river St. Lawrence, her passengers had a fine view of the town, situated, as it is, upon ground somewhat elevated above the river, and presenting a very handsome appearance. The St. Lawrence is about a mile and a quarter wide at this point. Upon the Canada side, opposite Ogdensburg, and situated upon a beautiful rising ground, is the town of Prescott, over the sign of whose Customs Warehouse the English arms, with the letters V. R., were the first indications noticed that the party had reached the British Provinces.

The sail upon the St. Lawrence, on board of the spacious and commodious steamer, was most delightful. The powerful engines of the "Niagara" forced her through the opposing current at a rapid rate, and the route led among the famous "Thousand Islands" and through scenery of the most picturesque and interesting description. Early in the evening the boat was gliding over the waters of Lake Ontario, and at dawn the fort at Niagara was in sight. Arrived at Lewiston, a portion of the Committee took passage in a steamer for Hamilton, situated about forty miles west from Toronto, and from its rapidly increasing commerce and wealth, popularly called the "Queen of the West;" while the rest of the Delegation left for Toronto on board the fine English steamer "City of Toronto," Capt. Dick. Fortunately, Capt. Cotten, an aid-de-camp to the Governor-General, was among the passengers, and the Committee having been introduced to him, arrangements were at once made with him in furtherance of the objects of their mission.

After a sail of about three hours, the city of Toronto was in sight, and its public buildings easily distinguished. On landing, the Delegation were received by the Mayor and members of the Corporation, and by several Cabinet Ministers of the Governor-General. The news of the intended visit of the Committee had preceded their arrival, and the authorities were prepared to welcome them. After a formal introduction, the authorities of Toronto accompanied the Deputation to their hotel, from the proprietor of which, Mr. Beard, the Committee received numerous and valuable attentions.

In a short time after the arrival of the Delegation, the Governor-General, through the medium of his aid-de-camp, assigned an early hour for an interview at the Government House. At the time appointed, the Committee waited upon Lord Elgin, and were received with a gratifying cordiality. Their letters of invitation and introduction were delivered, and the objects of their mission stated. The interview was one of the most agreeable character, and the Committee with great pleasure accepted the Governor's polite invitation to dine with him on the ensuing day.

Upon the afternoon of the arrival of the Committee, the band, attached to the regiment stationed at Toronto, played for the amusement of the public in the grounds of the Government House, which were thrown open for visitors; and though there was a large collection of people and no guards or police upon the ground, the most perfect decorum prevailed.

During the performance by the band, the piazza of the Government House was filled with distinguished personages. The Committee were there introduced to the members of the Cabinet and the Staff, officers of the army, and many members of Parliament.

The Hon. Sir Hew Dalrymple, commander of the 71st regiment of Highlanders, stationed at this place, politely offered to order a dress parade of his regiment, the next morning, for the especial pleasure of the Delegation. His politeness was readily accepted, and the city officers volunteered to conduct their guests to the barracks and parade ground.

The Mayor and Corporation accepted the invitation of the Committee to visit Boston on the occasion of the Railroad Jubilee, and the principal mercantile houses, to whom letters of introduction had been sent, were very much interested in the proposed festivities. Through the agency of the merchants, bankers, and public officers, the names of the most prominent merchants in Canada West were obtained, and invitations were forwarded to them.

The Parliament Houses were visited in the evening, when both branches were in session, and both engaged in debating the question of asking for a loan from the Imperial Parliament, for the construction of a continuous railway from Toronto to Halifax. The whole subject of railways, with their effects upon business, their advantages over canals, and all the matters incident to their establishment, were discussed. The speakers in both Houses made frequent allusions to the United States, and the experience of our own State and that of New England were often adduced, in support or in illustration of their arguments.

After devoting the next morning to business connected with their mission in Canada West, the Delegation met the City Authorities by appointment, and proceeded in carriages to the parade ground and barracks, situated about two miles west from the business portion of the city.

The 71st Regiment of Light Infantry, Highlanders, under the command of Col. Dalrymple, were formed in line inside the barrack enclosure. They marched to the parade ground, about half a mile from their quarters, and were drawn up in line, ready to receive the Governor-General. As the clock in a neighboring tower struck the hour appointed for the review, a trumpet announced the arrival of the Commander-in-Chief, Lord Elgin, with his Staff, who were received with the customary honors. The regiment was about 800 strong. After the review, many battalion manœuvres were performed with great exactness. The parade closed with a drill of the regiment as skirmishers, in which all the movements of light troops in presence of an enemy, the formation of squares to resist cavalry, and similar evolutions, were exhibited with great accuracy and fine effect.

The Provincial Institution for the Insane was next visited. The building occupied for this purpose, finely located, and having very large grounds connected with it, is about the size of the Massachusetts General Hospital, in Boston. It is a noble monument of the philanthropy of the Province. Internally, it is a pattern of neatness and good order, and contains all the most approved arrangements for warming and ventilating.

In returning to the city, the extensive grounds of the University were visited. One of the most gratifying circumstances, connected with the present social condition of Canada West, is the deep interest taken by all classes of the population in the subject of popular education. The last report of the Rev. Dr. Ryerson, the Superintendent of the Schools of the Province, states the number of public schools to be 3059; and the number of pupils 151,891. In Toronto, a fine building, situated in an open square of nearly eight acres, will be finished this year, for the Provincial Normal School. The building and land will cost $60,000. The corner stone was laid on the 2nd of July last, by Lord Elgin, who pronounced a most able and eloquent address upon the occasion, which has since been published and eagerly sought for. Dr. Ryerson, a devoted and eminent clergyman of the Methodist church, has, by his zeal and devotion to the cause of popular education, infused his own enthusiasm into the public mind to such a degree, that, last year, the people of Canada West voluntarily taxed themselves, for the salaries of teachers, a larger sum, in proportion to their numbers, and kept open their schools, on an average, more months, than the neighboring citizens of the great State of New York.

In the evening, the delegation dined at Elmsley House, the residence of the Governor-General. The party consisted of the accomplished host and hostess, Lord and Lady Elgin, their suite, the speakers of both branches of the Legislature, two members of the Cabinet and their predecessors, Sir Hew Dalrymple, an English Baptist Clergyman, whose name has escaped the writer's memory, Lieut. De Lancy Floyd Jones, of the U. S. Army, Hon. Charles Paine, of Vermont, Col. Schlatter, of Ogdensburg, and the members of the Committee. The conversation was confined to the topics naturally suggested by the mission of the Bostonians, the present happy relations existing between the two governments, and the progress made by the people of New England in the arts of peaceful industry.

After retiring from Lord Elgin's, and in accordance with arrangements previously made, the Committee, in company with the Cabinet Ministers, attended a brilliant levee at the residence of one of the principal citizens of Toronto. A numerous and elegant company were assembled, and the evening passed in a most agreeable manner.

The Committee were gratified to learn from Lord Elgin, that he would visit Boston, if the state of public affairs would allow him to leave the Province at the period of the commemorative festivities, and were charged by him with the following reply to the Mayor's note of invitation:

"TORONTO, AUG. 15, 1851.

SIR,

Your very kind and obliging letter of the 8th inst., has been handed to me by the Gentlemen of the Committee of the City Council who were charged with its delivery.

I am very sensible of the honor done me by the Authorities of the City of Boston, in inviting me to be the guest of the City on the occasion of the proposed Railway celebration. I feel moreover a sincere interest in the completion of the great lines of communication stretching from Boston towards the North and West, of which I witnessed the very promising beginning in the winter of 1846–7. I would, therefore, gladly, if it were in my power to do so, accept at once the invitation which has been so courteously conveyed to me by your Honor, and the Gentlemen of the Deputation. My time, however, is not altogether, as I have more fully explained to those Gentlemen, at my own disposal. I am compelled therefore to add that, much as I should desire to visit Boston, and to tender my thanks to yourself and the other authorities of the City, in person, my movements must depend on the state of public business within the Province.

I have the honor to be, Sir,

Your Ob't. Ser't.,

ELGIN AND KINCARDINE.

To His Honor, JOHN PRESCOTT BIGELOW,

Mayor of Boston."

The Cabinet ministers, many members of Parliament, officers of the army, and other official personages, also accepted invitations to be present at the celebration.

During the last morning of their stay, the Committee were visited by a large number of the principal merchants and bankers of the city. Members of Parliament, and of the Cabinet, furnished them with letters of introduction to several gentlemen in Montreal and Quebec. The officers of the Army and the mayor and officers of the Corporation called to pay their parting respects, and quite a deputation from various classes of society accompanied them to the steamer.

The Committee left Canada West fully impressed with the gratifying conviction that its citizens are earnestly desirous of cultivating the acquaintance of, and extending their business relations with, the people of New England. The mission of the Committee from Boston occurred at a most fortunate period, as the Provincial Parliament were then engaged in the discussion of the whole subject of internal improvements, and public attention was engrossed by the debates upon the subject.

Canada West is destined to be one of the most prosperous and wealthy portions of the American continent. Its climate and soil are as favorable to agriculture as the best portions of New York. The people have many sympathies with their brethren on the opposite side of the lake and river, and it is hoped that the influence which will be exerted by the increased facilities for intercommunication, will be productive of lasting good to all the parties interested therein.

The Delegation left Toronto, at noon, on Friday the 15th of August, for Kingston, where they arrived at day-break on the following morning, and whence, after having taken a hasty view of the city, they proceeded on their way to Montreal, distant one hundred and ninety-six miles. Reaching Montreal the same evening, the Delegation found the Mayor and members of the Corporation in waiting to give them an official reception, after which they were conveyed in carriages to the Hays House, where rooms had been engaged for them, and a splendid entertainment prepared. They were there again cordially welcomed by the Mayor, and handsome addresses were made to them by several gentlemen of the Corporation, which were responded to by members of the Committee. They then accepted an invitation to attend religious service at the Catholic Cathedral, on the following day.

On Monday, the Committee devoted the morning to the business of their mission. They found the men of business in Montreal quite enthusiastic in relation to the intended celebration. The principal bankers, importers and merchants gave the Committee a warm and hearty welcome, and assured them of their deep interest in all those great schemes of internal improvement, which connect the Canadas with Boston. Already the trade of Montreal has felt the beneficial results of the new and rapid means of intercommunication, and her merchants duly appreciate the importance of the roads which place her within a day's ride of Boston, and which no five months' frost can put under an embargo.

At noon, the Delegation met the Mayor and Corporation at their rooms, where Mr. Brinley, in their behalf, explained the objects of their mission, and, in behalf of the City of Boston, extended an invitation to the Corporation of Montreal, to honor the Railroad Jubilee with their presence. The Mayor replied, and for himself and his associates, accepted the invitation.

At this interview, the Committee received and accepted an invitation to visit the "Mountain," a favorite place of resort in the suburbs of the city. And, at the hour appointed, the Mayor and Corporation called at the hotel, and took up their guests. It was judiciously arranged, that but one member of the Committee should ride in each carriage, and that all political parties should be represented. This was the case in all the cities visited. The object was, that no erroneous impression should be made upon the minds of the strangers, and that the sentiments of Tories and Radicals, Ministerialists and members of the Opposition, French Canadians and Englishmen, should be adequately explained to each visitor.

The ride round "the Mountain" is through a fine country. North of the city, elegant and tasteful villas occupy the land. From the northern slope of the mountain, a magnificent panorama meets the eye. For miles and miles, the country is highly cultivated, and the scenery is superb. The valley of the Ottawa river can be distinguished for a great distance. To the South, the St. Lawrence is seen, and upon the opposite shore, the level country of Laprairie, while ranges of mountains in New York and Vermont bound the view in the southern and eastern directions.

Monklands, the name given to the mansion house at the Mountain, where Lord Elgin lived during his residence in Montreal, is finely situated, and surrounded by venerable woods. Its internal arrangements are upon a scale suitable for the residence of a great Pro-consul. After visiting the spacious apartments and extensive grounds, the company were ushered into an elegant hall, where a dinner was provided in a style worthy of the character of the city by whose authorities it was given.

At this dinner eloquent speeches were made, and appropriate sentiments given. The place, and the occasion, the past history and the present relations of the respective nations and races of men, who were thus assembled as friends and neighbors, afforded themes for eloquence, which were adequately improved.

On Tuesday, after passing the morning in the agreeable duty of receiving visitors from the various commercial, professional and official ranks of society, the Delegation, in company with the Mayor of Montreal, and a number of his associates in the City Government, visited several places of note in the city. The Catholic Cathedral was first examined, and the long journey to its tower performed. The top of the tower is 220 feet (the height of the Bunker Hill Monument) above the level of the street. A magnificent view of the city and its suburbs is obtained at that great elevation, and although the ascent is a laborious one, the visitor is amply repaid for his fatigue, by the extent, variety and beauty of the panorama which meets his eye.

Through the agency of their municipal guides, the party visited three of the principal nunneries in the city, and the rooms of the Bank of Montreal, in which last they were received with great attention by the Hon. Peter McGill, the President of the institution.

On the evening of Tuesday, the 19th of August, the Committee left Montreal on board a fine steamer, in order to make a short visit to Quebec—one of the oldest cities of North America, and one which abounds in historical associations of the most interesting character. Soon after their arrival on the following morning, they were visited by Dr. Sewell, the acting Mayor, and the objects of their mission were stated. A meeting of the Corporation was arranged, and the business connected with the visit transacted. A short time among the citizens of Quebec was all that was required to convince the strangers that its society was most polished and refined, and its people distinguished for urbanity, hospitality, and courtesy.

At noon the Committee received an official and very agreeable call from the municipal authorities, and regretted that their limited stay forbade their acceptance of the numerous invitations given them to partake the hospitalities of the city. The Corporation gratified them by accepting the invitation of the City of Boston.

The Quebec authorities then took the Committee to see the Citadel, Wolfe's Monument, the Plains of Abraham, and other objects of interest. On their way to the Citadel, they had an opportunity of witnessing part of the ceremony of "Guard Mounting." The review had just terminated, and as the guards broke off under their respective officers, and marched in various directions to the posts assigned them, they presented quite an animated and brilliant spectacle.

After passing through a long circuitous passage, with high walls upon each side, and with strongly fortified iron gates at each turn, they soon reached the heights of Cape Diamond, and were within one of the strongest fortresses in the world. The Citadel of Quebec was always a place of immense strength, and when it finally fell into the hands of the English, in 1759, after a seige of two months, it was by capitulation, and the works had received no injury.

In the afternoon the party, by invitation of the authorities, visited the celebrated Falls of Montmorenci, the ride to which is through a thickly settled agricultural district ; and on their return they were most hospitably and splendidly entertained at the mansion of Francis Xavier Paradis, Esq., City Councillor.

On Wednesday, August 20th, at 5 P. M., the Committee took the steamer to return to Montreal, where they arrived early on Thursday morning. They were visited at their hotel by members of the City Government, merchants, officers of the army, and professional gentlemen. The morning was devoted to the reception of these gentlemen, and to the completion of the correspondence connected with their mission in Canada.

Col. Horne, accompanied by several officers of the twentieth Regiment, most politely urged the Committee to remain and dine with the military gentlemen stationed at this place. This compliment was reluctantly declined, but an arrangement was made to visit the officers at their quarters, after the review, to partake of a collation.

At eleven o'clock, the Deputation, accompanied by the Mayor and several officers of the Corporation, visited the Champ de Mars, for the purpose of witnessing a review, which had been ordered out of respect to them. The troops were in line at the hour appointed. A detachment of the Royal Artillery was also upon the ground. After a few movements of the troops, Lieut. General Rowan, commander of the forces in British North America, arrived, accompanied by his Staff. He was very attentive to the Committee, and they were indebted to him for numerous favors. Gen. Rowan was in the battle of Waterloo, and, upon the parade ground, wore three medals which he had honorably earned. The review was very splendid, and was witnessed by a large concourse of people, who did not require either guards or police to keep them off the ground.

After the troops were dismissed, the Delegation, by invitation of the General, visited the island opposite Montreal, accompanied by the Montreal authorities, and explored the immense military storehouses, the extent and variety of the articles contained in which would surprise any one not familiar with the details of military expenditure. At the risk of encountering incredulity, one fact will be stated. Upon reaching the powder magazine, our party were supplied with moccasins for the purpose of passing through it. Some of the party declining to adopt the rule, which requires this precaution on account of occasional nails in boot heels, their military guide smiled, and stated that in case of accident, the nearest point of safety would be several miles distant. The quantity of powder stored in the magazine is upwards of five millions of pounds.

Immediately upon their return to the city, the Delegation visited the quarters of the officers of the twentieth regiment, where an elegant lunch was served. The display of porcelain and silver was very splendid; and nothing could exceed the brilliancy of the entertainment.

Upon their return to the hotel, the Committee found a large number of gentlemen waiting to escort them to the boat, on board of which they were to embark for home. When the boat left the quay, three hearty cheers were given for Boston and the Delegation. After an hour's sail across the river, the boat arrived at Laprairie, where the cars were taken for St. Johns. The party slept on board the steamer, and at six in the morning started for Burlington, and passed through a most beautiful region, the scenery of which is exceedingly varied and picturesque. The Delegation were accompanied from Montreal by Mr. H. D. Doane, the agent of the Rutland and Burlington Railroad. At Burlington they met Judge Follett, President of the road, who accompanied them to Bellows Falls, and by his courteous attentions rendered the ride a most agreeable one. The scenery along this route is magnificent. The train seems to pass through the mountains as if by magic—a new scene meets the eye at each moment, and every person who has once passed over this road must ever retain a pleasing remembrance of the extraordinary beauty of the Green Hills. At Bellows Falls, Mr. John S. Dunlap, the newly appointed Superintendent of the Rutland Road, joined the party, and accompanied them to Boston. Although the train was an hour late, owing to the detention of the steamer by adverse winds, it arrived at Keene at the usual hour. Between Bellows Falls and Keene, eight miles were travelled in ten minutes. The average speed during the day, over the Burlington and Rutland, Cheshire, Vermont and Massachusetts, and Fitchburg Roads, was thirty miles an hour, including stops. The officers of these roads were very polite and attentive to the Committee.

During their absence from Boston, the Committee travelled upwards of eighteen hundred miles, and had interviews with many hundred persons, in various walks of life. Though the labors of their mission were extremely arduous, far more so than would readily be conceived, yet they were rendered comparatively light by the courteous attention and frank hospitality with which the Committee were everywhere received; and they returned from Canada not only with the pleasing assurance that the primary object of their journey had been successfully accomplished, but with the delightful memory of the events of those few days deeply impressed upon their hearts.

As the time for the Jubilee approached, and it was known that the invitation extended to our friends in the British Provinces had been so cordially received, and that large numbers from other quarters would also be present, the general interest in the occasion became every day more obvious.

Mindful of the fact that, on all great occasions of public display, Boston had been accustomed to present the pupils of her schools as her brightest jewels, her especial pride, and that, without their presence, any display, however brilliant, would be incomplete, and fail to show the great fundamental element of her prosperity; the School Committee, in view of the contemplated celebration, unanimously adopted the following order, submitted by Francis Brinley, Esq., President of the Common Council:—

"*In School Committee, City Hall,*
Aug. 26, 1851.

Ordered, That Messrs. Wightman, Guild, Palmer, Tracy, and Thorndike be a Committee to confer with any Sub-Committee of the Joint Special Committee of the City Council on the proposed Railway Celebration, on the expediency of requesting the several grammar and primary schools to participate in the ceremonies of the occasion, with authority to make arrangements accordingly."

On Friday, September 5th, a large meeting of merchants was held at the Reading Room of the Exchange, for the purpose of taking measures to co-operate with the City Authorities in preparing for the celebration.

The meeting was called to order by Samuel Lawrence, Esq., and J. W. Paige, Esq. was chosen Chairman, and W. S. Eaton and Henry Lee, Jr., Secretaries.

J. Thomas Stevenson, Esq. made a brief address. He said that it was a matter of public knowledge that the city authorities, rightly appreciating the value of the social and commercial results which must flow from the completion of the great lines of railroad between this city and the Canadas, had proposed a public celebration of that event during three days of the present month. Not a three-days revolution, but a three-days rejoicing at the peaceful conquest which New England skill and New England enterprise have achieved over the barriers, which nature only seemed to have interposed between us and those whom we may now see, face to face, after a short and easy journey.

It is also well known that the Mayor of the City has extended numerous invitations to gentlemen, distinguished both in public and in private life, to be present and to participate in the festivities of that occasion.

This meeting had been called by a large number of our well known mercantile firms, at the suggestion of the Mayor, in order that all might co-operate in the proposed celebration, "to the end that it might be made in some degree commensurate with the importance of the events to be celebrated."

We all know that, in a country like ours, the constituted authorities cannot celebrate any event, as the citizens of Boston wish to see everything, that is good, celebrated, without the hearty co-operation of the people, whose agents they are.

A great number of persons will be here from the Canadas, and the cities of the lakes, and we have been called together for the purpose of making such arrangements as may be proper, that there may be extended to them the hospitality not only of our city, but of our houses and our homes. Many will be here for the first time. They are coming to see our city and its commercial advantages, both natural and artificial; and we all know how desirable it is to cultivate a personal acquaintance with those with whom we are about to open extensive commercial relations. There is always a satisfaction in having seen the countenances of those whom we trade with. It begets confidence, that great necessity of a commercial community. He rejoiced that so many guests were coming amongst us; many of them from inland cities and the shores of the lakes, for the first time in their lives to snuff the sea breeze, and to see where old Ocean kisses the continent, as he rests on the modestly ruffled bosom of our beautiful bay.

In the full assurance that the merchants of Boston would extend to them a cordial and a hearty welcome, and enable them, when they leave us, to say that their *lines* had fallen in pleasant places, he would offer the following resolutions:

Resolved, That the establishment of railroad communication between this city and the Canadas, and Great Lakes, is an event in which the commercial community is deeply interested, as it is calculated to work great and beneficial changes in the business relations of the people of both nations; and that as the advantages which must result from these new means of intercommunication will be mutual, it is a fit subject of mutual congratulation and a proper occasion for a common celebration.

Resolved, That the city government, having made the necessary arrangements for a proper celebration of the event by appropriate ceremonies to take place on the 17th, 18th, and 19th instant, it will be alike our duty and our pleasure to extend the right hand of fellowship and all hospitalities to those who may visit us on that occasion."

The Hon. Benjamin Seaver then rose and said:

MR. CHAIRMAN,—

I second the motion of my friend, Mr. Stevenson, and cordially respond to his appropriate remarks, and the resolutions offered by him. I am aware, sir, that it is not necessary that another word should be spoken to ensure the unanimous adoption of the motion, but I feel desirous of saying that this is no ordinary occasion to the merchants of Boston. That great consummation so long desired by us all, the final completion of the great lines of railway uniting our city with the Canadas and the great West, is of too much importance to us, and to Massachusetts, not to be celebrated in some public and appropriate way, and I think that our city authorities deserve our thanks for the manner in which they are preparing to notice this event. Our thanks, too, are especially due to His Honor, the Mayor, and to the Committee of Arrangements for their admirable address to our citizens, which embraces in so small a compass so much valuable and reliable information. Sir, I am sure that there will be a very general willingness manifested to co-operate with the City Government in carrying out the plan they have adopted. It is alike creditable to them and to us. Let us all, then, do what we can to render the anticipated visit of our Canadian friends interesting and pleasant to them. I hope that the resolutions will pass unanimously.

The question was then taken, and the resolutions were unanimously adopted.

Mr. Seaver then moved that the officers of the meeting be requested to communicate the doings thereof to the City Authorities, and to co-operate with them, in behalf of the merchants, in any measures which they might take for carrying out the contemplated celebration in a proper manner.

This motion was carried, and, on motion of Mr. Lawrence, the meeting then dissolved.

The general arrangements for the occasion had now been so far made, that, on the 8th of September, the City Government were able to make the following announcement:

CITY OF BOSTON.

GRAND RAILROAD JUBILEE.

ORDER OF ARRANGEMENTS.

The City Government announce the following as the proposed arrangements for celebrating the final completion of the great lines of railway communication between Boston, the Canadas, and the Great West, and the establishment of American lines of steamers between Boston and Liverpool.

The festivities will occupy *three days*, to wit :—the 17th, 18th and 19th of September.

Wednesday, September 17th. On this day the distinguished invited guests of the city will be received with appropriate honors, and escorted by a military body and the City Government to the houses provided for them.

In the afternoon of this day, the various public institutions of the city, and points of interest in its vicinity, will be visited, and the members of the City Government will devote the day in attention to their guests.

Thursday, September 18th. On this day there will be a grand excursion in Boston Harbor, and the various objects of interest therein will be visited. For this purpose, suitable steamers will be engaged and collations and music provided.

The shipping in the harbor will be decorated for the occasion.

Friday, September 19th. On the morning of this day there will be a civic procession, escorted by the Boston Brigade, the route and details of which will be announced hereafter. The children of the public schools will take a prominent part in the proceedings of this day.

In the afternoon, a banquet will be given by the City Government in honor of their invited guests, which will be held under a pavilion on Boston Common.

On the evening of this day, the public buildings of the city will be illuminated, and a display of fireworks made from various parts of the city and harbor.

Per order of the Committee of Arrangements,

JOHN P. BIGELOW, *Mayor.*

On the evening of Tuesday, September 9th, on the invitation of the City Committee of Arrangements, a large meeting of the mechanics and artizans of the city assembled at the City Hall, to decide upon the part they would take in the proposed procession on the 19th. The Hon. Jonathan Preston was called to the Chair, and Edward H. Brainard and J. W. T. Stodder appointed Secretaries. Sub-Committees, of two from each of the trades, and from the government of the Mechanics' Association, were chosen to confer with those engaged in the different branches of industry, for the purpose of arranging a procession to exhibit, not only specimens of mechanical work, but the processes by which they are manufactured. At a meeting of the Sub-Committees, held on the following evening and fully attended, it was ascertained that representations of twenty or more different branches of industry would appear in the procession of the 19th, with emblematical designs, and be accompanied by bodies of workmen; and a resolution was adopted, pledging the best efforts of all present, to make the mechanical exhibition as extensive and varied as the limited time would allow. A vote was also passed, to invite manufacturers and artizans from the neighboring cities and towns, to join in the display, and a committee of five was chosen to confer with the committee of the City Council. The meeting then adjourned, to meet at the same place on the next Friday evening, to hear the final reports of the various Sub-Committees. Many of the most influential mechanics of the city were present, and the proceedings of the meeting indicated that quite an imposing demonstration would be made by this important portion of the community.

On the same evening, a meeting of the Mercantile Library Association was also held, at which a circular from the committee of the City Council, inviting the Association to join in the intended procession, was read by the President. After brief, but eloquent speeches, by Messrs. George S. Blanchard and Charles G. Chase, a resolution was unanimously adopted, accepting the invitation, and requesting the Government of the institution to make all necessary arrangements for taking part in the ceremonies.

It was the universal and ardent desire of the citizens of Boston, that the President of the United States should honor the festival with his presence.

To the invitation extended to him by the City, he at first felt obliged, in consequence of the pressure of public duties, to return an undecisive answer, yet leaving room for the hope that circumstances might be such as to allow of his ultimate acceptance of it. To strengthen the assurances he had received of the pleasure, which a visit from him would confer, Francis Brinley, Esq., on the part of the City Government, proceeded to Washington, and the gratifying intelligence was received through him before the end of the week preceding the Jubilee, that the President had accepted the invitation, and, accompanied by a part, at least, of his Cabinet, would leave Washington for Boston in the early part of the ensuing week.

As soon as it was ascertained that the President had accepted the invitation of the City, a Committee of the General Court, acting under a resolve passed at its last session, in the hope that he might visit the Commonwealth during the current year, immediately adopted the necessary measures to give him a suitable reception.

The Committee consisted of the following named gentlemen, viz. On the part of the Senate: Henry Wilson, President; Charles T. Russell, of Suffolk; Edward L. Keyes, of Norfolk; Erasmus D. Beach, of Hampden; Alexander De Witt, of Worcester; Whiting Griswold, of Franklin; William A. Hawley, of Hampshire.

On the part of the House: Nathaniel P. Banks, Jr., of Waltham, Speaker; Caleb Cushing, of Newbury; Samuel H. Walley, of Roxbury; Ensign H. Kellogg, of Pittsfield; John Mills, of Springfield; James S. Whitney, of Conway; J. Thomas Stevenson, of Boston; John Branning, of Monterey; William Schouler, of Boston; John Milton Earle, of Worcester; Nathaniel B. Borden, of Fall River; Almerin L. Ackley, of Auburn; Everett Robinson, of Middleboro'; George O. Brastow, of Somerville; Sirson P. Coffin, of Edgartown.

Acting in conformity to the same Resolve, the Governor of the Commonwealth issued the following General Order:—

[OFFICIAL.]

COMMONWEALTH OF MASSACHUSETTS.

Head Quarters, Boston, September 15, 1851.

[GENERAL ORDER, NO. 9]

As by a resolve of the Legislature of this Commonwealth, at their last session, His Excellency the Governor was authorized and requested to tender to the President of the United States, if he shall visit this Commonwealth during the present year, the customary hospitalities and the respectful congratulations of the State; and as, by the same resolve, a Committee of the Legislature was authorized to make all suitable arrangements, in the name and behalf of the State, for the proper reception of the President; and as the said Committee, in the expectation that the President will visit this Commonwealth during the present month, has requested His Excellency, the Governor, to tender to the President a military escort, and to take such other measures as circumstances may render expedient and proper, to carry the intention of the Legislature into effect:

His Excellency, the Commander-in-Chief, orders that the following troops be hereby detailed for parade, escort, and review; and they will assemble on Boston Common on Wednesday, the 17th inst., at 9 o'clock, A. M.

The First Brigade, under command of Brigadier General Samuel Andrews.

Companies C, D, and G, of 4th Regiment of Light Infantry; Companies C, D, and E, 5th Regiment of Light Infantry; Companies B and C, 8th Regiment of Light Infantry—

To constitute a regiment, under the command of Colonel J. Durell Greene, of the 4th Regiment of Light Infantry, who will order his field and staff.

Companies A, B, E, and C, 6th Regiment of Light Infantry; Companies A, C, and I, 7th Regiment of Light Infantry; Company B, 5th Regiment of Light Infantry—

To constitute a regiment, under the command of Col. Nathan P. Colburn, of the 7th Regiment of Light Infantry, who will order his field and staff.

Company of Rifles, annexed to the 1st Regiment of Light Infantry, and company of Rifles G, annexed to the 5th Regiment of Light Infantry, to constitute a Battalion, under the command of Major William Saunders, of the 6th Regiment of Light Infantry.

Major Edmund A. Parker, of the 5th Regiment of Light Infantry, is detailed to act as Major of the regiment, under the command of Col. Greene.

The above two regiments of Light Infantry and Battalion of Rifles, will constitute a Brigade, under command of Brigadier General Henry Wilson, of the 3rd Brigade.

The whole to constitute a Division, under the command of Major General B. F. Edmands, who will report to Head Quarters for instructions.

The Divisionary Corps of Cadets of the 1st and 2nd Divisions, will constitute a Battalion under the command of Lieut. Col. Thomas C. Amory, who, with his command, will report at Head Quarters at 10 o'clock, A. M., on Wednesday, 17th inst.

Capt. John B. Sandford, of Company B, 4th Regiment of Artillery, is ordered to fire a salute on the arrival of the President at Fall River.

The Acting Quarter Master General will furnish commutation in money instead of rations.

All General and Field Officers, with their Staff, who are not detailed for duty, are requested to report themselves at Head Quarters, in uniform, not mounted, at 2 o'clock, P. M., in order to attend the Review of the troops. All officers and troops ordered for duty, named in the above order, will govern themselves accordingly, without waiting for the regular transmission of orders. Major Generals Sutton, Hobbs and Edmands will promulgate this order in their respective Divisions.

By command of his Excellency

Geo. S. Boutwell, *Governor,*
and Commander-in-Chief.

Ebenezer W. Stone, *Adjt. Gen.*

The President, accompanied by the Hon. Charles M. Conrad, Secretary of War, and the Hon. Alexander H. H. Stewart, Secretary of the Interior, left Washington on Monday for New York, where, on his arrival late in the evening, he was met by Alderman Holbrook and Francis Brinley, Esq., a Committee of the City Council of Boston, who were in waiting to receive him and escort him thence to Boston. After a short delay, the party went on board the steamer "Bay State," and reached Newport at 10 o'clock, A. M., on Tuesday. The Hon. William B. Lawrence, Lieutenant Governor of Rhode Island, and Acting Governor, had issued orders, directing an artillery company to fire a salute on the arrival of the boat, and to escort the President to his quarters at the Bellevue House. In the evening, a sub-committee of the joint Committee of the Massachusetts Legislature, consisting of the Hon. Edward L. Keyes, the Hon. Nathaniel P. Banks, Jr., and Col. William Schouler, and with them Lieut. Cols. J. T. Heard and Daniel Needham, Aides-de-Camp of the Governor, and the Hon. George Lunt, United States Attorney for this District, reached Newport. The Committee having been introduced to the President, and cordially received by him, Col. Schouler, on their behalf, addressed him as follows:—

SIR,—

The Legislature of Massachusetts, at its late session, in anticipation of a visit from the President of the United States, passed, by a unanimous vote, certain resolves, requesting his Excellency, the Governor, to tender to the President "the customary hospitalities and respectful congratulations of the State." A Committee, consisting of members of the Senate and House of Representatives was also appointed, "to make all necessary arrangements for the proper reception of the President." We have been sent upon this pleasant duty, and to make known to you these facts, and to assure you of the profound satisfaction which we feel, and which the people of Massachusetts feel, in this your visit to our State. We have come to conduct you to within our own borders, where you will be met by the other members of the Committee, and by thousands of patriotic and intelligent men, and warmly welcomed to Massachusetts; a State ever ready and desirous of extending her welcome and her hospitality, to those who "deserve," as you do, sir, "well of the Republic." The occasion which you are to honor with your presence, is one of deep interest to the people of Massachusetts. It is to mark the completion of a long chain of railroads, connecting the Canadas with Massachusetts, and the great Lakes with the Ocean, and the commencement of a line of steam vessels between the capital of New England and Liverpool. These form an epoch in the history of our State, from whence we hope to make an advance step in commercial and social prosperity, and thus add to the stability and the value of this great Union, by uniting in closer bonds the interests and affections of the people. Your presence among us at any time, would be to us most pleasant, and all would unite to do you honor; but you are doubly welcome to us now, as it will afford our people an opportunity of attesting, at one and the same time, their joy at this triumph of American skill and enterprise, and their high appreciation of one, who, by his wisdom and his virtue, has rendered illustrious the American name.

To this Address, the President replied, in substance, as follows:

SIR,—

For the invitation to visit the State of Massachusetts conveyed to me through you, and for the flattering terms, as unexpected as they are undeserved, in which that invitation has been expressed, permit me to return my sincere thanks.

You have alluded, sir, to the completion of the long lines of railway connecting the Canadas and the Great Lakes with Massachusetts and the Ocean, as one of the causes which have occasioned this invitation at this time. However gratifying it might be to me to come amongst you at any time, it is peculiarly so to be present at the celebration of such an event; for, I confess, I feel a deep interest in whatever is connected with the prosperity and the happiness of any part of our Common Country.

Massachusetts has done as much as any portion of the United States, to extend and multiply facilities for trade and intercourse; and I am glad, Sir, that she has now stretched forth her iron arms to the great West and the Canadas. Although I am not, Sir, in favor of annexation, in a certain sense of the term, (for I think we have already territory enough,) yet I am entirely in favor of all the means by which States and Countries can be bound together by ties of mutual interest and reciprocal commercial advantage.

You have also spoken, Sir, of the establishment of a line of American Steamships between your principal city and foreign ports. This too is a subject in which I take a deep interest. I rejoice in all measures which extend and increase our means of intercourse with foreign countries, and strengthen and enlarge our foreign commerce.

It must have been noticed that the great improvement which has taken place in our relations with one another, and with other countries, is owing principally to the rivalry between our great cities; and this is a generous rivalry.

New York, as you know, has already completed a great work, which extends her trade to the West; and, in whatever part of our land these enterprises are begun, we all feel a deep interest in their success, because they serve to multiply among us the resources of living, and, by giving us mutual interests and making us better acquainted with one another, they must strengthen the bonds by which we are joined together in common union.

Permit me, again, to thank the Governor and the Commonwealth of Massachusetts, for the kind invitation they have extended to me, and to assure you, Gentlemen, of the great pleasure I feel in accepting it.

Lt. Col. Heard, one of the Aides-de-Camp to the Governor, then addressed the President as follows:—

MR. PRESIDENT,—

His Excellency, the Governor of the Commonwealth of Massachusetts, having learned with pleasure that you contemplate visiting that State, has instructed us, a portion of his personal military Staff, to wait upon you at this place, and tender to you the congratulations and hospitalities of the Commonwealth. A part of the militia will be under orders, near and at the line of the City of Boston, to escort you to the lodgings which, he understands, the Authorities of that city have provided for you.

His Excellency has also instructed us to tender to you a review of the troops composing the escort, on Boston Common, at such hour as may be convenient to you. And he has directed us to attend you in person to the capital of the State, if that should meet your pleasure.

The President, in reply, accepted the invitations of the Governor, excepting that relating to a review of the troops, to which he hesitated to give a decisive answer at that time. But, upon its being represented to him that an early answer on this point was desirable, so that the troops might be kept under orders for the purpose, he promptly accepted this invitation also. He was then requested to state what would be his pleasure as to the manner in which he would make the review; whether in a carriage, on horseback, or on foot. He replied, "Not certainly in a carriage; it seems to me it should be done either on foot or on horseback: I think on horseback is the better way. I will review on horseback, provided I am sure of a good horse." The last remark was made jocosely and excited a general smile.

The President then introduced his visitors to his lady—remarking that she was prevented, by a temporary lameness, from rising to greet her guests. In a short time the interview terminated, and the President was then ushered into a beautiful ball-room, where a large number of the ladies of Newport were assembled to welcome him.

In the meanwhile, the City resounded with "the stirring notes of preparation," and every thing betokened the near approach of the long-expected day. The extreme beauty of the weather, the busy activity displayed in the decoration of the streets, the mustering of military companies, the throngs of strangers from all parts of the land,—every train bringing accessions of welcome visitors,—and the certainty that the President of the United States, and the Governor-General of Canada,* were on their way hither, all gave promise of a full realization of the most sanguine anticipations.

The Hon. Daniel Webster, the Secretary of State, though, on account of his health, unable to accept the invitation, (which had been extended to him personally by the members of the Committee of Invitation) to participate in the public festivities, had come to the City for the purpose of meeting the President, and of joining in the reception to be given him by the Commonwealth at the State House.

In the course of the day [Tuesday,] a telegraphic despatch was received by the Mayor, announcing that a large number of Canadians, including the City Authorities of Montreal, Toronto, Cobourg, and other places, were on their way to Boston. A Committee was forthwith deputed to receive the guests, and twelve carriages were despatched to the Lowell Railroad station, to convey them to their respective hotels. Lowell street was handsomely decorated in honor of the strangers, and the

* Lord Elgin had written to the Mayor from Niagara Falls, subsequently to his letter in the text, that he should arrive in Boston by the Western Railroad on the 15th. The operators of the Telegraph, at every principal point on the line, kept the Mayor advised of his Lordship's arrival at, and departure from, the same.

English and American flags, becomingly arranged in festoons, were displayed near the depot.

Among the many distinguished persons who had already reached the City were the following—viz.:

At the Revere House—The Hon. Daniel Webster; the Hon. H. H. Killaly, Assistant Commissioner of Public Works; Mr. Solicitor General McDonald; the Hon. Messrs. Justices Alwyn, Day, and Mondelet, of Montreal; Mr. Justice W. K. McCord, of Quebec; Col. B. C. A. Gugy, M. P. P.; N. Dumas, Esq., M. P. P.; W. H. Scott, Esq., M. P. P.; D. Ross, Esq., M. P. P.; D. M. Armstrong, Esq., M. P. P.; J. Scott, Esq., M. P. P.; W. McFarland, Esq., M. P. P.; H. Smith, Esq., M. P. P.; W. B. Richards, Esq., M. P. P.; Benjamin Holmes, Esq., member for the city of Montreal; A. Jobin, Esq., member for the county of Montreal; the Hon. S. Crane, of the Legislative Council; the Hon. John Molson, of Montreal; and the Hon. Francis M. Hill, Mayor of Kingston.

At the Winthrop House—the Hon. Charles Wilson, Mayor of Montreal; Aldermen A. McFarlane, J. Grenier, J. B. Homier, S. Benjamin, and P. Lynch, and Messrs. O. Frechette, N. S. Whitney, J. Leeming, J. B. Bronsdon, J. A. Montreuil, E. Lamarche, and E. Atwater, of the Council; Hon. Adam Ferrie, M. P. P.; J. P. Sexton, Esq., City Clerk; J. A. B. McGill, Esq., City Surveyor; Major H. Elwell, George Desbarats, Esq., Queen's printer, and Mr. Justice John McCord, of Montreal; and Major H. P. Bourchier, of Kingston.

At the Tremont House—the Hon. N. F. Belleau, Mayor of Quebec; Col. Horne and other officers of the 20th regiment of Infantry; Capt. the Hon. H. F. Keane; Lt. A. M. Chisholm, 42d regiment Royal Highlanders; Deputy Asst. Com. Gen. G. J. Webb; Senior Surgeon Chisholm, Royal Artillery; Dr. Maitland, Royal Rifles; Drs. Rutherford, and Barrett, Medical Staff—all of Canada; the Hon. E. Twisdton, of England; and the Hon. A. N. Skinner, Mayor of New Haven.

At the United States Hotel—Sir Allan N. MacNab; the Hon. James Colman, Mayor of Dundas; Lieut. Col. Cartier; Lieut. Col. Lelan; G. B. Lyon, Esq., M. P. P.; Mr. Sheriff E. C. Thomas; the Hon. Mr. Boulton, M. P. P.; A. Gauthier,

Esq.; the Hon. P. B. De Blaquiere, M. P. P.; Capt. Duvergny; Capt. Boulange; Lieut. Andy—all of Canada.

At the Pavilion—Major Jecklan, of Three Rivers; Mr. Wheelcott; Mr. J. R. Wright; W. B. Lindsey, Esq., Clerk of the Legislative Assembly—all of Canada.

During the evening, the Committee of Reception divided themselves into three parties,—one of which entertained the Mayor and City Council of Montreal at the Winthrop House; another, the Mayor of Quebec and Suite at the Tremont House, and the third, at the latter hotel, the officers of the 20th regiment.

Many of those who arrived in the late trains, unable to find accommodations at the public houses, which were now filled to overflowing, were entertained at private mansions, many of which had been hospitably thrown open for their reception.

The proprietors of the Athenæum notified the City Council that all the guests of the City, during the Jubilee, would be welcomed to that Institution; and the Horticultural Society, whose annual exhibition, always beautiful and attractive, was to take place during the week, extended a similar invitation.

All things were now ready for the opening day of the Jubilee, and, that the next morning's sun might rise in his loveliest smiles over the City, was the hope which filled all hearts, as his setting beams threw their "splendor of azure and gold" over the western skies.

FIRST DAY OF THE JUBILEE.

And the hope of the evening was realized. The morning of Wednesday, September 17th, was clear and bright, and at an early hour the streets of the city were alive with the bustle of preparation for the festivities of the day. Every thing betokened an auspicious beginning of the Jubilee.

The main features of this first day were the arrival of the President of the United States and his Suite, their reception by the City and State Authorities, and the Military Review on the Common.

After breakfast, at Newport, the President, accompanied by

the Secretaries of War and the Interior; the Hon. Mr. Bradley, of the Post Office Department; the Hon. Mr. Crampton, Charge d'Affaires of Great Britain at Washington; Francis Brinley, Esq., President of the Common Council, and Mr. Holbrook, of the Board of Aldermen, of Boston; Mr. Tallmadge, United States Marshal for New York; Mr. Devens, United States Marshal for Massachusetts; Mr. Borden, of Fall River; Mr. John O. Sargent, editor of the Washington "Republic," and the Legislative Sub-Committee, took the steamer "Canonicus" for Fall River. At that place, the following members of the Legislative Committee were waiting to welcome the Chief Magistrate to the soil of Massachusetts: Messrs. Henry Wilson, President of the Senate; Charles T. Russell, of Suffolk; Whiting Griswold, of Franklin; and William A. Hawley, of Hampshire, of the Senate; and Samuel H. Walley, of Roxbury; James S. Whitney, of Conway; J. Thomas Stevenson, of Boston; Almerin L. Ackley, of Auburn; and George O. Brastow, of Somerville, of the House.

At Fall River the shipping in the harbor had been decorated with flags, and, on the arrival of the "Canonicus" a national salute was fired by the troops. The President was then conducted on board the steamer "Empire State," where he was met by the Committee, and addressed by its chairman, the Hon. Henry Wilson, as follows:—

Mr. President,—

The Legislature of Massachusetts at its last session, as you have already been officially informed, with entire unanimity, passed a resolution requesting the Governor to tender to you, whenever you should see fit to visit us, the hospitalities of the Commonwealth. In compliance with that vote we are here to welcome you to Massachusetts, and to offer you a warm, cordial and enthusiastic greeting—in the name of her people—of her whole people. I welcome you, Sir, as the Chief Magistrate of the Republic, and assure you that you will receive from the people here the same cordial reception that they gave to your illustrious predecessors.

You, Sir,—a citizen of that great State which borders on our own—are not unfamiliar with our history, our character, or our institutions. You know the skill of our artizans, and you know that their prosperity has been achieved and maintained—not by the bounty or the protection of the government, but by their own educated, intelligent and free labor. You have heard of our common schools, where ingenuous youth first learn those lessons of obedience to the laws, and of respect for those principles of freedom and equality which lie at the foundation of our institutions. You are acquainted with the excellence of our charitable institutions, where the care-worn and weary sons and daughters of men find repose and shelter from the storms of life. We bid you welcome, Sir, to our Commonwealth, and trust that in your visit, you, and the distinguished gentlemen with you, who are your constitutional advisers, may receive, as you will all give, the highest gratification.

Your visit, Sir, is to us fortunate and agreeable, combined as it is with the celebration of the completion of a system of railroads which connects the Atlantic with our inland seas, and the dwellers on the seaboard with the teeming millions of the imperial West. The same system connects us with the Canadas, and it adds greatly to the pleasure of the occasion, that the authorities of those Provinces, with large numbers of their inhabitants, will be present at our celebration, a meeting with whom cannot but tend to cultivate harmony and sympathy of feeling between us, and to eradicate prejudices growing out of past events—a result, which, should they, in the Providence of God, cease to be a portion of the British Empire, would prepare them willingly to become an integral part of our ever-extending Republic.

Permit me, Sir, in conclusion, again to tender to you a respectful and cordial welcome to the State of Massachusetts, and to testify to you the personal regard and good wishes which each one of the Committee entertains towards you, and to assure you that the whole people of this State cherish an unwavering loyalty to the Union, the Constitution, and the great principles of liberty and equal rights for all men, and that amid the storms of free discussion, they have an unshaken confidence in the stability of our institutions, the maintenance of our republican government, and the ultimate triumph of the democratic ideas on which it was established.

To this address the President replied as follows:—

MR. CHAIRMAN AND GENTLEMEN OF THE COMMITTEE,—

This unexpected and cordial expression of your kind feelings towards me is highly gratifying, and is deeply appreciated by me. I feel that this enthusiastic welcome is not so much intended for me, as to do honor to the high office which it is my fortune to fill, and as such I receive it.

I regret, Gentlemen, that this is the first time I have ever visited this place;—all that I see around me is new to me. But,

Gentlemen, I know and I appreciate the character of the people of Massachusetts. I know well what they have done for our country, for liberty and for civilization, and I believe that nowhere else is there a deeper conviction that the blessings we enjoy are owing, mainly, to the constitution under which we live ; and that nowhere else is there a firmer determination to be faithful to the constitution. And this beautiful city before us, is, we all feel, indebted, for whatever makes it most delightful to look upon, to the intelligence and to the patriotism of its citizens, and to their faithful maintenance of law and order.

It was with great reluctance, and solely on account of my public duties, that I felt obliged at first to decline the invitation I received to visit Boston on this occasion. To my great satisfaction, however, I have since found it not inconsistent with public duty to accept that invitation, and the pleasure is greatly enhanced by meeting my fellow citizens of Fall River here to-day; and now, feeling grateful, Gentlemen, for the kind invitation extended to me by you on behalf of the State, I proceed to accept with pleasure the proffered hospitalities of your metropolis.

Permit me, Gentlemen, for myself and in behalf of those associated with me in the government, to thank you for the cordial and courteous greeting you have given us.

At the conclusion of the President's reply, he, with his Suite, was conducted by the Committee to a very handsomely decorated car provided for his reception by the Railroad Company, and in a few minutes the train was on its way to Dorchester. At Bridgewater and other stations the President was repeatedly cheered by the crowds who had gathered to greet his arrival. At about half-past ten o'clock, the train, drawn by the large locomotive "Hingham," which was decorated with flags and evergreens, reached the Harrison Square Station-house in Dorchester, where an immense multitude, on foot, on horseback, and in carriages, were waiting its approach. On alighting from the car, the President was warmly welcomed by the Hon. Marshall P. Wilder, Chairman of the Selectmen of the town, in behalf of its inhabitants. Mr. Wilder addressed him as follows : —

Mr. President,—

In behalf of the ancient town of Dorchester, I bid you welcome. In behalf of the County of Norfolk, the land of the Adamses, which has furnished its full share for filling the high office which you now sustain—in behalf of the people whose institutions have taught us to respect the laws and constitution of our country, and to unite together for the preservation of our glorious Union, I greet you. I am not permitted, sir, to occupy a moment of your time, and I again bid you a cordial—a right hearty welcome. Welcome. Welcome. Welcome.

To this salutation the President replied, and said:

Mr. Chairman and Citizens of Dorchester,—

For myself and in behalf of the gentlemen who accompany me on this excursion, I desire to tender to you our profoundest thanks for this cordial reception. I am happy—extremely happy—to meet you, Citizens of Dorchester, in view of those heights upon which your fathers stood in arms, and opened the way for the establishment of a constitution, which you at this day, I doubt not, are prepared to defend. This is consecrated ground, for here repose the ashes of one of the leaders of the Revolution.

I am greatly pleased, also, to witness this gathering of ladies, the beauty of Dorchester;—God bless them!

Again, Sir, permit me once more and most heartily to thank the citizens of Dorchester for this flattering reception.

At the conclusion of this brief address, the attentive silence which had been preserved during its delivery was broken by resounding cheers, and the firing of a national salute. Flags waved in the breeze from every eminence in the vicinity. The ladies—the beauty of Norfolk County—graced the occasion by a large attendance. They filled the windows, covered the hill-sides, thronged the balcony of the Mattapan Bank, and even made their appearance upon the roofs of the buildings in the immediate vicinity.

The National Lancers, Capt. T. J. Pierce, were present to do escort duty, and made a most brilliant appearance. They numbered one hundred and eleven strong, and were accompanied by the Suffolk Brass Band.

The railroad track and the different roads forming a junction with it were kept well sprinkled by the authorities of Dorchester; and, by the liberality of Enoch Train, Esq., the route from Dorchester to the Roxbury line had been watered in the morning, so that, although a bountiful supply of dust was furnished by the trampling of the hundreds of horses which preceded the carriages containing the distinguished visitors, the public had the satisfaction of knowing that a great deal more had been prevented from displaying itself.

The platform upon which the President alighted from the car was carpeted and adorned with evergreen, bunting, and other decorations, and by the side of it was the barouche appropriated for conveying him to the city. This carriage, furnished from Niles's stable, was exceedingly handsome, and was drawn by six elegant grey horses.

After a short delay, the President, accompanied by the Hon. Henry Wilson and two of Governor Boutwell's Aides-de-Camp, took his seat in his barouche, and in the next, which was drawn by four beautiful bay horses, and also furnished by Niles, were seated the Secretary of the Interior and the Secretary of War, accompanied by the Hon. Charles Devens, Jr., U. S. Marshal, and the Hon. Charles T. Russell.

Next followed some fifteen carriages, containing the members of the Legislative and Municipal Committees, and other gentlemen of distinction.

A detachment of the Lancers, twelve in number, mounted on fine grey horses, and commanded by Lieut. Smith, served as a body guard to the President.

The procession marched through Park street to Neponset Turnpike, up Adams street, over Meeting-House Hill, into Boston street, and through Mount Pleasant and Eustis streets, to the line of Roxbury. A very large number of vehicles of all descriptions, containing many of the good citizens of Dorchester and the neighboring towns, followed in the rear, and, along the whole route, the President was greeted with the most enthusiastic cheers, accompanied by the waving of thousands of handkerchiefs by as many fair hands—which he acknowledged by gracefully bowing alternately on either side. On Meeting-House Hill there was an array of nearly fifteen hundred of the school children of Dorchester, accompanied by their teachers and the School Committee, and formed in lines on either side of the street, so that the procession might pass between them. The children had their hats and bonnets neatly decorated with flowers and wreaths, and each school was designated by an appropriate banner. As the President passed the children, they seemed to vie with each other in uttering the loudest hurras. Many of the houses and most of the public buildings along the route, both in Dorchester and Roxbury, were gaily decorated with banners and other appropriate indications of the gladness with which the people welcomed their Chief Magistrate.

When the procession reached the line, on Eustis street, which separates Dorchester from Roxbury, there was a halt, and the distinguished guests were surrendered by the Dorchester authorities to those of Roxbury. The President and his associates were there addressed by His Honor, Mayor Samuel Walker, in a short and appropriate speech, as follows:

MR. PRESIDENT,—

In the name, and in behalf, of the citizens of Roxbury, I have the honor to tender to you a most hearty welcome to their city.

I congratulate you on your fortunate selection of this opportunity to visit the metropolis of New England—to join in the commemoration of the triumph of science and art over the obstacles of nature—to witness the mighty achievements of human industry, guided by intelligence, in levelling mountains, bridging seas, and thereby uniting nations in the closest bonds of interest and affection.

We make no attempt to vie with our sister city in an ostentatious display; we make no military parade; we present no scenes of historic interest for your inspection; but, Sir, we receive you with joy, and feel honored by your presence.

To these words of welcome and congratulation, the President returned the following reply:

MR. MAYOR,—

Permit me to return to you, and, through you, to the authorities and the people of Roxbury, my profound acknowledgements for this cordial reception. I cannot doubt its sincerity, when I see your streets lined with citizens and strewn with flowers, and meet the bright eyes of woman beaming kindly on me from every quarter.

I regret that the time is so brief that I cannot refer to the many interesting associations connected with the history of Roxbury. In reference, however, Sir, to your comparison of this city to your great neighbor, Boston, I may say, that, although you do not equal her in population, yet for beauty of scenery your city can hardly be surpassed; for miles my eyes have been delighted with the elegance of your country seats. But especially have I been delighted with the sight of the many happy youthful faces that remind me of your common schools, those nurseries of intelligence and virtue.

Permit me again, Sir, to thank you, for myself and in behalf of my associates, for your kind and cordial reception.

The column, now strengthened by the addition of a fine cavalcade of about three hundred of the citizens of Roxbury, proceeded to the Boston line amidst the most enthusiastic demonstrations of joy. Guns were fired, the bells rang loudly and merrily, and the air was rent with shouts of welcome to the President.

On the Neck, at a short distance from the Line, and awaiting the arrival of the President, were the Mayor of Boston, the Committee of Reception, and the guests of the city, attended by mounted Marshals, as follows:

Chief Marshal—Major General John S. Tyler. Aids—Major John C. Park, Col. Frederick W. Lincoln, Major Joel Scott, Major C. H. Appleton, Major Lewis W. Tappan, William H. Foster, Esq., Col. Enoch Train, Col. John L. Dimmock, B. E. Bates, Peter Butler, Jr., Ives G. Bates, Edward F. Hall, John D. W. Joy, Charles T. Savage, F. Lyman, Henry C. Lord, Pliny E. Kingman, J. B. Wheelock, E. Train, Jr., T. W. Pierce, D. W. Childs, Frederick A. Allen, Farnham Plummer, Stephen Rhoades, H. F. Blodgett, G. F. Train, Albert Bowker, Charles F. Lougee, Beza Lincoln, Granville Mears, J. M. Wightman, F. W. Lincoln, Jr., T. H. Leavitt, John P. Ober, Jr., J. B. Richardson, F. L. Winship, Charles E. Wiggin, W. H. Learnard, Jr., Alpheus Hardy, G. F. Woodman, F. G. Whiston, George Wheelwright, J. Russell Bradford, G. A. Batchelder, M. Field Fowler, H. W. Cushing, and H. L. Richardson.

At the same place, also, and drawn up in line, were the troops detailed by the Commander-in-Chief as an escort of honor to the President of the United States, and under the orders of Major General Edmands, from whose command the escort of Lancers had been detailed to receive the President at Dorchester.

DIVISION OF MASSACHUSETTS VOL. MILITIA,

Commanded by Maj. Gen. B. F. Edmands.

Lieut. Col. Francis Boyd, Division Inspector.
Maj. Benjamin C. Howard, Division Quarter Master.
Maj. Charles G. King and Maj. John L. Plummer, Aides-de-Camp.

The Division was composed of the following Brigades:—

FIRST BRIGADE,

Commanded by Brig. Gen. Samuel Andrews.

Maj. P. Stearns Davis, Brigade Inspector.
Capt. Daniel Sharp, Jun., Brigade Quarter Master.
Capt. Henry C. Brooks, Aid-de-Camp.
William Baker, Jun., Acting Aid-de-Camp.

The first Brigade was composed of a corps of Cavalry, the National Lancers, the 5th Regiment of Artillery, and the 1st Regiment of Light Infantry

FIFTH REGIMENT OF ARTILLERY,

Commanded by Col. Robert Cowdin.

Lieut. Col. Henry W. Usher. Maj. Caleb Page.
Lieut. Frederick A. Heath, Quarter Master.
Dr. Charles E. Buckingham, Surgeon's Mate.

Boston Artillery,	Company	A,	Capt.	Thomas H. Evans.
Columbian "	"	B,	"	Elijah Thompson.
Washington "	"	C,	"	William W. Bullock.
Roxbury "	"	D,	"	Moses H. Webber.

FIRST REGIMENT OF LIGHT INFANTRY,

Commanded by Col. Charles L. Holbrook.

Lieut. Col. John C. Boyd. Maj. James A. Abbott.
Lieut. Thomas E. Chickering, Adjutant.
" T. Lewis Robinson, Quarter Master.

Boston Light Infantry,	Company	A,	Capt.	Ossian D. Ashley.
New England Guards,	"	B,	"	Josiah P. Bradlee.
Pulaski Guards,	"	C,	"	Albert J. Wright.
Boston Light Guard,	"	D,	"	George Clark, Jun.
City Guards,	"	E,	1st Lt.	David Pulsifer, Com'g.
Boston Fusileers,	"	F,	Capt.	William Mitchell.
Washington Light Guard,	"	G,	"	Thomas Savory.
Winthrop Guard,	"	H,	"	William C. Cassell.

Norfolk Guard,	Company I,	Capt. Abijah S. Merriam.
Mass. Volunteers,	" L,	" Jeremiah B. Moore.
Warren Infantry,	" M,	1st Lt. Rob't C. Nichols, Com'g.
National Lancers,		Capt. Thomas S. Pierce.

A BRIGADE,

Commanded by Brig. Gen. JOSEPH ANDREWS.

Maj. D. Goodwin Lang, Brigade Inspector.
Capt. Francis W. Bigelow, Brigade Quarter Master.
Capt. J. G. Chase, Aid-de-Camp.
Lieut. John G. Willis, and
Nehemiah Brown, Jun., Acting Aides-de-Camp.

This Brigade was constituted for the occasion, and embraced two Regiments of Light Infantry and a Battalion of Rifles.

A REGIMENT OF LIGHT INFANTRY,

Commanded by Col. J. DURELL GREENE.

Lieut. Col. Horace Williams. Maj. Edmund A. Parker.
Lieut. N. A. M. Dudley, Adjutant.
" Samuel J. Ladd, Quarter Master.
Lieut. Josiah Porter, Paymaster.
Dr. Henry B. C. Greene, Surgeon.
William A. Allen, Quarter Master Sergeant.

LIGHT INFANTRY.

Comp.	C, 4th Regt.	(Cambridge City Guards)	Capt.	Geo. A. Meacham.
"	D, " "	(Charlestown City Guard)	"	Geo. P. Sanger.
"	G, " "	(Woburn Phalanx)	"	Wm. T. Grammar.
"	C, 5th, "	(Lowell Phalanx)	"	Thos. G. Farmer.
"	D, " "	(Lowell City Guards)	"	Swan L. Lesure.
"	E, " "	(Acton Davis Guards)	"	W. E. Faulkner.
"	B, 8th "	(Worcester Light Inf.)	"	Edward Lamb.
"	C, " "	(Worcester City Guards)	"	John M. Goodhue.

A REGIMENT OF LIGHT INFANTRY,

Commanded by Col. NATHAN P. COLBURN.

Lieut. Col. Thomas A. Parsons. Maj. Solon Dike.
Lieut. Henry Merritt, Adjutant.
" George O. Carpenter, Quarter Master.
" William H. P. Wright, Paymaster.
Dr. Josiah Norcross, Surgeon.

Salem Light Infantry,	Comp. A, 6th Lt. Inf.,	Capt.	Wm. C. Endicott.
Salem Mec. Lt. Inf.	" B, " " "	"	Benj. R. White.
Marblehead " "	" C, " " "	"	Jos. Gregory.
Beverly " "	" E, " " "	"	Jos. W. Hildreth.
Winchester, " "	" A, 7th, " "	"	Fred. O. Prince.
Stoneham, " "	" C, " " "	"	Lyman Dike.
* Lawrence " "	" I, " " "	"	Jos. M. Dodge.

BATTALION OF RIFLES,

Commanded by Major William Saunders.

Jesse B. Edwards, Adjutant.

Mech. Riflemen,	(annexed to 1st Lt. Inf. Reg't.,)	Capt.	S. G. Adams.
Marlborough Rifle,	" 5th " " "	"	Daniel Pope.

FOR SALUTE DUTY ON 17TH OF SEPTEMBER.

Fall River Artillery,	Com. B, 4th Artillery,	Capt.	John B. Sandford.
Charlestown "	" D, 1st "	"	Ezra G. Huntley.

The troops were accompanied by numerous and well appointed bands, including all those belonging to the city, and a large number from other places.

The Mayor and his Suite were drawn up on the east side of Washington street, while the west was occupied by the long line of troops composing the escort.

The scene which was presented to the eye, at the moment (12 o'clock), when a discharge of artillery announced that the President had reached the line, was singularly beautiful and imposing, and perhaps in no part of the City could a spot have been selected, so well adapted, as that, to give effect to the ceremony which was about to be performed. Commencing at the line, a broad avenue, lined on either side by a row of noble elms, stretches down towards the heart of the City, in which direction, the view from a gentle elevation in the avenue near the line, is unbroken for more than half a mile, when a graceful curve terminates the vista.

* Company B, of the 5th Regiment of Light Infantry, "the Pepperell Light Infantry," was represented by its Captain, George Thomas Bancroft, its 1st Lieutenant and Orderly Sergeant. The privates did not receive notice of the "Order" in season to appear.

Stretching across from tree to tree or from house to house, gay lines of flags were floating in the breeze, while the ample sidewalks were thronged with the crowds who had eagerly assembled to see and to welcome their President. A wide space in the centre of the avenue, flanked, on the one hand, by the train of carriages containing the authorities and the guests of the City, and, on the other, by the military companies composing the escort, was kept open; and towards this now approached the President with his Suite, escorted by the Lancers, with their bright uniforms, glancing spears and floating pennons. Having advanced, amid the pealing of cannon, the shouts of the multitude, the waving of handkerchiefs, and the inspiring sounds of martial music, within the line of the escort, the troops gave the military salute, and the President's barouche was drawn up by the side of that in which the Mayor was seated.

The Hon. Henry Wilson, President of the Senate, who was in the President's carriage, now rose, and presented the President to Mr. Mayor Bigelow, who welcomed him to the City in the following appropriate and eloquent manner:—

SIR,—

The people of Boston now crowd her gates to receive, with tokens of honor, the great head of the Republic, and, in their name, I bid you welcome to this metropolis. We regard it as a happy omen that we receive you on the spot where our fathers gathered to hail the coming of Washington, in the first year of his presidency. The contrast exhibited, between that period and this, is striking and instructive. The salutations extended to the first President were the offering of only eighteen thousand inhabitants, —the welcome, tendered to his successor this day, is the voice of a population of one hundred and forty thousand. The ruler, who was then received, administered the affairs of less than four millions of people, who had but lately emerged from the smoke of battle for independence, and were just beginning, under the auspices of liberty and union, to take rank among the nations of the earth. You, Sir, we acknowledge as the Executive Chief of a population of twenty-five millions, living in the enjoyment of an amount of prosperity and happiness, almost unparalleled in the history of the world.

By a remarkable coincidence, which doubtless has occurred to yourself, you visit us on the anniversary of the completion of the

Federal Constitution. It is a day peculiarly fitting for our reception of him, whose authority as the Federal Chief Magistrate, is derived from that great compact. The day has also a special interest for this city,—for it is the anniversary of its settlement. While the occasion thus calls to mind the Philadelphia conclave and the Pilgrim colony, I trust that you will recognize in the character of our citizens and their institutions, the happily blended influences of the puritan and the patriot.

You have recently visited Virginia, and now stand upon the soil of Massachusetts. The names of those States recall the story of the Revolution, and the patriotic part, sustained by each of them in its momentous scenes. Your reception in the Old Dominion indicates her fealty to the Union, and the principles on which it rests. This day will furnish evidence of the fidelity of the Bay State, also, to that Union, and those principles, by the manner in which her people will testify their regard for the faithful administrator of the Constitution and the Laws.

It has been the custom of war, Sir, for the inhabitants of captured cities to bring forth the keys and lay them at the victor's feet. We greet your approach with a nobler tribute than was ever proffered to conciliate a conqueror's mercy. The hearts of our people are here, to welcome their civic father, with grateful and affectionate respect, to the homes and firesides of his children. [Enthusiastic cheering.]

To this address the President replied in substance as follows:—

Mr. Mayor,—

I receive from you, as the executive organ of this proud City, this welcome to me and my associates, with profound gratitude and emotion.

You have alluded to the fact, that this is the anniversary of the day on which the Constitution was completed, and you have also alluded to the visit of General Washington to this City. What a change has taken place since the time when he *first* visited this City, not for the purpose of receiving the cordial congratulations of her citizens, but for that of defending her against the great and then adverse power of the mother country. If my memory serves me aright, that son of Virginia, he who connected the fate of that State with yours, when appointed, at Philadelphia, Commander-in-Chief of the armies of the United Colonies, set out forthwith from that place for the seat of war. History tells us that he travelled from Philadelphia to this vicinity in eleven days, and that on his arrival the good people of Watertown gathered together and congratulated him on the speed of his journey.

What has brought about this change? Why is it that the distance which it took him eleven days to travel over, and that, too, when a most critical state of affairs called for the utmost speed, has now been passed over by me, as a matter of pleasure, in almost as many hours? It is owing, in great part, to the intelligence of your citizens, who have also opened avenues of commerce to the western world, which is now, through them, pouring into your lap her rich treasures. You have stretched, too, your Briarean arms to the capital of my own State, and laid her under contribution, and have now reached even to the Canadas, and made them also contributors to your still increasing wealth.

These evidences of civilization and intelligence, the greeting which I have everywhere received since I stepped upon the borders of your State, and the welcome now so cordially extended to me by this City, convince me, that the Constitution which received its fiat at the hands of Washington, on the 17th of September, in the year 1787, will, at this day, be maintained by you, at all hazards and at every sacrifice. [Loud, long-continued, and enthusiastic cheering.] I not only see in the intelligence of your citizens the moral power, but I see, in the troops before me,—a military display of which Boston may well be proud,—the physical force to accomplish this purpose. [Cheers.]

It only remains for me, Sir, to repeat my sincere thanks for the kind and flattering reception you have extended to me and to my associates.

Upon the conclusion of his address, the President took a seat in the open barouche of the Mayor,—who alone rode with him during the march of the procession. The carriage was then driven back to the head of the escort, so as to give the President a favorable opportunity to view the military. By this move, which drew the spectators up towards the Roxbury line, the column of our citizen soldiery was thrown more open to the inspection of Col. Horne, and a large number of other officers of the British army; who, dressed in their brilliant uniforms, accompanied the Mayor, and attracted great attention. The division next countermarched before the President, and then the line of march was taken up. The route was down Washington street, through East Dover street, to Harrison avenue, down Harrison avenue, through Beach to Lincoln street, and through Summer, Washington, and Court streets, to the Revere House. Throughout this whole distance a dense crowd lined the streets, and the President was greeted with the heartiest cheers. Every window and balcony commanding a view of the procession was filled with ladies and children, and the roofs of the houses were covered with men. Streamers were stretched across the streets, flags were floating at every turn, the eye could find no rest from the incessant waving of white handkerchiefs, and the whole route was in the highest degree bright and gay with the emblems of rejoicing.

To notice all the decorations which gave to the streets, through which the procession passed, such a joyous aspect, would now be almost impossible, as a record of the more prominent ones only has been preserved. All, however, were characterized by good taste, and each, however unpretending, contributed something to the general beauty of the display. The following imperfect description may serve, nevertheless, to give some idea of the reality.

At Harrison Square, in Dorchester, the place where the President and Suite alighted from the cars, there was a fine display of banners, streamers and emblematic devices. On one side of the railroad was erected a scaffolding and frame work, covered with an awning and ornamented with tastefully festooned streamers and rosettes of evergreen. The depot was surmounted by the Stars and Stripes, and other handsome decorations. Stretched from the depot to the house and flagstaff opposite, was a rich display of American flags, and across the street a flag bearing the word "UNION."

Leaving the Square, the first object that greeted the eye was a handsome arch erected across Park street, bearing the words, "WELCOME GUEST." In its centre was a very pretty wreath of flowers, and the pillars of the arch were wound around with streamers and bands of oak leaves.

On Eustis street, Roxbury, over the beautifully situated mansion of John S. Sleeper, Esq., editor of the Journal, floated a large American flag, and in front of his tasteful grounds were erected temporary platforms, which were occupied by a large delegation of the fair daughters of our sister city.

Many other houses attracted particular notice for the neat and tasteful arrangements of the various standards which floated from the windows. Long and brightly colored streamers hung in graceful festoons from the buildings, and had a fine effect.

Passing down Washington street, the residence of D. Hamlin, Esq., presented a striking appearance. A line of beautiful flags was thrown across the street, and the columns in front of the house were entwined with streamers.

The house of Dr. Willard, fronting on Blackstone square, in which the fountain was in full play and glittering in the sun, was handsomely dressed with a variety of tasteful ornaments.

Immediately below, on Washington street, the house of Mr. Lougee was ornamented with streamers and pennons, and a line of flags was run across the street, embracing the Union Jack, and the American colors, and between both, the inscription—

WELCOME! PRESIDENT FILLMORE!

At the house of Mr. David Pulsifer, a golden eagle held in his beak long streamers, a large American flag floated from one of the windows, and graceful festoons and gay pennons waved over the balustrades.

The buildings of Isaac Cary, Esq., and Mr. John M. May, were ornamented with much taste. Flags were suspended across the street, and upon the building of Mr. Cary, decked with streamers, was the inscription—

PRESIDENT FILLMORE—THE PRESIDENT OF THE NATION, AND NOT OF A PARTY.

On the balustrade was displayed the motto—

IN OUR UNION IS OUR STRENGTH.

At the corner of Dover street and Harrison avenue, a line of flags was suspended across the street, and a large single flag was displayed by Major Frederick K. Tyler. The view, on turning into Harrison avenue, was very animating. Here, as on the other streets, crowds filled the sidewalks, and gave a lively appearance to the scene. Mr. Silas Allen displayed a full length portrait of Washington, with the legend, "SACRED TO LIBERTY!" Three large flags, French and

American colors, were suspended across the street, the centre banner bearing the words—

"WELCOME! OUR PRESIDENT!"

The house of P. E. Gay, Esq., was adorned with a portrait of the Goddess of Liberty, and an array of banners and streamers joined the sides of the avenue. The motto—

ON EARTH PEACE AND GOOD WILL.

was displayed from one of the upper windows.

On the building of Mr. Warren, No. 8, Harrison avenue, was an emblematic portrait of Justice, while the usual line of flags was suspended across the front. Underneath, and on the house was inscribed,—

ANGLO-SAXONS.

From the Armory of the Boston Light Infantry, on Washington street, was suspended the American flag, bearing, on one side, the name, and the date of the organization, of the company—and on the reverse, its ever memorable motto,—

"DEATH OR AN HONORABLE LIFE."

The China Tea Store was finely decorated with a large number of flags and streamers. Partridge & Co. displayed a large American flag. Mr. James H. Foster stretched a line of colors across the street. The flag of the Whig Reading Room next met the eye, bearing upon it the names of "WINTHROP and GRINNELL." The store of Mr. Armington, merchant tailor, was very tastefully ornamented. From the upper windows of the building at the corner of State and Washington streets, were exhibited a number of small and neat American flags. The office of the "Commonwealth" newspaper was decorated in a similar manner.

Passing up Court street, from "Thompson Hall," the Armory of the City Guards, near the head of Hanover street, were displayed several lines of flags and streamers.

The route ended at the Revere House, where was seen one of the finest displays of the occasion. From the flagstaff on its lofty roof floated, together, the Stars and Stripes and the Union Jack. From each corner of the main building was displayed an American flag. The portico in front was trimmed with excellent taste. From each corner was suspended, in graceful festoons, the English and French flags, meeting in the centre the Stars and Stripes, which overhung the others as if to bind them together in close embrace. Small flags were displayed from other parts of the building. From the house, across to the Bowdoin Square Church, was thrown a line of flags, embracing those of England, France, and the United States. The latter bore the inscription—

"Of one Blood, all Nations."

And on the reverse,

"Peace shall Preserve what Liberty Bequeathed."

Along the entire route, as the eye glanced down the streets on each side, it was greeted with the sight of flags and streamers, intermingled in many instances with the green foliage of the trees, and making with them a most exhilarating show.

On the arrival of the column at the Revere House, at half past two o'clock, the President was received by a battalion of Cadets, detailed by the Commander-in-Chief to attend as a guard of honor at the quarters of the President, and under the command of Lieut. Col. Thomas C. Amory. The battalion consisted of—

First Division—Boston Independent Cadets, Lieut. Col. Thomas C. Amory.

Second Division—Salem Independent Cadets, Capt. Samuel B. Foster.

The President was then escorted to his quarters by Mr. Mayor Bigelow, and introduced to the members of the Board of Aldermen and of the Common Council. The military escort was then dismissed until the hour fixed for the review on the Common. Large delegations from Salem, Lowell, Cambridge, and Charlestown, were presented to the President, and invited him to visit those cities.

The demonstrations of welcome, made from the Revere House and other buildings upon Bowdoin square, on the arrival of the President, were of the most enthusiastic character. The windows were bright with smiling faces, and the Square and every avenue leading to it closely packed with a thronging multitude. Deafening cheers went up continually from that mass of men, while the noiseless welcome of women everywhere greeted the eye, and the President gracefully and heartily acknowledged both.

At the Revere House, the President met the Hon. Daniel Webster, Secretary of State, who had come from his farm at Marshfield, (where he was making his usual summer visit) for the purpose of meeting President Fillmore and his associates in the Cabinet, on this occasion.

After the reception of His Excellency, George S. Boutwell, Governor of the Commonwealth, the President and the members of his Cabinet were escorted to the rooms of the State and City Committees, and there partook of a collation provided by those Committees.

At half past three o'clock, the President and Suite and the Legislative Committee left the Revere House, and, escorted by the Independent Cadets of Boston, and the fine company of the same name belonging to Salem, proceeded to the State House.

The galleries and the body of the House of Representatives were filled to overflowing long before the arrival of the President. Seats had been reserved for the President and Suite, for the Governor and Council, and for the Legislative Committee of Arrangements. In the body of the House were many of the Overseers, and members of the Faculty, of Harvard University, officers of the Army and Navy, and many distinguished citizens of our own and other States.

At a quarter before four o'clock, the Governor and Council entered the Hall, and took the places which had been assigned to them. The cheering, outside, now indicated the President's approach, and in a few minutes he entered, accompanied by Mr. Webster, Mr. Stuart, Mr. Conrad, and the Legislative Committee. The audience rose to receive them. As soon as silence was restored, General Wilson presented the President to Governor Boutwell, who addressed him as follows :—

Mr. President :—

It is my agreeable duty, in accordance with the unanimous vote of the Legislature, and in the name of the people of Massachusetts, to tender to you a generous welcome to the territory and the hospitalities of this Commonwealth.

And we wish to extend to those distinguished sons of other States who are associated with you in the administration of the national government an equal welcome. Nor will we forget, on this occasion, to welcome and honor him whom Massachusetts has honored through a large part of her constitutional history.

The words of welcome are upon my lips, but the sentiment is in the hearts of the people.

They respect the purity of your private life ; they appreciate the duration, variety and elevated character of your public services ; and, finally, they welcome you as the chief magistrate of the American republic.

We invite you to a more intimate acquaintance with the people of Massachusetts—to an examination of their mechanical and manufacturing skill and success, and to a nearer view of their commercial and agricultural resources and power.

We shall gladly open to your inspection our institutions of different orders for the reformation of the guilty—our asylums for the care and restoration of the deaf, the dumb, the blind, and the insane—our schools, academies, and colleges, established and maintained for the education of the whole people.

And especially do we desire to direct your attention to the system of railways, whose net-work has been spread over Massachusetts and New England within the last twenty years.

We trust that you will see, in that system, not only evidence of past accumulation of wealth, but also clear indications of future growth and prosperity.

Nor shall we attempt to conceal from you the darker side of our character : for the poor, the ignorant, and the vicious are still found amongst us.

But we desire to assure you, that, on this occasion, we forget all names and distinctions, but the honorable one of *American citizens ;* that in the future, as in the past, Massachusetts will prove true to the Constitution and the Union ; that she will know no North, no South, no East, no West, but only the Republic, one and indivisable.

And for yourself, Sir, allow us to hope that your public life may be agreeable to you and beneficial to the country—and that in your hours of retirement you may enjoy the usual rewards of a virtuous, private and public, career.

President Fillmore replied as follows:

Governor of Massachusetts,—

Under no circumstances could I have received such a welcome as this through the executive head of this great State, without feeling the deepest emotions of gratitude. From the moment I reached the borders of your State, I have every where met with a welcome which I could not have anticipated.

You have said, Sir, that your institutions of every kind are open to the inspection of myself and of those associated with me. It is a gratification to me to be permitted to look into the institutions of this State, the most flourishing, perhaps, of any in the Union. You have said, Sir, that Massachusetts is prepared to sustain the Constitution and the Union. Sir, as I passed through this city and saw its streets lined for miles with a dense multitude of people, and witnessed the perfect order that every where prevailed, I could not for a moment believe that this community, though often excited, could ever be brought to commit treason against the United States. [Applause.]

Sir, it has been my duty,—sometimes a painful one,—to execute the laws of the Union upon those who did not approve of them. This must inevitably be the case with all who occupy the position which I now hold. But, Sir, I see manifested in the faces of this intelligent community that which assures me, that so far as this City is concerned, and I believe so far as this State is concerned, this duty, however painful it may be, may hereafter be performed with ease. [Applause.]

Sir, I congratulate you on the proud distinction your State has acquired from the prosecution and completion of her great works of internal improvement. You have stretched out your railroads to the North and invited her Commerce; and she is now pouring her tribute into your lap. May you and those associated with you long live to enjoy this rich blessing. You have taught your sister States that although you do not possess the power of inviting commerce by canals, you can yet stretch forth your iron arms, reach the remotest cities of the Union, and bring hither their wealth and their productions.

Sir, it does not become me to express for them the emotions of those who accompany me. They can speak for themselves far better than I can speak for them. Permit me, however, in conclusion, to say that I receive this testimony of respect from the City of Boston and the State of Massachusetts not so much as a testimony of respect to myself, as an evidence of their devotion to our Union and to our glorious Constitution, and of their determination to maintain them. [Loud and prolonged cheers.]

As soon as the President had concluded his remarks, Mr. Webster was presented to the Governor by Benjamin Stevens, Esq., Sergeant-at-Arms. He was greeted with great cheering by the audience, and spoke as follows:

MAY IT PLEASE YOUR EXCELLENCY,—

This occasion is not mine. Its honors or its duties are not due to, or from me. The State, the great State, the old State, the old patriotic Bunker Hill and Faneuil Hall State of Massachusetts, has invited the President of the United States within her borders. To your honored person, and to your honored office, may it please your Excellency, this visit is paid. Nevertheless, I am a good deal touched by your Excellency's allusion to me and to the length of my public service.

As I have said, Sir, the occasion belongs to the President, and to those of his Cabinet who are strangers. Thank God, I am no stranger here. [Applause.] I am of Massachusetts—bone of her bone, and flesh of her flesh, [cheers] and I would rather rejoice in taking a part with you, may it please your Excellency, as the Governor of the State, and my fellow citizens who surround you, in paying honor to the President of the United States, than in acting any part, or in demanding any part, toward myself. [Cheers.]

And, may it please your Excellency, I wish, in the first place, to say that, from the bottom of my heart, I wish entire success to your administration of the great affairs of this State. Into whosesoever hands these affairs may fall, if they are fairly and impartially administered, those hands shall have my hand in their support and maintenance. [Applause.]

In the next place, I wish to say that I devoutly wish that the great interests of the Commonwealth may prosper. Our interests are various. They are complex. We have a million of people living on a very small surface—on a sterile soil, and beneath an inclement sky; and yet we are full of happiness, and all are, as we say in the country, "well-to-do in the world, and enjoying neighbor's fare." [Cheers.] Now, that must be owing to wise legislation. It must be owing to great economy and prudence among the people. It must be owing to a system of education. It must be owing to something that is not in the earth, nor in the sky, but in the soul and heart of man, woman and child. [Renewed cheers.] And these, I hope, will prosper.

I not only hope that every local concern of this great Commonwealth, under your administration, and those of your successors, may prosper, but above all, *above all*, a sentiment I can never repress, and hardly postpone, my ardent prayer is, that this whole country, bound together as it is by ties of interest, of affinity, of association, may continue to be so bound forever. Those ties can never be broken until that thing shall happen, which I trust will never happen, under God's blessing, until the Constitution of the country shall prove a curse to it. [Prolonged applause.] Never! *Never!* NEVER!

Why, what is it that supports all these interests? What is it? Here is a mass of commerce. Who protects it? Here is a vast interest in manufactures. What protects it? Here is a coasting trade running from Newburyport round to California. Who protects it? What laws? What government? In short, wherever we turn our eyes, we see that this State is not only an agricultural State, but a commercial State, a manufacturing State, a State mixed up with all the interests that belong to society; and beyond all these visible and demonstrable interests, there are a vast many Yankee notions besides; with all these we live under the laws of the general government, and should perish if those laws were abrogated. [Applause.]

Sir, you have alluded to the period in which I have passed some part of my life in the administration of the affairs of the country. The years of human life wear away, Sir. I shall perform such services for no such other length of time. But with every increasing year, and day, and hour, the more I contemplate *the history of this country, the great destiny of this country, the* more I see it and behold it, as stretching from sea to sea, and from the rivers to the ends of the earth, the more I see it exhibit the American genius at home and abroad, the more I see what exhibitions of skill have astonished Europe in this our day, and in this our summer, the more I am surprised and gratified. Why, Sir, the bitterest, ablest, and most anti-American press in all Europe, within a fortnight, has stated that, "in every thing valuable, in every thing that is for human improvement, exhibited at the World's Fair, the United States go so far ahead of every body else as to leave nobody else in sight." It is like the position of Jove among the gods. Jove is first and there is none second. And in another paper, of much influence in the councils of Great Britain, the editor says, "The time is coming" (he might almost have said, "and now is,") "when America shall command the ocean, and both oceans, and all oceans." This results partly from the skill of individuals, partly from the untiring ingenuity of the people, and partly from those great events which have given us the ocean of one world on one side, and the ocean of the other world on the other. They appear to have filled the minds of men with astonishment. It has brought to my mind an incident in the life of an eminent Bostonian, not now living, Mr. John Lowell. He was an ardent admirer of the achievements of the American

Navy, and perfectly enthusiastic in regard to the extent to which the naval power of the United States might be carried. After the war of 1812 he was in England, and, dining with some friends, he gave utterance, in a playful manner, to his high and almost unbounded hopes and expectations on this point. One of the gentlemen said, "Well, Mr. Lowell, your country may, for aught I know, reach that height of elevation which you predict, but I trust we Europeans may yet be able to cross the seas." "Certainly," replied Mr. Lowell, with such promptitude and facetiousness of manner as to set the table in a good tempered roar, "certainly, Sir, certainly, but do not wonder if some day you shall hear us say, 'by our leave, Gentlemen.'" [Applause.]

May it please your Excellency, I hope that all health, happiness and prosperity will attend you henceforward through life. [Enthusiastic cheers.]

The Hon. C. T. Russell then presented to the Governor the Hon. Alexander H. H. Stuart, the Secretary of the Interior, who was warmly received, and made the following remarks:

May it please your Excellency,—

The very complimentary manner in which you have been pleased to allude to my friend on my left (Mr. Conrad) and myself, seems to demand at our hands a word of response and of thanks. I tender to you, Sir, my most cordial acknowledgments for the welcome you have given us. This, Sir, is the first time that my foot has ever rested on the soil of New England. [Hear, hear.] But I trust, Sir, it will not be the last. [Applause.]

I have seen to-day many things to admire, and which have afforded me instruction. I have seen the network of railroads to which you have alluded, which are now penetrating to the remotest parts of our country. I have seen, as I traversed your territory, the hardy yeomanry of your Commonwealth. And here, Sir, permit me to say that, in all my travels throughout this wide confederacy, I have never yet seen the same evidences of intelligence, of industry, of prosperity, and of every thing that renders the condition of man delightful in this life. [Applause.]

I have seen bands of children lining our way for miles, who had come from your glorious common schools to tender their welcome to the President of the United States. [Cheers.] I felt, Sir, that it was well that they should be there. I felt that they would learn lessons of national patriotism, and have them deeply implanted in their hearts. [Renewed cheers.] I felt that the very fact that they looked upon—not the Chief Magistrate of Massachusetts,—but, the Chief Magistrate of this broad confederacy, extending across this wide continent, would teach them to raise their eyes above the horizon of Massachusetts, so as to take in the interests, and the honor, and the glory of this whole Republic. [Cheers.]

Sir, my friend on my right [Mr. Webster] told us just now, that this was not a day devoted to him; that it was devoted to the strangers. Sir, if he intended to allude to me as one of the *strangers*, I deny the application of the term. [Applause.] Sir, it is true that I never before stood upon the soil of Massachusetts! But, Sir, can Virginia be a stranger to Massachusetts? [Enthusiastic applause.] No, Sir! I feel that, as a Virginian, as a son of that glorious old Commonwealth which stood side by side with Massachusetts in the darkest hour of the Revolution, I am no stranger within her borders. [Loud cheers.]

Sir, when I saw the evidences, to which I have alluded, of your prosperity and of your advancement in every thing that promotes national happiness, I felt not one sentiment of envy. No, Sir! I felt that while all these things belonged to Massachusetts, they belonged also to the Union—they belonged also to *me!* [Sensation.] Sir, I shall go back to Virginia, as I said before, instructed. I shall be able to teach my venerated old mother some few lessons of the modern mode of growing into prosperity. I trust that the few hours I have spent here have not been uselessly spent. But I must acknowledge that I have felt something like humiliation when I contrasted the condition of my own Commonwealth with that of Massachusetts. She has a climate and a soil superior to yours. She has a population in many of their traits your equals. [Applause.] But she has not understood the true principles of practical economy. You have taught her a lesson. I will be the bearer of it to her when I return to my home. [Cheers.]

But while I acknowledge our inferiority to your noble State in many things, there are others in which I feel that she is at least your equal. If you have your Bunker Hill, we have our Yorktown! [Loud applause.] If you have had your Hancock and Adamses, we have had our Jefferson and Madison. [Increased applause.] If you have had your Daniel Webster, [reiterated applause] we have had our Patrick Henry. [Stunning cheers.] And towering high above them all we have had *our* and *your* WASHINGTON! [Irrepressible enthusiasm.]

Sir, there is one other thing in which I will not yield the palm even to Massachusetts. In loyalty, in true devotion to the Constitution and to the Union, you may rely upon it, Virginia has no superior. [Hear, hear.] She will stand by them to the last hour of her existence. She will neither repudiate the guarantees of the Constitution, nor will she do aught that can tend to weaken the bonds of our glorious confederacy. [Cheers.]

Pardon me, Sir, for having detained you so long, and accept the sincere expression of my thanks. [Prolonged applause.]

The Hon. CHARLES M. CONRAD, the Secretary of War, was then presented to His Excellency, by J. T. Stevenson, Esq., and spoke as follows :—

MR. GOVERNOR :—

Although the remarks of my friends and fellow-laborers, who have just addressed you, might seem to render it superfluous, I cannot, nevertheless, resist the temptation to offer also the feeble expression of my thanks and my acknowledgments for the cordial greeting which I have received from you, and from the citizens of the State of which you are the organ, from the moment we entered its borders. I need not assure your Excellency, that I have not the vanity to impute this warm, and, I might almost say, this enthusiastic greeting at your hands, to any personal merits of my own. Associated, as I am, in the Cabinet with men far abler and far older than myself, having at its head your illustrious fellow-citizen, [turning towards the Hon. Daniel Webster,] a man who combines the logic of Aristotle with the eloquence of Tully, I feel that, while I am ready to take my full share of all the responsibility that may attach to the station which I have the honor to occupy, I can claim but a very small portion of any merit that may belong to it. But, Sir, I view these manifestations simply as demonstrations of respect for the office which I have the honor to hold. Viewed in that light, viewed as indications of the attachment of the people of this great Commonwealth to the Union, and to the institutions of the country, I assure you most sincerely that they are far, very far more gratifying to me than viewed as manifestations of any personal regard to myself, however pleasing that might be. [Applause.]

Mr. Governor,—My friend who has just addressed you, disclaimed for himself the title of a " stranger." I think I may with equal right disclaim that title. [Applause.] I have not, it is true, the honor of coming from a State, which, like Virginia, has been a partner with Massachusetts in the perils and dangers of the Revolution. But, Sir, I come from a State, which counts, among her best and most virtuous and enlightened citizens, many who came from both of those States. I think, Sir, that a citizen of New Orleans may well claim some acquaintance with the citizens of Boston. Connected, as we are, by ties, not only of common kindred, but by the social intercourse and commercial relations that bind us daily more and more closely together, I cannot feel, when I tread the soil of Boston, that I am on the soil of a foreign land. [Cheers.] Neither is this my first visit to your City or to your State. I have heretofore, on one or two occasions, as a private individual, enjoyed the hospitalities of your citizens; and I assure you that every visit, that I make to your State and to its beautiful capital, is a source of new pleasure and satisfaction. At every new visit that I make to both, I perceive new evidences of that industry, that enterprise, that public spirit and that philanthropy, which may be said to be their prominent characteristics, and, I am happy to add, new indications of their continued and increasing prosperity.

I need not say to the citizens of Massachusetts, and above all, Mr. Governor, I need not say to you, and to the enlightened audience which I now have the honor to address, how much of this prosperity is due to the preservation of that Union which the Commonwealth of Massachusetts contributed so powerfully to establish, and which I am sure she will also, at all times, be ready, as powerfully to assist in maintaining. [Applause.] All that I can now do, Mr. Governor, is to express, as I do, the sincere wish that this prosperity may continue as long as the Union continues, and that both may be perpetual. [Applause.]

As soon as Mr. Conrad had concluded, the Hon. C. T. Russell announced that, in consequence of the proposed review of the military upon the Common, the President would be obliged to forego the pleasure of a personal introduction to the assembly.

The ceremony of reception at the State House having thus terminated, the President, accompanied by Governor Boutwell and his Staff, consisting of Adjutant General Stone, and Lieut. Colonels Heard, Chapman, Williams and Needham, and by General John S. Tyler, Chief Marshal, and the other Marshals of the day, and escorted by the Battalion of Cadets, proceeded thence to the Common, at the foot of which, on the Parade Ground, the troops were already drawn up in line awaiting his arrival. As he passed down Beacon street, and through the gate at the corner of Charles street, discharges of cannon announced his approach, and, in a few moments after his arrival, leaving his escort, and followed only by the Governor and Staff, and the mounted Marshals, he appeared in front of the line, mounted upon a superb black charger, which he managed with graceful ease, at the same time, as he passed along, acknowledging the hearty salutations which burst from the excited thousands who thickly crowned all the rising grounds that almost encircle the field. Having reached a position nearly opposite the centre of the line, he was saluted by the General in Command, accompanied by whom and Staff, he rode along the whole front,—saluted by each regiment as he passed,—and returned by the rear to the same position. The line now broke into column, and, preceded by the Lancers, marched in review before the President, and after passing around the entire parade ground, formed into line again as before ; each regiment occupying the same relative position as in the procession of the morning.

The President, with the Governor and Staff, now retired from the field, and was escorted to his quarters at the Revere House ; and the troops were dismissed, after having received the thanks of General Edmands for the manner in which they had discharged the duties of the day.

Besides the President, and the Governor and Staff, a large number of distinguished persons were on the field at the time of the review, many of whom, including several officers of the British army, were in uniform. The authorities of the City were also present, together with several officers of the Army and Navy of the United States.

The review, to which the beauty of the weather gave additional effect, was regarded as one of the finest military exhibitions ever witnessed in this part of the country. In fact the appearance of the troops, throughout the day, was in the highest degree creditable to them. The British officers expressed themselves in terms of generous admiration of our citizen soldiers, and the President said that the military display was the finest he had ever witnessed.

The festivities of the day were brought to a close by a dinner, given, at the Revere House, by the City Government, to the President and Suite and the distinguished guests, from the British Colonies, and from different parts of our own country. At half past eight o'clock in the evening, the company took their seats at the tables in the main dining hall, which was tastefully decorated in honor of the occasion. The dinner was sumptuous and elegantly served.

Mr. Mayor Bigelow presided. Upon his right sat the President of the United States, and on his left, the Governor of the Commonwealth. Sir Allan McNab and the other distinguished men, civil and military, from Canada, occupied seats at the central table, while the other guests, representing the two countries, were seated at the side tables.

The President, in consequence of great fatigue, left the hall at an early hour, accompanied by the Mayor, at whose request, Mr. Alderman Rogers then took the Chair. His appropriate address, upon assuming it, was followed by others from the Hon. Francis Hincks, the Prime Minister of the Governor General of Canada, Gen. Edmands of Boston, Col. Horne, the senior British officer present, the Hon. Benjamin Seaver, Sir Allan McNab, the Hon. Joseph Howe, Provincial Secretary of Nova Scotia, Ex-Gov. Paine of Vermont, John P. Putnam, Esq., of Boston, Mr. Justice Alwyn, of Canada East, Col. Ezra Lincoln, the Hon. Josiah Quincy, Jr., and Col. Wm. Schouler, of Boston, Gen. Leslie Coombs, of Kentucky, the Hon. Henry Wilson, and the Hon. W. B. Lawrence, Acting Governor of Rhode Island.

These festivities closed, at about eleven o'clock, with nine cheers for Her Majesty, Queen Victoria, and nine more for the President of the United States.

During the whole day, which had now so agreeably come to an end, the streets of the city were thronged with hilarious, yet well-conducted crowds, and each train of cars arriving brought large and welcome additions to the already great number of strangers within our gates. Among the new comers, was His Honor, John G. Bowes, the Mayor of Toronto, accompanied by several Aldermen, members of the Council, and others of the principal officers of that city.

No accident or disorder occurrred to disturb the general harmony and joy; the anticipations of the day were fully realized, and its observances left on the minds of all, who shared in or witnessed them, impressions simply delightful.

SECOND DAY.

The distinguishing features of the Second Day of the Jubilee, Thursday, September 18, were the Excursion down the Harbor of Boston; the arrival and reception of Lord Elgin, the Governor General of British North America, and his Suite; and the Levees given in the evening at private residences and other places in honor of the distinguished guests of the City.

A serene and cloudless sky continued to smile upon the festivities, while the summer blandness of the air drew forth into the streets still greater crowds than those which had constituted so striking a feature of the day preceding, and additional banners and other tasteful and showy embellishments lent their gaiety to the scene.

The water-side, near the spot where the parties embarked on board the steamboats for the excursion down the harbor, presented a most enlivening sight. The wharves and the vessels and their rigging were covered with a dense mass of spectators. The ships were decked in their gayest apparel, and hundreds of masts, flinging to the breeze their ensigns and streamers, gave a vivid idea of that extensive commerce whose interests are so intimately connected with the event over which all were rejoicing. The wide expanse of the harbor, with the multitudes of small craft upon its heaving bosom, the clear blue sky and the bright sun over head, giving life and splendor to all, made up a picture which has not been surpassed in its characteristic features by anything of the kind among us.

At an early hour the guests invited to the excursion began to move toward the T wharf, the place of embarkation, and until half-past ten, the time of starting, the avenues leading in that direction were thronged. The steamers engaged for the excursion were the S. S. Lewis, (which was kindly placed at the disposal of the City Government for this occasion by her owners,) the Benjamin Franklin, the St. Lawrence, the Mayflower, the Naushon, and the John Taylor. To these were added the revenue cutters Hamilton and Morris.

The arrival of the steamer S. S. Lewis had been anxiously looked for, for several days, and the announcement that she had come to anchor off East Boston in the morning, and would be in readiness to perform the part assigned her in the excursion, was highly gratifying to all. She arrived below in the night, having made the passage from the Delaware Breakwater in forty-seven hours, running time.

The number of guests invited, and nearly all of whom embarked on board these several vessels, was between three and four thousand, distributed nearly as follows, viz.:

In the S. S. Lewis, Capt. Cole, - - -	200
" " Benjamin Franklin, Capt. Sears, - -	500
" " St. Lawrence, Capt. Cyrus Sturtivant, -	800
" " Mayflower, Capt. Elijah Beal, - -	800
" " Naushon, Capt. H. W. Freeman, - -	500
" " John Taylor, - - - - - -	200
" " Morris, Capt. Walden, - - - - -	150
" " Hamilton, Lieut. Burroughs, - -	150

These figures indicate the number of tickets originally issued for the excursion. Before the party left the wharf, however, the number was probably swelled to 3500 or 4000.

By about half-past ten o'clock, the several boats, with the exception of the S. S. Lewis, having each received on board the guests assigned to them, moved from their moorings into the open harbor to await the arrival and embarkation of the President at East Boston, at the terminus of the Grand Junction Railroad, for the formal opening of which road on this day, in the presence of the Chief Magistrate of the Nation, appropriate preparations had been made.

In the meanwhile, the larger portion of the party which was to embark on board the S. S. Lewis had assembled at the Mayor and Aldermen's room, in the City Hall. At a quarter before ten o'clock, his Honor the Mayor,—escorted by Mr. City Marshal Francis Tukey and his Aids, all mounted,—proceeded, in a barouche, from the City Hall to the Revere House, and there received the President and Messrs. Conrad and Stewart. Francis Brinley, Esq., in another barouche, received the Hon. Mr. Crampton, Charge d'Affaires of Great Britain at Washington, and the Hon. Francis Hincks and the Hon. William Young, of Canada. Other carriages, containing Governor Boutwell and Suite, Mr. Marshal Devens, and distinguished visitors from the Canadas, followed, and all successively proceeded to the depot of the Boston and Maine Railroad. The remainder of the party, destined for the S. S. Lewis, took carriages at the City Hall and proceeded directly to the depot, accompanied by members of the Board of Aldermen and Common Council. A train of five long cars, drawn by the engine "Essex," and handsomely decorated for the occasion, was in readiness to receive the party on its arrival.

As soon as all were seated and everything ready, the word was given, and amid the cheering of the crowd the cars started for East Boston, via the Grand Junction Railroad. The train left the depot at five minutes past eleven o'clock, and arrived on the depot grounds of the company at twenty-five minutes past eleven. Upon the entrance of the cars on the track of the new road, the party was greeted by a grand salute, fired by the citizens of Malden, and, when the train crossed the line between Chelsea and East Boston, two cannons pealed forth their thunder tones in quick succession. Just upon the line across the track was erected a handsome arch, decorated with evergreens and flowers, and bearing on the front the inscription,—

BOSTON AND THE CANADAS, UNITED BY BONDS OF IRON.

And on the reverse,—

"UNION IS STRENGTH."

At the head of the pier, upon which the train stopped, was a similar arch, bearing the following inscription:

GRAND JUNCTION RAILROAD, UNITE ALL, SERVE ALL.

And on the reverse,—

LIVERPOOL, BOSTON, AND THE CANADAS.

The arches were got up in good taste, and added greatly to the still life of the picture.

As the train reached the pier,—the terminus of the road,—a national salute was fired from the wharf of the Cunard Steamship Company. From the cars the party proceeded to the new ferry-boat of the Eastern Railroad Company, on the deck of which was stationed the Boston Brass Band, playing the tune, "Hail Columbia," and, amidst the roar of artillery and the cheers of the rejoicing multitudes lining not only the wharves, on the East Boston side, but all the wharves and the shipping in Boston proper from which a view of the enlivening scene could be obtained, the President and those who accompanied him, were conveyed on board the S. S. Lewis, which, bearing the English flag at her fore, and the Union Jack at her mast-head, and with the Stars and Stripes floating from her mizen, was impatiently riding at anchor in the stream.

The party was soon transferred to her decks, the anchor was hove up, and the noble ship moved majestically down the harbor, preceded by the cutters "Hamilton" and "Morris" as her escort, and followed by the Benjamin Franklin, the St. Lawrence, and the other boats in succession.

As the cutters, towed, one on each side, by the John Taylor, passed by the President's ship to take their places in the van, they fired a national salute of twenty-one guns.

And now the whole pageant was moving gracefully and gaily down the animated harbor, whose waters, hardly ruffled by the soft air, were glittering in the sun, and on either shore the thousands of delighted spectators were giving vent to their enthusiasm in oft repeated cheers which, mingled with the gladsome roar of artillery, added the last and perhaps not the least effective element to the sympathetic enthusiasm of the hour.

The President was accompanied on board the steamer by the gentlemen who came with him from Washington. Governor Boutwell was attended by his Aids, Lt. Cols. Chapman, Williams and Needham, and also by Adjutant General Stone. The Mayor did not go on board the ship, but returned to the city proper, to be in readiness to attend to other guests who were expected in the course of the day.

Among the other distinguished strangers on board the S. S. Lewis, were the Hon. Mr. Crampton, the Hon. Francis Hincks, the Hon. Joseph Howe, the Hon. William Young, Speaker of the House of Assembly of Nova Scotia; Col. Gugy, of Montreal, a member of the Provincial Parliament; Col. Horne, Capt. Nye, 20th Reg., Capt. Stevens, R. N., Lieut. Butler and Mr. Parkinson, of the 20th Regiment, R. A.; Capt. Keene and Lieut. Noble, from Toronto, of the Royal Corps of Engineers; Capt. Sweedenham, and Mr. Thompson, of the 54th Regiment; and Mr. Hughes, of the Quartermaster's Department, from Quebec.

Commodore Downes, the commanding officer at the Charlestown Navy Yard, the venerable Capt. Percival, of the U. S. Navy, Capt. Tucker, of the U. S. Army, the Hon. Amasa Walker, Secretary of the Commonwealth; the Hon. John H. Clifford, Attorney General; ex-Lieutenant-Governor Reed; Lieutenant Governor Cushman—all the Governor's Council but one; Richard Frothingham, Jr. Esq., the Mayor of Charlestown; Judge Phelps, of Vermont, ex-Senator of the United States; many members of the Senate and House of Representatives of Massachusetts; members of the City Government, and persons occupying various official stations, were also of the President's party, participating in, and contributing to the enjoyment of the occasion.

Among the guests on board the propeller Benjamin Franklin were the Hon. N. F. Belleau, Mayor of the city of Quebec, Messrs. Councillors Paradis, Lepper, Dorval and Lampson, the Sheriff, W. S. Sewell, Esq., and the Clerk of that city, F. X. Garneau, Esq., Capt. Alleyne, of the Royal Navy, Messrs. Dunn, Pemberton, and Patterson, eminent merchants, and Joseph Hamel, Esq., Surveyor, of the same city; the Hon. Messrs. Scott, Robinson and Holmes, of the Provincial Parliament, and the Hon. Judge Mondelet, and Messrs. Larkin,

Molson, and Townsend, of Montreal. The Authorities of the Commonwealth and of the City of Boston were represented by the Hon. Henry Wilson, the Hon. Charles Hudson, Surveyor of the Port, and Col. Ezra Lincoln and Benjamin Beal, Esq., of the City Council. The Hon. Isaac Livermore, of Cambridge; the Rev. Dr. Beecher, and his son, the Rev. Edward Beecher; the Hon. Leslie Coombs, of Kentucky; the Hon. Mr. Clark, member of Congress, from New York, and many other distinguished gentlemen, were also present.

On board the St. Lawrence were John G. Bowes, Esq., Mayor of Toronto, Dr. Nelson, of Montreal, and many other Canadian gentlemen, whose names cannot now be ascertained; Daniel N. Haskell, Esq., of the City Council, several members of the School Board, and other distinguished citizens and strangers.

Among the guests and persons of distinction on board the Mayflower, were Sir Allan N. McNab, the Hon. R. Matheson, of Perth, Canada West; the Rev. J. Jenkins, of Montreal; J. J. Burrowes, Esq., of Kingston; E. P. Campbell, Esq., of Argyleshire, Scotland; John Counter, Esq., ex-Mayor of Kingston; Capt. Gildersleeve, Charles Hales, Esq., and Anthony Drummond, Esq., Agent of the Montreal Bank, of Kingston; and Mr. George Debarats, of Montreal, Queen's Printer. From St. Catharine, Canada West, Rev. R. Shanklin, Thomas Colton, Esq., George Kent, Esq., Mr. Thomas Burns, Messrs. Thomas R. and William H. Merritt, Mr. William A. Chisholm, and Mr. Andrew Horton. From Toronto—George A. Philpotts, Esq., George B. Wells, Esq., and George Beatty, Esq., of the Council. From Hamilton—Messrs. John O. Hatt, Thomas Davidson, E. B. Freeman, and E. W. Brown; and the Hon. J. C. Park, of this city; Col. J. D. Greene, and Staff, of the 4th Regiment, Massachusetts Infantry; Lt. Col. Boyd, of the 1st, and Lt. Col. Abbott, of the third.

The staunch little steamer Naushon had on board her full share of distinguished guests, whose names, however, have not been reported.

The parties on board the cutters Morris and Hamilton, and

the steamer John Taylor, which, as the vessels were united together, formed in reality but one, included a large number of guests from Halifax, Montreal, Toronto, and other places in Canada, and from New York and Philadelphia. Among them were Mr. Sheriff Boston, of Montreal, Mr. D. W. Gilkison, of Brantford, Ca.; Col. Crittenden, of the U. S. Army; Judge Rice, of the District of Augusta, Me.; Col. Cowdin, of the Regiment of Artillery; Lieut. Hedden, of the New York City Guards; and Col. N. A. Thompson, and Lieuts. Pulsifer and French, of the Boston City Guards.

As the flotilla moved slowly down the harbor, the attention of all on board was attracted by the various objects of interest with which it abounds.

On passing Fort Independence, the party on board the S. S. Lewis was greeted with a national salute.

It had been the original intention to carry the President as far as Minot's Ledge, in order to give him an opportunity to witness the scene of the late melancholy disaster; but owing to his other engagements, it became necessary to return at an earlier hour, and at a short distance this side of the lower Light the Lewis put about to return. At this moment the other steamers, crowded with passengers, passed close by her, dipped their ensigns, and saluted the President with loud and repeated cheers, which were returned with equal heartiness from the Lewis, and all then came up the harbor.

During the excursion, the President, accompanied by Capt. Cole, inspected every part of the Lewis, and expressed his admiration of the numerous improvements which have been introduced into this model of a vessel. Every one on board was struck with the facility and steadiness with which she moved through the water.

It is worthy of comment, and of the highest praise, considering the few hours her officers and agents had had for preparation, that every thing belonging to her was in such admirable order, and that all the arrangements for the fete were so complete and satisfactory.

As she drew near the city, the company were invited to partake of an elegant banquet which had been spread in the spacious cabin. Francis Brinley, Esq. presided, in the absence of the Mayor, and announced the following toast, which was received with enthusiasm:

"The President of the United States."

As it was understood that there were to be no speeches on the occasion, the President only bowed in acknowledgment of the cheers given by the company.

The Hon. J. H. Clifford, Attorney General, then gave,—

"Her Majesty, the Queen."

Benjamin T. Reed, Esq., proposed the health of—

"His Excellency, the Governor of the Commonwealth."

The Hon. George Lunt, United States District Attorney, proposed,

"The members of the Cabinet accompanying the President."

Each toast was received with three hearty cheers.

Immediately after dinner, the President and Suite landed at the Navy Yard, accompanied by Commodore Downes, and were received with a national salute from the heavy battery of the yard. The corps of Marines, under Capt. Pope, were drawn up to receive him, and presented arms as he passed. The President and the guests, who left the Lewis at Charlestown, then entered the carriages in attendance, and, after being driven round Bunker Hill Monument Square, proceeded to Boston, and alighted at the Revere House.*

Entertainments had been also provided for the companies on board the other boats, to which ample justice was done. The crowd on board the Benjamin Franklin was so great that anything in the way of ceremony was impossible, but still every one appeared to be greatly pleased with the trip.

In the cabin of the St. Lawrence a long and well furnished table was spread, to which the strangers were first invited, as the number on board was far too large to be accommodated at once. After the company had again assembled on deck, addresses were made by Mr. Mayor Bowes, of Toronto, Dr.

* After the President left them, the company on board the S. S. Lewis again sat down at the dinner table, under the auspices of H. J. Gardner, Esq., of the Council, and made and heard several very eloquent and agreeable speeches, of which it is much regretted that no report has been preserved.

Nelson, of Canada, and Daniel N. Haskell, Esq., of the City Council, the last of whom, at the conclusion of his remarks, introduced Samuel A. Walker, Esq., to the company. Mr. Walker made a humorous and diverting speech, and sang an amusing song, in which he ingeniously introduced the names of the Mayor and Aldermen and members of the Common Council. On landing at the wharf, the citizens formed themselves into a procession, and escorted their guests to Court square, where, after three hearty cheers, the party separated.

Several happy speeches were made, and patriotic sentiments offered, on board the steamer Mayflower, and the festivities were enlivened by the music of McDonald's fine Cornet Band. On the return of the party, the New Englanders escorted the Canadians to their hotels, and, on arriving at the Revere House, cheers were proposed and most heartily given, for the passengers of the Mayflower in 1620, and the passengers of the Mayflower in 1851.

The steamer Naushon, though small, bore well her part in the maritime exercises of the day, and gave great satisfaction to all on board. When nearing the wharf, on the return, her passengers wrote and signed a complimentary letter to her commander, Capt. H. W. Freeman, expressing their sense of his courteous demeanor during the excursion.

The Revenue Cutters, Morris, Capt. Walden, and Hamilton, Lieut. Burroughs, commanding, were gaily and appropriately decorated with flags and pennants flying from each mast.

Upon the fore-yards of the Morris, on either side, were two beautiful flags of the Spanish and Dutch nations. At the summit of the mainmast floated the revenue flag. Between the mainmast and the foremast, extending from the top to the deck, were various signals, and the Stars and Stripes floated from her gaff. On board, the company were entertained with a sumptuous collation : sentiments were offered, songs sung, and the hilarity and mutual good feeling of all found, in other ways, also, suitable expression.

On board the Hamilton, speeches were made by Col. Thompson and Mr. Dunham of the Common Council, which were very handsomely responded to by Mr. Sheriff Boston, of Montreal, and A. Gilkison, Esq., of Brantford, Canada.

The beautiful and unique appearance of the Cutters as they moved through the waters, one on each side of their peaceful companion,—half concealed by the smoke of their own cannon, which at short intervals pealed forth a gladsome salute,—contributed as much to heighten the general effect of the scene, as the courteous attentions of their commanders added to the comfort and enjoyment of those who were assigned to their care.

Thus terminated the aquatic portion of the pageant, which, for its novelty, the beautiful appearance it presented, the enthusiasm with which it was entered into, and the delightful feelings, which it gave to all who participated in it, only needed the additional observance, alluded to by the Mayor, of dropping a "golden ring" into the sea, as a token of the happy union, which had now been consummated between the waters of the Atlantic and the rivers and lakes of Canada and the West, to recall to mind the gorgeous Venetian ceremony of wedding the City to the waves of the Adriatic.

Amongst the various schemes which had been devised to give interest to the excursion, was a Regatta off Point Alderton, at Hull, which had been intended to take place on the approach of the fleet. As the President's arrangements did not allow of his going that distance, and spending the time which a view of the race would have required, the Regatta was witnessed by a smaller number of spectators than had been anticipated. But notwithstanding this disappointment, the parties who were present at the trial of skill highly enjoyed the exhibition.

The morning did not promise much, as there was no wind; but by the time of starting, there was a fine breeze from the south east. The judges' boat, the yacht Raven, proceeded down the harbor at about ten o'clock, in tow of the steamer Hornet. She arrived S. E. of the Graves before eleven, and was anchored at the appointed place.

She was suitably decorated for the occasion. From the jib stay was suspended the Union Jack, at the fore topmast head the British ensign, and below the flag of Denmark, the yacht's signal; at the main, the American Union Jack, pure white ground with a crimson star; below the flag of France, and at the topping-lift, the American ensign.

The judges were, Benjamin C. Clark, and Geo. B. Upton, Esqs., and Capt. Matthew Hunt.

After the arrival of the Raven at the scene of operations, the steamer was despatched to the harbor to bring down the yachts, which intended to enter.

At 12 M., the signal gun was fired from the Raven, and soon after, the boats, for the first race, formed in line.

There were four competitors for the first race—all boats belonging to Hull, viz.:—

Odd Fellow, - - - - -	5 tons.
Gift, - - - - - - -	5 "
Susan, - - - - - - -	8 "
Charade, - - - - - - -	9 "

The signal gun was fired at 2h. 49m., and the boats went off in fine style. The station boat was placed about four miles to the N. E. of the Graves; the boats all rounded her, and came back in the following order by the judges' boat;—

The Gift, in - - - -	$56\frac{1}{4}$ minutes.
" Charade, - - - -	$57\frac{1}{2}$ "
" Susan, - - - -	61 "
" Odd Fellow, - - -	66 "

The boats were allowed 30 seconds a ton, for difference of tonnage; though after making this allowance, they took the prizes in the order of their coming in.

It will be seen that they made excellent time, the distance sailed, being about eight miles.

The prizes fell into good and grateful hands. The Gift (a very pretty boat) won the President's Goblet. In presenting it, the judge said, "Capt. Cobb, you are already the possessor of one beautiful Gift—the city of Boston makes you the owner of another."

The Charade took the second prize, an elegant spy-glass—being the second she has won lately. The judge said, "Captain, you have already taken one glass—the city of Boston tenders you another. It is not often she give her friends a glass too much."

The Susan, a modest looking little boat, took the third prize, a highly finished brass compass. The judge, in passing it over, said, "Captain, you have worked hard and skilfully to win a prize, and have COMPASS-ed your wishes."

In the meantime, as soon as the small boats had left, the large ones were immediately formed in line; the bay, at this time, was literally covered with boats of every description; the steamer Hornet arrived with five or six yachts in tow, nearly all of which at once entered; there were many other large boats plying around, which did not enter; among others we noticed the beautiful Coquette, the Hornet, Witch, Gazelle, Grace, Rattler, Alida, Bride of the Billow, Mary, and Minna.

The signal gun was fired at thirteen minutes past three. The breeze had now freshened, and gave promise of a fine race. Precisely at the moment, the following yachts started:—

Neptune,	10 tons,	of Marblehead,	Capt.	Gregory.
Edward Eddy,	12 "	Salem,	"	Smith.
Excelsior,	10 "	"	"	Wallis.
Triumph,	20 "	Hingham,	"	Souther.
Cygnet,	31 "	Boston,	"	Healey.
Pearl,	32 "	Salem,	"	Martin.
Quarantine,	43 "	Boston,	"	Berry.
Flirt,	43 "	Boston,	"	Manning.
Mystery,	46 "	Salem,	"	Perkins.
Surprise,	53 "	Boston,	"	Thayer.

The race was from the judges' boat, outside the Graves, round Egg Rock, back to the place of starting. The wind thus made it a dead beat back from Nahant. The Neptune started in beautiful style, and rounded Egg Rock among the first; but in beating back the larger boats showed their superior qualities on a wind. The judges' boat was rounded in the following order:—

Quarantine, - - - - - -	2h. 01m.
Flirt, - - - - - - -	2h. 02m.
Cygnet, - - - - - - -	2h. 03m.
Pearl, - - - - - - -	2h. 05m.

Mystery,	- - - - -	2h. 07m.
Excelsior,	- - - - -	2h. 11m.
Neptune,	- - - - -	2h. 17m.
Triumph,	- - - - -	2h. 20m.

In about ten minutes after the arrival of the last boat, the prizes were awarded by B. C. Clark, Esq., the Chairman of the Committee, as follows:—

The "President's Pitcher," (value $100,) to the Cygnet. The second prize, "a spy-glass," (value $20,) to the Excelsior, and the third, "a set of colors," to the Pearl.

The winners appeared to value the prizes highly, not on account of their intrinsic value, but as tokens of attention and regard from the city of Boston.

Thus ended one of the most beautiful and exciting regattas ever witnessed in Massachusetts Bay. The skill, evinced in getting up the exhibition, was only equalled by the perfect harmony and gôod feeling which marked its progress and its close.

The scene was lovely in the extreme; the sun was shineing in an unclouded sky, and the waters of our beautiful bay sparkled and danced in his beams, as if rejoicing to add their abounding share to the attractiveness of the scene. The whole harbor was dotted with vessels, which were adorned with gay flags, and filled with persons who, overflowing with the spirit of enjoyment, continually gave and received vociferous cheers and friendly salutations as the vessels passed and repassed each other.

In the afternoon, the expectation of the arrival of Lord Elgin, the Governor General of British North America, drew a great concourse of spectators to the Western Railroad depot, eager to see and welcome him. The Mayor, attended by several members of the City Government, was on the spot to receive the distinguished guest. At a quarter past five o'clock, the train, bearing his Lordship and Suite, arrived. The multitude welcomed him with hearty cheering as he stepped from the cars and stood upon the platform in the wide space, in the open air, to the south of the depot. Mr. Mayor Bigelow then tendered to him a public welcome, and the hospitalities of the City, in the following address :—

Your Excellency :—

In the name of my fellow citizens, I welcome you to the metropolis of New England. We recognise you, not only as the ruler of extensive and important provinces, but as the principal representative, on this continent, of the venerated land of our ancestors. It is told of Samoset, the Indian Chief, that his first salutation to the Pilgrims at Plymouth, was "welcome, welcome, Englishmen." Such was the greeting of the old warrior to those, who were to invade the hunting-grounds and extinguish the council fires of his race. With a better augury for the future, it becomes me on this occasion, to repeat that salutation, and say, "welcome Englishmen and their fellow subjects," who come to us under circumstances so auspicious for our own and their prosperity.

There is a special interest connected with your Excellency's visit at this time, gracing, as it does, with your presence, the establishment of a social and commercial alliance between this city and the Canadas. Lines of intercommunication have been opened, by which the products of your provinces may find speedy and convenient transit to the sea. The railways, which unite us, are works more truly admirable than the wondrous avenues which radiated from Imperial Rome—avenues for facilitating the march of invading armies, or the return of triumphal chariots laden with the spoils of desolated countries. Our own iron pathways, the result of scientific labor and skill unequalled by ancient times, are devoted to far different objects. They unite in friendly relations the inhabitants of widely separated regions—minister to their mutual wants—diffuse abroad the means of knowledge—"and scatter plenty through a smiling land."

Our festival may be considered, in some sort, as the celebration of a conjugal union between Canada and the Ocean. We can dispense with the golden ring, which was used in the espousals of Venice with the waters of the Adriatic; for this union is effected by bands of iron, which at once attest its perpetuity and strength. My Lord, the more intimate connection, which hereafter is to subsist between the people whom you govern and the Atlantic states, is perhaps, in no small degree, a pledge and a guaranty of perpetual amity between the British and American nations. The memory of their fratricidal conflicts is fading away, and the history thereof, I trust, is completed forever. The record of their generous rivalry, for pre-eminence in the arts of peace, is now opening, and is destined to exhibit the brightest pages in the annals of their common race. Such, I am confident, are the anticipations and hopes of the people for whom I speak, and they enhance the pleasure with which they salute you as their welcome and honored guest. [The address of the Mayor was seconded by the enthusiastic cheers of the multitude.]

To this address Lord Elgin made the following reply:—

MR. MAYOR AND GENTLEMEN:—

I am quite overcome by this kind and cordial reception; but, Gentlemen, I have been travelling all day, and my throat is so full of dust that you will excuse me if do not attempt to follow the Mayor in his most eloquent address.

But there is one thing he has said, which I cannot allow to pass unnoticed. He has suggested that we should consider this celebration the "conjugal union of the Canadas with the Ocean." Whatever may be my object in coming to Boston, I assure you, Sir, that I do not come to "forbid the bans." [Hear, hear, and cheers.]

I appreciate most highly the sentiment of personal regard, which you have so kindly expressed towards me; and still more highly do I appreciate the assurances you have given me of your respect and consideration for my Sovereign and my Country, and for that great rising Canadian people, upon whose prosperity and welfare my hopes and my feelings and my wishes are all centred.

Gentlemen: I come here upon the hospitable invitation of the city of Boston, but prompted also—I must confess it—by the desire to show by this act of mine rather than by mere words,—because I know that this mode of expression is the more emphatic and more intelligible of the two—to show by this act, my conviction that it becomes us, Americans and Britons—I put the Americans first,—[hear, hear, hear,]—Americans and Britons,—descended as we are from the same stock, inheritors of the same traditions, and, unless I grievously misconstrue the signs of the times, with duties and responsibilities, as respects the future, not widely dissimilar,—to be ready at all times, and all places, and more especially at this time, and upon this soil of North America, to cultivate toward each other feelings of brotherly love and mutual friendship. These are my feelings, and I therefore gladly accept your proffered kindness. [Cheers.]

Lord Elgin then took a seat in an open barouche, with the Mayor, and, together with his Suite in other carriages, was escorted by the Independent Cadets, (the Governor's Guard,) to the Revere House. The cortege passed through Lincoln, Summer, Winter, Tremont, and Court streets, and Lord Elgin was frequently cheered as he passed by the multitudes, who lined the streets. Nothing could be more respectful, at once, and cordial than his reception.

The inhabitants of Boston are led both by instinct and education to treat any stranger with courtesy, any guest with kindly hospitality, and,—in spite of an ancient feud or two, remembered every day with less of acrimony, and more of the sentiment of half-affectionate respect for the gallant antagonist,—every Briton as a brother. It is most agreeable, to every true-hearted American, to watch the rapid and ever onward process of "re-annexation" in mind and heart, which is going on between this country and her political and intellectual mother, and natural and almost necessary ally. It would be invidious at present to particularise the statesmen of our own country, to whom we are in a large measure indebted for the public manifestation of this universal feeling, but it is not improper, it is in fact a duty, to say, that to such eminent men of Great Britain as Sir Henry Bulwer, the citizens of Boston, and, we believe, the people of the United States, as Anglo-Saxons, as Christians, and as men, feel themselves under very great obligations. That gentleman's "bad speeches," as he alone ventures to call them, not only rank with the best of their class, as oratorical performances, but actually tend more powerfully to promote a kindly union among the nations of men, upon the basis of mutual justice, kindness and forbearance, than the more elaborate efforts of a greater number of Peace Congresses than has yet had to be counted, though the propriety and utility of those conventions are to be estimated at a high rate. It is also an agreeable duty to assign to Lord Elgin his honorable place, at the side of Sir Henry, in the same admirable career. Some of these considerations doubtless had their influence in the minds of the assemblage which so cordially welcomed his Lordship. And it was probably remembered, that he was born in that Scotland, which more than any other country resembles our own New England,—that classic land of our childhood, whose Covenanters, the true cousins, in spirit and in faith, of our own "persecuted remnant" of Puritans, are almost as dear to our early memories, as the Pilgrims themselves; and, despite our strong disposition to recalcitrate against hereditary honors, it probably was not altogether forgotten, that he is a representative of that Bruce of Bannockburn, whose fame is part of our own inheritance, and the story of whose life is interwoven with our first-impressed recollections. It is no small compliment to his Lordship, to say that the crowd, knowing who he was and what he was, were not disappointed in the personal appearance of one around whom so many associations at that moment clustered. Although somewhat under the middle height, his figure is portly and dignified. He resembles in face and in person the late John Quincy Adams, though,—if the expression may be used,—projected upon a bolder scale. His very handsome countenance indicates extraordinary intellectual power, refined culture and habitual command over other men, at once, and his own impassioned nature; and in his eye and his mouth are seen, each in a strongly marked degree, grave and earnest thought, the consciousness of power, and the sense of great responsibility, all struggling with almost irrepressible humor, half comic, half sarcastic, but always racy and vigorous. There is also expressed in his face indomitable courage, and anything but a fondness for opposition. He does not look as if he could readily bring himself to yield to anything in the shape of opposing force. He is in the prime of life, (born July 20th, 1811,) and evidently enjoys vigorous health.

His bearing was in the highest degree frank, courteous and manly. His person and deportment, obviously struck the people most favorably, and he was greeted with three enthusiastic cheers upon alighting at the Revere House.

He was at once ushered into the gentlemen's parlor, and introduced to President Fillmore, by Mr. Mayor Bigelow. The meeting of the President of the United States and the highest officer of Great Britain in North America, to rejoice together over the beneficent triumphs of peace and the addition of new facilities to the friendly intercourse of the two nations, was an occasion of peculiar interest and of the happiest augury.

His Lordship's Suite, consisting of his brother, Lieut. Col.

Bruce, whose face was remarked as peculiarly expressive of refined culture, and Lord Mark Kerr, the Hon. George Waldegrave, Sir A. N. MacNab, Solicitor General McDonald, and Messrs. Hincks, Drummond, Taché and Price, all of them men of very gentlemanlike bearing, were also formally introduced to the President and Messrs. Conrad and Stuart, by Alderman Rogers, after which some two hours were passed in the presentation of citizens who desired to welcome the Chiefs of two contiguous lands.

At a later period in the evening, Mr. Webster welcomed Lord Elgin and his Suite. There were no formal speeches, but a simple, cordial, friendly greeting.

After the retirement of Lord Elgin, the President and Messrs. Stuart and Conrad were introduced to all the Canadian gentlemen by Alderman Rogers. Subsequently, the President went to the ladies' parlor, where he was introduced to a large number of ladies, with whom he passed an agreeable hour. During all these ceremonies there was a great crowd of people in Bowdoin Square, and when the fireworks were displayed, a general shout of approbation resounded through the area.

At the Tremont House, a dinner was given by the City Authorities to the officers of the British Army then in Boston, as a token of cordial welcome. The Adjutant General of the Commonwealth and other principal officers of the Massachusetts Militia were present, and the evening was passed in the interchange of expressions of mutual respect. Numerous other entertainments were also given, at public houses, to the guests of the city.

In the evening, the Mayor held a Levee at his mansion, in Temple street, at which were President Fillmore, Lord Elgin and Suite, the Secretaries of War and the Interior, members of the Canadian Cabinet, Judiciary and Parliament, officers of the British Army, Gov. Boutwell and other principal officers of the State, the members of the City Government, and a large number of eminent citizens of various trades and professions. Two bands of music were in attendance,—one of them being stationed in the street, to salute the arrival and departure of distinguished guests in an appropriate manner. As the President and the Governor-General were successively announced by "Hail to the Chief," and "God save the Queen," the dense multitude in the street repeated the welcome with enthusiastic cheers.

Other levees were given by Mrs. Harrison Gray Otis, in Mount Vernon street, Philip Greely, Jr., Esq., Collector of the Port, in McLean street, the Hon. Robert C. Winthrop, in Pemberton square, and the Hon. Samuel A. Eliot, in Beacon street, all of which were honored with the presence of President Fillmore and Suite, and Lord Elgin and Suite.

A grand Military Ball was also given in the evening, at Union Hall; it was a most agreeable gathering, and passed off with great eclat. Among the distinguished persons present were Lord Elgin, Sir Allan McNab, Capt. Lord Mark Kerr, Lieut. Col. the Hon. R. Bruce, Mr. Solicitor General McDonald, Mr. Solicitor General Drummond, Mr. Inspector General Hincks, the Hon. Mr. Killaley, the Hon. Mr. Taché, M. P. P., Col. Fitzgerald, Major Brooks, Col. Horne, the Hon. Capt. King, R. E., Mr. Parkinson, of the 3d Regiment, Judge McCord, Col. Gugy, Mr. Sheriff Thomas, the Hon. W. H. Boulton, M. P. P., Capt. Jones, of the 54th Reg., Lieut. Chisholm, of the 42d Reg. Highlanders, in the splendid and peculiar uniform of the corps, Capt. Stimpson, of the 20th Reg., Dr. Chisholm, of the Medical Staff, and Messrs. Young, McDonald, Mills, Cameron, Ross, Radcliffe, Odell, Bourchette, Merritt, F. Merritt, Bell, Philpotts, McKenzie, Jones, Hart, Patrick, and others, of Canada.

Among other distinguished men who were present, were Gov. Boutwell and Staff, ex-Gov. Paine, of Vermont, the Hon. N. P. Banks, Jr., the Hon. Josiah Quincy, Jr., Major General Edmands, Col. Sherman, of the U. S. Flying Artillery, Gen. J. S. Tyler, and Francis Brinley, Esq.

Many ladies from Canada also lent their charms to grace the festive occasion.

At the entrance of Lord Elgin, the national air of England was played by the Germania Musical Society.

The Viceroy was introduced to many of our citizens in the hall. After remaining half an hour he retired, expressing himself as much pleased with his visit.

The ball was under the management of Gen. S. Andrews, Col. R. Cowdin, and Col. C. L. Holbrook.

At the Masonic Temple, the Grand Lodge of Massachusetts entertained their Provincial brethren in a most liberal manner. A large number of distinguished Masons were present, among whom were Sir Allan McNab, Judge McCord, of Quebec, and William Henry Boulton, Esq., of the Provincial Parliament. E. A. Raymond, Worshipful Grand Master, of Massachusetts, presided, and, after much good music, the hospitalities of the fraternity were extended by Rev. George M. Randall, Deputy Grand Master, in a neat and appropriate address, which was replied to by Sir Allan McNab, Provincial Grand Master of the Grand Lodge of Canada West, on behalf of his brethren present. The company then adjourned to the spacious ante-room adjoining the Lodge, where refreshments had been prepared.

After an hour's interchange of friendly sentiment, the company separated, congratulating each other on the great event which brought them together.

In the afternoon, the City Greys, of Bath, Me., Capt. E. K. Harding, were received at the Maine Depot, and escorted to South Boston by the Pulaski Guards, accompanied by the Charlestown Brass Band.

On the arrival of the Company at the draw of the upper bridge, a salute was fired by a detachment of the Boston Artillery, under the direction of Capt. Thomas H. Evans.

The Greys were escorted to their camp, (in the rear of the Guards' Armory,) which was called "Camp Harding," in honor of their Commander. Supper was served for the two companies in Lyceum Hall. At eight o'clock in the evening there was a Promenade Concert in the Armory, after which fireworks were let off from the camp-ground under the direction of Mr. William Beals, Pyrotechnist.

A beautiful exhibition of fireworks was given in the evening, in front of the Revere House, by Mr. Stevens, the proprietor, in honor of President Fillmore and Lord Elgin. Besides the usual display of rockets, bombs, Roman candles, and the like, there were several set pieces;—one of which was a representation, in colored lance work, of a Steamship, decorated with flags flying from her masts and peak.

The grand finale consisted of the Crown and Eagle beneath the English and American flags, between which were seen the Clasped Hands of Friendship.

A most brilliant display of fireworks was made by the citizens of East Boston, in honor of the opening of the Grand Junction Railroad. It took place at 7½ o'clock, and was greatly admired by the thousands who witnessed it from both sides of the harbor. The reflection of the fires from the intervening waters gave additional splendor to the view from the city proper. Besides the display on the grounds of the company, bon-fires were lighted on Eagle Hill, and at the residences of many of the citizens were private exhibitions of much beauty.

Such were the scenes of the Second Day of the Jubilee. No accident or untoward event occurred to mar the general joy, and the sun, as he sank in smiles behind the western hills, gave the pleasing assurance that the coming day would be enlivened by the same genial rays which had thus far given to the pageant so much of its brilliancy, and contributed so largely to the comfort and enjoyment of the gathered multitudes.

THIRD DAY.

The morning of Friday, September 19th, the last day of the Celebration, disappointed no fondly indulged hope, but dawned brightly and beautifully, filling the hearts of thousands with joy and gladness, and exciting the highest anticipations of pleasure. And all that the morning promised was fully realized; no cloud dimmed the mild splendor of the sun; no harsh breath from the east chilled the air. From sunrise to sunset the weather was glorious, and entire success crowned all the proceedings of the day.

The Banks, the Custom House, the Market House and most of the stores in the business part of the city were closed, and the occasion was observed by all classes of citizens as a holiday. The streets were thronged, from early dawn to midnight, with dense masses of happy people in holiday attire, and on no previous occasion, perhaps, in the history of the city, had so large a multitude been gathered within her limits;—yet order and decorum every where prevailed, and "gladness ruled the hour."

The distinguishing features of this day's doings were the Procession, the Dinner on the Common, and the Fireworks and Illuminations in the evening; and for all these, preparations had been made upon a becoming scale.

The appearance which the city presented, as the hour for forming the procession drew near, was animating in the extreme. In all the streets through which it was to pass, the sidewalks were every where crowded—sounds of martial music from time to time rose on the air—flags, streamers and evergreens, mottoes, inscriptions, and all manner of fanciful devices adorned the buildings—and groups of smiling and lovely faces filled the windows and looked down from the balconies. The whole scene was one of exceeding beauty, such as one would look upon again and again, "that he might call it up when far away."

To the general regret, a sudden, though happily not serious, indisposition prevented the President from joining in the procession;—he, however, had, in consequence, a far more favorable opportunity than he otherwise would have had, of seeing the whole display as it passed the Revere House; and it was a display well calculated to impress a stranger with a vivid idea of the character and resources of the city.

The hour named for the formation of the Procession was 9 o'clock, A. M.; but, owing to the unforeseen delays incident to the arrangement of so large a body of men, and so extensive a collection of the products of industry, some of them of the most ponderous description, it was nearly 11 o'clock before all was in readiness to move.

The Procession was composed of eleven divisions; and its route was from the City Hall, in School street, through Tremont, Court, Cambridge, Chambers, Green and Pitts streets, Haymarket square, Blackstone, Clinton, and South Market streets, Merchants' row, State, Washington, Dover and Tremont streets, to the corner of Park street, where it entered the Common, and passed, through lines of school children, up the Park street, down the Beacon street and through the Charles street Mall, to the Boylston street gate where it was dismissed.

FIRST DIVISION.

The vanguard consisted of a line of twelve policemen extending across the street, under the direction of officers Osborn and Sleeper.

Francis Tukey, Esq., City Marshal.

Aid, Officer Spurr.	Aid, Officer Butman.

MILITARY ESCORT.

Brigadier Gen. Samuel Andrews, of the first brigade first division, commanding, and Staff, viz:—

Major P. S. Davis, Brigade Major; Capt. Henry C. Brooks, Aid; Capt. Daniel Sharp, Jr., Brigade Quarter Master, and William Baker, Jr., Acting Aid-de-Camp.

SUFFOLK BRASS BAND.

The National Lancers, Capt. T. J. Pierce.

The Fifth regiment of Artillery, under Col. Robert Cowden, Lieut. Col. H. W. Usher; Major Caleb Page; Lieut. Samuel S. Chase, Adjutant; Lieut. Frederick A. Heath, Quartermaster; Dr. Phipps, Surgeon; Dr. C. E. Buckingham, Surgeon's mate.

BOND'S CORNET BAND.

Boston Artillery, Capt Evans.
Columbian Artillery, Capt. Thompson.
Washington Artillery, Capt. Bullock.
Roxbury Artillery, Capt. Webber.
Concord Artillery, Capt. Wood.
Charlestown Artillery, Capt. Huntley.
The last two companies annexed to the fifth regiment for the occasion.

The First Regiment of Light Infantry, under Col. C. L. Holbrook; Lieut. Col. John C. Boyd; Major James A. Abbott; Lieut. Thomas E. Chickering, Adjutant; Lieut. Thomas L. Robinson, Quartermaster; Lieut. Caleb T. Curtis, Paymaster.

KENDALL'S BRASS BAND.

New England Guards, Capt. Bradlee.
Boston Light Guard, Capt. Clark.
Washington Light Guard, Capt. Savory.
Boston Light Infantry, Capt Ashley.
City Guards, Lieut. Pulsifer commanding.
Norfolk Guards, of Roxbury, Capt. Merriam.
Massachusetts Volunteers, Capt. Moore.
Warren Light Infantry, Roxbury, Lieut. Nichols commanding.
Boston Independent Fusileers, Capt. Mitchell.
Winthrop Light Guard, Capt. Cassell.
Pulaski Guards, Capt. Wright.
Mechanic Riflemen, Capt S. G. Adams.

Next came a fine battalion of two companies from Rhode Island and Maine, under command, for the occasion, of Col. J. D. Greene of the 4th Infantry; Lieut. Col. Horace Williams; Maj. Edmund A. Parker; Dr. H. B. C. Greene, Surgeon.

BATH BRASS BAND.

Providence Light Infantry, Col. W. W. Brown commanding.
Bath City Greys, Capt. E. K. Harding.

Gen. JOHN S. TYLER, Chief Marshal.

Aids.	Aids.
Major John C. Park,	Major Joel Scott,
Col. John L. Dimmock,	Major Charles H. Appleton,

William H. Foster, Esq.

FLAGG'S BRASS BAND.

The Committee of Arrangements in carriages.

These weres ucceeded by the Mayor and Aldermen, and Common Council of this city.

SECOND DIVISION.

B. G. BATES, Chief Marshal.

Aids.	Aids.
Enoch Train,	I. G. Bates,
Peter Butler, Jr.	J. W. Ward,

Edward F. Hall.

BAND.

Secretaries Conrad and Stuart, accompanied by Mr. Alderman Rogers, in a barouche drawn by six white horses, and flanked by detachments of the Independent Cadets. [The Mayor was not in the procession,—being occupied in arrangements concerning the exercises at the Pavilion.]

Lord Elgin, and his Suite, consisting of the Hon. Col. Bruce, Private Secretary and principal Aid-de-camp, and Lord Mark Kerr, Aid-de-camp, accompanied by Francis Brinley, Esq., in a barouche drawn by six white horses, and flanked by a detachment of the Independent Cadets.

Gov. Boutwell and Aids, as follows:—Lieut. Cols. J. T. Heard, C. W. Chapman, and H. A. Williams; followed, in another carriage, by Adj't. Gen. E. W. Stone, and Lieut. Col. D. Needham.

Acting Gov. W. B. Lawrence, of Rhode Island, Major Sherman of the Flying Artillery, and Col. Pitman.

Canadian Ministry:—The Hon. Francis Hincks, Inspector General; the Hon. E. P. Taché, Receiver General; the Hon. J. H. Price, Commissioner of Crown Lands; and the Hon. George Waldegrave.

Lieut. Gov. H. W. Cushman, the Hon. Joseph Bourret, Commissioner of Public Works, and the Hon. Henry Wilson, President of the Senate.

Members of the Executive Council; the Hon. Messrs. Isaac Emery, E. K. Whitaker, and J. B. Alley, and the Hon. A. Abbot, ex-representative in Congress, from Andover.

Messrs. George W. Pike, Rodolphus B. Hubbard, Philo Leach, and Noah Gibson.

Mr. Gilkison, of Brantford, Canada; Capt. Allyne, R. N., Quebec; W. H. Ponton, Esq., Mayor of Belleville; James Ross, Esq., of Belleville.

The Hon. Amasa Walker, Secretary of the Commonwealth; Charles B. Hall, Esq. Treasurer; David Wilder, Jr., Esq., Auditor; and T. H. Campbell, Esq., Auditor of Illinois.

Sir Allan N. McNab, M. P. P.; the Hon. H. H. Killaly, Assistant Commissioner of Public Works; Mr. Robinson, of Canada; and Ex-Gov. Paine, of Vermont.

The Hon. William Morris, M. L. C.; Rev. Dr. E. Ryerson, Superintendent of the Department of Education, C. W.; the Hon. Samuel Mills, M. L. C., of Canada.

The Hon. Robert C. Winthrop, Mr. Attorney General Clifford.

Solicitor General McDonald; the Hon. W. B. Richards, M. P. P.; Mr. Sheriff Thomas, Mr. Sheriff Smith, Mr. Sheriff Camell.

George Brown, Esq., the Hon. James Hall, M. P. P.; the Hon. Robert Bell, M. P. P., of Canada; accompanied by Symmes Gardner, Esq., of Boston.

The Hon. Mr. Goodenow, the Hon. Mr. Hebard. Halifax; Col. B. C. A. Gugy, M. P. P.; the Hon. W. H. Boulton, M. P. P.

His Honor, John G. Bowes, Mayor of Toronto; Aldermen Wakefield and Beard, Mr. Recorder Duggan, and the Rev. Barnas Sears, Secretary of the Massachusetts Board of Education.

Messrs. Lepper, and Lampson, of the City Council, Quebec.

Joseph Hamel, City Surveyor, and A. Dorval, Esq., Councillor, Quebec; Aldermen Thompson and Ridout, Toronto.

William Weller, Esq., Mayor of Cobourg; Messrs. D. E. Boulton, C. H. Morgan, and R. H. Throope, and Dr. Beatty, of the same place.

George L. Allen, Esq., the Police Magistrate of Toronto; Alderman Whittemore, and Messrs. Councilmen Price, Ritchey, and Platt, of Toronto.

Mr. James Brown, Canada; William Mattice, Esq., Mayor of Cornwall, C. W.; J. Lane, Esq., Clerk C. C., Barrie; A. T. McCord, Esq., Chamberlain, and Mr. Councilman Hayes, Toronto.

Messrs. Graveley, Strong, and Jeffrey, Cobourg; Messrs. Strobridge, and Bunnell, Brantford.

Alderman Dempsey, George L. Allen, Esq. Chief of the Police, and John Watkins, Esq., of Toronto, and W. Patterson, Esq., Quebec.

James Cotton, Esq., Toronto; J. Brouseau, Esq., and Dr. Kimlin, of Quebec; and J. H. Larkin, Esq., Montreal.

The Hon. Charles Wilson, Mayor of Montreal; the Hon. N. F. Belleau, Mayor of Quebec; Alderman McFarlane, Montreal.

Mr. Councillor Weeks, Hamilton; W. G. Cassels, Esq., Toronto; Dr. E. J. Barker, Kingston; and W. Lampson, Esq., of City Council, Quebec.

Messrs. Frechette and Bronsdon, of City Council, Montreal; Alderman Magill, Hamilton; Duncan McFarlane, Esq., Toronto.

W. L. Distin, Esq., Alderman, and J. Moore, Esq., Councillor, Hamilton; J. G. Ridout, Esq., Toronto; Messrs. C. Berczy, and J. C. Pyper, Canada.

J. Trilles, M. Davis, and R. McElroy, Esq's, City Council, Hamilton; G. E. French, Esq., Washington, D. C.

The Hon. Tappan Wentworth, Lowell; J. H. Williams, Esq., and C. Willis, Esq., Boston; T. Trask, Esq., Salem; Alderman J. M. Williams, Hamilton; Gen. McLean, C. T. Gwinnell, Esq.

Hon. Alex. McLean, M. P. P.; Roderic W. Cameron, Esq., and A. Mathewson, Esq., Hamilton.

Aldermen Lynch, and Grenier, and Councillors Leeming and Atwater, Montreal.

S. Morrill, Esq., Mayor of London, C. W.; J. Lister, Esq., of the City Council, Hamilton.

Sir Robert Campbell, Montreal; and Messrs. Lane, Adams, and Richards, Canada.

Messrs. Manning, Brunskill, Robertson, and Urquhart, Toronto.

J. P. Sexton, City Clerk, and S. J. Lyman, Esq., Montreal.

The Hon. A. N. Kinsman, Mayor of New Haven; the Hon. E. Flower, Mayor of Hartford; F. Crosby, Esq., Boston.

The Hon. R. Matheson, M. P. P.; George P. Lawson, Esq., Halifax; Dr. G. C. Ardouin, Quebec.

THIRD DIVISION.

AMERICAN BRASS BAND.

HENRY C. LORD, Chief Marshal.

Aid.	Aid.
P. E. Kingman.	J. B. Wheelock.

The Hon. Charles Hudson, Naval Officer of Port of Boston; G. H. Miller, Esq., Collector of Port of Salem; S. D. Whitney, Esq., Consul to Venezuela; S. Bryant, Esq., Consul to Equador; William Elliott, Esq., British Vice Consul.

The Hon. Messrs. Kuhn, Keyes, Hubbard, and others of the Senate of Massachusetts.

Mr. Chief Justice Wells, and Messrs. Justices Hoar and Mellen, of the Court of Common Pleas, followed by about twenty members of the House of Representatives.

FOURTH DIVISION.

J. W. PIERCE, Chief Marshal.

Aid.	Aid.
D. W. Childs.	F. A. Allen.

SOUTH DEDHAM BRASS BAND.

Officers of the Army and Navy.

Capt. Nye, 20th Regiment; Capt. Stevens, R. N.; J. R. Pilkington, R. E.; Capt. Percival, U. S. N.; Capt. Jugall, Lieut. W. H. Noble, R. E.; W. A. Holwell, Ordnance Storekeeper, Quebec; Dr. Rutherford, Medical Staff; Dr. Maitland, C. P. R.; Capt. Kerr, R. E.; Capt. Marjory, 54th Regiment; Dr. Wright, U. S. N.

Senior Surgeon Stewart Chisholm, Royal Artillery; Dr. John Graham, British Army; Lieut. Archibald M. Chisholm, 42d Royal Highlanders; Dr. Delany, U. S. N.

Capt. Hawkes, Royal Regiment; William Gaudet, Commissioner of Staff; Mr. Shane, 54th Reg't; Lieut. W. A. Parker, U. S. N.

Lieut. Lutzens, 20th Reg't.; Lieut. O'Brien, 54th Reg't.; Assistant Com. Gen. Webb; Commissary John Pope, U. S. A.; Mr. Kean Buchanan, U. S. A.

FIFTH DIVISION.

Farnham Plummer, Chief Marshal.

Aid. Aid.

Stephen Rhodes. H. F. Blodgett.

This Division was composed chiefly of invited guests from Canada and the other Provinces, on foot. Among the gentlemen present we noticed the following: His Honor, the Mayor of Halifax, and Alderman More; Ex-British Consul Buchanan; the Hon. J. T. Williams, Ex-Mayor of Port Hope; the Hon. E. Hale, Sherbrooke; Mr. Justice T. C. Aylwin, C. Q. B.; the Hon. John Molson, President of the Champlain and St. Lawrence Railroad Co.; Mr. William Molson, Director of the St. Lawrence and Atlantic R. R. Co.; the Hon. William B. Robinson, M. P. P.; Dr. Hallowell, Professor in Trinity College, Toronto; Judge Mondelet and son, of Montreal; Mr. Sheriff Treadwell, of Prescott Co.; B. Delisle, R. N.; W. B. Richards, Esq., Queen's Counsel, and M. P. P. for Leeds; Mr. Charles Scheller, Deputy Clerk to the Crown; A. Jobin, Esq., M. P. P.; Henry Smith, Esq., M. P. P., for Frontenac; John Egan, Esq., M. P. P.; Messrs. Weeks and Labadie, Notaries Public, Montreal; William Lunn, Esq., and son, Montreal; B. Chamberlain, Esq., Advocate; William McDonald, Esq., Lachine; Mark Burnham, Esq., Port Hope; Mr. J. Gamble, Municipal Office, Montreal; Mr. Charles Geddes, Montreal; Dr. G. Russel, Toronto; Dr. Munro, Montreal; A. J. Alexander, M. D.; Dr. Mount, Montreal; Messrs. M. Cassiday, J. F. Peltier, and T. Cherrier, Members of the Bar, and the Hon. Judge Day, S. Court, Montreal.

Quite a number of prominent railroad capitalists and directors also appeared in this division. Among them were observed Samuel A. Walker, Esq., E. Hasket Derby, Esq., Mr. Hammond, and others.

SIXTH DIVISION.

Albert Bowker, Chief Marshal.

Aid. Aid.

C. F. Lougee. Beza Lincoln.

This Division was composed of the officers of the different departments of the City Government, past Mayors, Aldermen and Common Councilmen: also of members of the City Governments of other Cities of the United States, Officers and Clerks of various City Institutions, past resident Physicians, and others. Among them were, the Hon. J. H. Ayer, Mayor of Lowell; the Hon. Geo. Hood, Mayor of Lynn; the Mayor of Lawrence, and the Hon. Mr. Skinner, of New Haven.

The Seventh Division, constituting by far the most prominent, as well as the most interesting feature in the procession, and representing the various trades and mechanical pursuits of the city, will be specially noticed in another place. Such a display, as this Division made, was certainly never before equalled in our City, and it surpassed even the highest expectations of the most sanguine.

It placed in a striking light the industrial resources of Boston, and the elements of its prosperity ; and, in the variety, beauty, and magnitude of its exhibitions, surprised many even of those who had been all their lives familiar with the industry of the city. As no exhibition of this kind in our streets ever equalled this, so no one certainly ever gave more pleasure, or received more marked proofs of unqualified commendation and approval, from the thousands, both citizens and strangers, who were the delighted spectators of it; and it called forth from President Fillmore the expression, that, although he knew Boston "had its Merchant Princes, he had not known till then, that it had its Mechanic Noblemen of Nature."

EIGHTH DIVISION.

ALPHEUS HARDY, Chief Marshal.

Aid.	Aid.
G. F. Woodman.	F. G. Whiston.

This Division was composed of the officers and members of the Mercantile Library Association, numbering nearly 1000 persons, under the Marshalship of Mr. John Stetson, aided by Messrs. Levi L. Wilcutt and Henry C. Allen, and of a delegation of the Students of Harvard University. The Association was accompanied by the Weymouth Brass Band, and, as usual when they appear in a body, made a very fine appearance.

Harvard College was largely represented, and the delegation of students was accompanied by the Mechanics' Brass Band. The Senior Class was marshaled by C. W. Upham, with D. C. Tremble, and J. Porter as aids ; the Junior Class, by G. H. Sargent, with C. F. Livermore and W. Davis, as aids ; the Sophomore Class, by R. C. Winthrop, Jr., with B. J. Jeffries, and J. B. Dickson, as aids ; the Freshman Class, by J. Hayes, with H. Walker, and A. Agassiz as aids. A plain banner, with the simple inscription

HARVARD.

was borne by A. W. Thaxter, aided by W. P. Phipps and G. W. Norris.

NINTH DIVISION.

George Wheelwright, Chief Marshal.

Aid.	Aid.
G. A. Batchelder.	J. R. Bradford.

This Division was composed of the children of the Warren Street Chapel School, drawn in thirty-two wagons, under the marshalship of John S. Freeman. The wagons were tastefully decorated with evergreens and flowers, and the young masters and misses, to the number of about 500, had their hats, bonnets and heads wreathed with evergreen. The exhibition was arranged so as to represent the four seasons, commencing with Spring, and terminating with Winter, and was one of the most pleasing features of the procession. The children were dressed in costume appropriate to the seasons which they represented. Those in the rear wagons were in no danger of suffering from cold, judging from the material which composed their garments. In the last wagon of the train, were seated, on the trunk of a tree, Master Sidney Fisher, and Miss Elizabeth J. Foster, dressed in ancient costume, and having the appearance of a venerable couple, which character they sustained in the most appropriate manner. Over their heads, was a banner bearing the motto,

"Peace be with you."

The body of this wagon was filled with large lumps of alum, making a capital *fac-simile* of ice, and giving great effect to the show.

TENTH DIVISION.

M. Field Fowler, Chief Marshal.

Aid.	Aid.
J. B. Richardson.	H. W. Cushing.

At the head of this Division was the German Gymnastic Society, Mr. Meier, Marshal. They numbered about 30 persons, and bore the German flag.

Other Societies followed in the order mentioned below, each bearing its banner :—

The Bay State Lodge of the Grand United Order of Odd Fellows, No. 814.

The Scots Charitable Society, led by Alexander Macgregor, all wearing plaid, and some the emblematic feather.

The Mutual Relief Society, John Madigan, Marshal.

The Young Catholic's Friend Society, Wm. F. A. Kelly, Marshal.

The St. Mary's Mutual Benefit Society, Owen Harrington, Marshal.

The Irish Protestant Mutual Relief Society, John Hagan, Marshal.

The Laborer's Aid Society, James O'Neil, Marshal.

[The members of this Society were uniformly dressed in black hats, blue frocks, and black pantaloons.]

The Father Mathew T. A. Society, Berthold Taylor, Marshal.

The St. Nicholas Total Abstinence Society, of East Boston, Martin Burke, Marshal.
The St. John's Mutual Relief Total Abstinence Society, of East Boston, D. W. Campbell, Marshal.
The St. Vincent Total Abstinence Society, Thomas Carberry, Marshal.
The Father Mathew Mutual Benevolent Total Abstinence Society, of Charlestown, James O'Brien, Marshal.
The St. Joseph Total Abstinence Society of Roxbury, James Kilduff, Marshal.

ELEVENTH DIVISION.

C. J. SAVAGE, Chief Marshal.

Aid.	Aid.
Enoch Train, Jr.	F. Lyman.

This Division was composed of our hardy and muscular truckmen, to the number of 110, dressed in their neat white frocks, black hats and trowsers, mounted on their noble horses, and under command of Col. Thomas Bancroft.

The whole procession terminated with a cavalcade, which though not very numerous, made a very respectable appearance.

It is difficult to make any very accurate estimate of the number of those who took part in the procession; but some idea of it may be formed from the fact that the time occupied in passing any given point was fully two hours, and that its length could not have been less than three and a half miles. The streets through which it passed were kept entirely free from carriages, and had been swept and sprinkled with water. The sidewalks along its whole route were filled by a compact yet perfectly orderly mass of delighted spectators, while from every window, balcony and portico, and even from many roofs, clusters of happy faces looked down upon the moving pageant. As the distinguished guests of the city came in view they every where met a most cordial and enthusiastic reception. Cheer followed cheer continually, while from window and balcony the animated looks, bright smiles, fluttering silks and waving handkerchiefs of the ladies added a poetic grace to the scene. The greeting, so heartily given, was warmly received and gracefully reciprocated. The ever ready shout of welcome which attended the progress of Lord Elgin, in particular, was indicative, not only of the friendly feelings entertained towards the nation he represented, and of respect for the high station he filled, but it was a spontaneous testimony of the personal interest in himself which his frank courtesy and noble bearing had inspired.

The streets, through which the procession was to pass, had been profusely and tastefully ornamented. Although any description, which can now be given of their various decorations, can convey but a faint impression of the reality; yet their beauty, number and appropriateness contributed in so great a degree to the splendor of the pageant, that an attempt must be made to indicate their character. The account which follows, imperfect as it is, may in some measure answer this purpose. It is given in the order of the route of the Procession, commencing with the City Hall.

THE CITY HALL.

This building was only ornamented on the southern side, facing School street. Over the general passage-way to the building, a large arch was erected, the columns of which were inscribed with the names of the thirty-two railroads of Massachusetts, centering in Boston. On the face of the arch, as viewed from the south, a train of cars was represented in full motion, and the motto—

GRAND RAILROAD JUBILEE,

SEPT. 17TH, 18TH, 19TH, 1851.

On the reverse was the inscription,—

THE CANADAS AND THE GREAT WEST.

PROSPERITY TO ALL.

The emblem, enclosed by the inscription, was a steamship ploughing her way through the ocean.

From the highest windows of the central front, lines of large and well arranged banners extended to the east and west. The Stars and Stripes, the red cross of St. George, and flags with the armorial bearings of the Canadas, gave a fine appearance to the building. Starred streamers and pennons, of various colors and tastefully garlanded, hung from the various windows. On the balcony in front was an equestrian portrait of Washington, of life size, with the inscription,—

WASHINGTON,

"THE FATHER OF OUR COUNTRY."

And beneath,—

THE MARCH OF IMPROVEMENT!

Over the eastern entrance from School street was a medallion, inscribed,—

"E PLURIBUS UNUM."

1851.

and surmounted by a golden Eagle grasping in his talons the national colors. Over the western entrance, another medallion showed the old Pine Tree Flag of Colonial Massachusetts, with the word and the date,—

PLYMOUTH!

1620.

From each medallion waved a heavy flag, with silver stars on a ground of azure.

TREMONT STREET.

On reaching Tremont street, the Albion Hotel, richly decorated, first attracted the attention of the spectator. From it lines of flags of different nations were stretched in various directions, and festoons of streamers were arranged across its front. Along the balustrade, commencing on Beacon street was the following inscription:

GRAND RAILROAD AND STEAMBOAT JUBILEE.

BOSTON, SEPTEMBER 17TH, 18TH, 19TH, 1851.

[Two hands interlocked.]

WE GREET OUR FRIENDS.

BOSTON, 1630. BOSTON, 1851.

OUR MARCH IS ONWARD.

The Museum building was beautifully decorated with almost numberless flags of various nations, and streamers in great profusion. Across the street in front were several large flags, and from the staffs which surmount the building, lines of the same graceful drapery were extended to the corners. The display, generally, at this point was very good.

COURT STREET.

Across Court street, at the head of Hanover, the City Guards threw out a medallion bearing their name, and flanked on either side by American flags. From Chilson's Block to the house opposite, was extended a line of English and American flags, festooned with streamers, and connected together by a band bearing the following couplet:

"Thus, with the glorious *Stars* forever bright,
Shine, radiant *Cross*, in undivided light."

BOWDOIN SQUARE.

Next came the Revere House, whose tasteful decorations have already been described as amongst those which added so much to the attractiveness of the scene on the occasion of the President's arrival.

In the square, however, other flags and streamers had been suspended, which added much to the beauty of the show.

CAMBRIDGE AND HANCOCK STREETS.

Passing down Cambridge street, as the eye wandered up Hancock street, it was greeted with a fine display. At different places were American and English flags floating in friendly union. The front of Dr. Bigelow's residence, besides supporting lines of flags which extended across the street, was very tastefully decorated with red, blue and white pennons, in the centre of which was the inscription,—

HAIL TO OUR CITY'S NOBLE GUESTS.

At the junction of Cambridge and Chambers streets there was a very profuse display of flags, marine signals, streamers, and other gay bunting.

CHAMBERS STREET.

In Chambers street, the residences of Rev. Dr. Barrett and Newell Harding, Esq. were tastefully festooned. In front of the residence of Mr. George Cook a very neat arch was formed with American and English flags, in the centre of which was placed a portrait of Queen Victoria. The house was also decorated with a complete set of Marryatt's signals. The portico of the block opposite, occupied by Messrs. Prince, J. Fowle, and G. W. Lewis, was also very prettily trimmed. On the corner of Cambridge and Eaton streets, the house of Mr. Edwin A. Raymond was well decorated. Mr. Raymond very tastefully introduced into his decorations a fine engraving of Washington. Flags across the street completed the display at this point.

PITTS STREET.

In Pitts street, in front of the houses of Messrs. Brewster, Knight, Elliot, Sibley, Cheever and Barry, were several lines of flags and streamers. Across the street was an American flag, bearing the motto,—

OUR GUESTS AND OUR COUNTRY.

The fronts of Nos. 4, 5, and 29, were also decorated.

HAYMARKET SQUARE.

Haymarket square and the Depot of the Boston and Maine Railroad, were profusely ornamented with flags and streamers. Across the entrance of the Square from Union street, was displayed, in large letters, the word,—

WELCOME!

BLACKSTONE STREET.

Along Blackstone street, between Haymarket square and Hanover street, there were several lines of flags. In Hanover street, in front of the printing office of G. C. Jenks, No. 86, were displayed two banners, each twenty-five feet in length. On one of them was printed, in large letters, the word,—

OREGON.

suggestive of that prodigious embryo, the great Pacific Railroad. On the other,—

HARVEST.

significant not only of the beautiful season, but of the bountiful fruit now yielded to the city by the network of railways spread over the State. Crossing Hanover, a very brilliant show was made of the American, English and French flags. Suspended across the street was the following motto:

"BIEN-VENU, CAMARADES."

The fronts of Nos. 50 and 52 were abundantly trimmed. Messrs. Parker & White, Benjamin Wilder, Field, Converse & Co., Wm. Lovejoy & Co., O. H. Underhill, and Tuttle & Higbee, also decorated their several premises. The New England House was well trimmed, and also threw across the street a line of flags, the central one of which bore the inscription,—

WE WELCOME OUR PRESIDENT.

CLINTON STREET.

In Clinton street there was a large exhibition of American flags and streamers. Reed & Wade's store was tastefully decorated. A bronze bust of the Hon. Daniel Webster occupied the middle window of the second story, immediately below the other windows of which, were models of clipper ships. Among the many flags across the street was one which showed unequivocal evidence of having seen service.

COMMERCIAL STREET.

Across Commercial street, from the Eastern end of Faneuil Hall Market to the opposite building, was a line of American flags. In the centre was a large spread eagle, admirably carved in wood, and gilded. At this point the members of the procession caught a glimpse of a portion of the shipping in the harbor, which was profusely and gaily decorated with flags, pennons, streamers, and other characteristic bunting, adding much to the brilliancy of the spectacle; while on the other side, was Faneuil Hall Market, whose interior presented a beautiful appearance. Along the passage-way, on either side, was one continuous line of streamers, of various colors, festooned and blended together with much taste. At the various entrances these lines of streamers were intersected with the American flag, arranged in graceful arches. Several of the stalls were also trimmed with good taste. Directly under the clock in the centre of the Market, were the following inscriptions :—

"OUR COUNTRY: IN ALL THAT IS GOOD, LET ITS COURSE BE ONWARD."

On the reverse,

OUR NATION AS IT IS: OUR MARKET AS IT WAS.

SOUTH MARKET STREET.

The long block of granite buildings on the South side of South Market street was ornamented with a rich profusion of flags and streamers. The proprietors of "Quincy Hall," also made an excellent display.

STATE STREET.

State street at its junction with Merchants' row, looked very finely. Not only was there an abundance of flags, but they were tastefully arranged. Nos. 87, 89 and 91, looked exceedingly well. In front of the Merchants' Exchange was a line of beautiful banners. In this building are the offices of the Ogdensburg and Rutland Railroads, the completion of which was, in so large a measure, the occasion of the celebration. Very appropriately therefore, the Directors of these roads exhibited, drawn across the street, a very large map on which were represented the New England States, New York, Ohio, Pennsylvania and Upper Canada, with Lakes Ontario, Erie, and Huron. On the map were traced the different lines of railroads which have been constructed, and at the bottom of it was the inscription :—

THE WEST AND CANADA TO BOSTON, VIA OGDENSBURG, VERMONT CENTRAL, AND RUTLAND AND BURLINGTON RAILROADS.

From the Old State House, flags were suspended across the street on each side of the building. On the north side, the fronts of Redding & Co's. store, the Journal office, and Eastburn's printing office, looked very finely. The telegraph station on the top of the building was trimmed with the usual good taste of its proprietors, and presented a fine appearance. The Traveller, Bee, and Times offices on the south side, were ornamented with flags and pennons. In one of the windows of the "Bee" building was a medallion, bearing this inscription :—

THE PEOPLE'S PRESS PAYS HOMAGE TO THE PEOPLE'S PRESIDENT.

In front of the Times office, across the street, was a large American flag, bearing the words :—

WELCOME ! CANADIANS.

Above the portico at the eastern end of the Old State House, was erected a grand triumphal arch, on which was inscribed the words :—

"LIBERTY, EQUALITY, FRATERNITY."

WASHINGTON STREET.

On Washington street, in front of Adams & Co's. Express office, was a very large American flag, flanked by smaller ones, and bearing these inscriptions :—

"No pent up Utica contracts our powers—
The whole unbounded Continent is ours."

On the reverse, the words of Puck,—

"WE'LL PUT A GIRDLE ROUND THE EARTH IN FORTY MINUTES."

The fronts of Nos. 107 and 109 were fittingly decorated. In front of No. 129, was displayed in large letters, the word

WELCOME !

The occupants of Nos. 129, 134 and 136, displayed good taste in decorating their several buildings. In a window in front of No. 162, mounted upon a pedestal, was a bust of Washington.

In front of Thomas J. Atkins' store, was a miniature statue of Samuel Adams. James G. Hovey's store was also tastefully ornamented. Shorey & Co. made a very liberal display of streamers. The front of No. 176 was covered with American flags, very handsomely arranged. From a window in the second story, projected a balustrade, which was hung with streamers ; in the centre of it, was a very handsome gilt vase, filled with flowers, and on each corner, an alabaster lion. The display here was very fine. Tucker & Brothers' store, the China tea building, Wheelock & Wells, and A. Kinsley's store, were well decorated. From the armory of the Boston Light Infantry, floated the Stars and Stripes. At the head of Summer street, a line of flags and streamers combined in excellent taste, extended across Washington street. Across the street, from No. 348 to No. 401, was a plain white flag, bearing the inscription,

BOSTON AND CANADA UNITED,
1851.

From the Liberty Tree Block to Boylston Market, waved a line of flags, with the inscription :—

MAGNA CHARTA AND THE DECLARATION OF INDEPENDENCE.

On the reverse :

"ON EARTH, PEACE AND GOOD WILL."

From William Brown's drug store, on the corner of Eliot street, were suspended the words,

WE WELCOME YOU ALL.

Mr. Matthews' store, No. 507, bore on its front, the mottoes :

ENGLAND AND AMERICA.
PERPETUAL PEACE.
THE QUEEN,—THE PRESIDENT.

The balustrade above, was gracefully festooned, and had in its centre an excellent bust of President Fillmore. Building No. 563, was decorated in front, and had a line of colors across the street. The balustrades of Nos. 322, 324, 326 and 328, were covered with flags and streamers, and filled with ladies. The occupants of the fine block on the south easterly corner of Washington street and Indiana place, did well their part. Upon an American flag across the street, in front of the building, was the noble inscription :—

"THE UNION NOW AND FOREVER, ONE AND INSEPARABLE."

and along the balustrade,

THE UNION AND THE CONSTITUTION, THE TWO GREAT LIGHTS IN THE AMERICAN FIRMAMENT.

Over the entrance to Orange street, was a very happy design. An iron arch was prettily trimmed with the American flag and streamers. Beneath the crown of the arch was a shield, surmounted by a small gilt eagle. Underneath was the inscription,

A HEARTY WELCOME TO ALL.

On the right, surrounded by stars:

"UNITED WE STAND."

On the left:

PEACE.

The building on the corner of Castle street, was very prettily festooned—as were also Nos. 665 and 667.

DOVER STREET.

Dover street far eclipsed all others in the beauty and extent of its decorations. Along its entire length, on both sides, the buildings were hung with streamers, grouped together with rosettes and wreaths of flowers and evergreens—while from the windows and across the street were thrown out innumerable flags of various nations, at short intervals between which, mottoes were suspended. The first one, near the head of the street, was

WELCOME! PRESIDENT FILLMORE.

On each side of this, were the American and English flags. Along the balustrade of the handsome block of swelled front buildings, on the right hand side, were the names of the Presidents, from Washington to Taylor, in ornamented letters. Directly over the entrance to No. 80, between the names of J. Q. Adams, and Monroe, was the inscription:—

RAILROADS MAKE US ONE.

Over the entrance to No. 82, was inscribed,

"THE UNION FOREVER."

In front of No. 73, opposite, was displayed the motto,

OUR GUESTS FROM THE BRITISH SOIL.
WE BID THEM WELCOME
TO YANKEE LAND.

and from a window a medallion bust of FILLMORE, surrounded by a wreath of flowers. The second display across the street consisted of a representation of a steam engine, under full headway, around which were the following inscriptions.

On the right :—

THE GREAT PEACE MAKER.

On the left :—

STEAM POWER, ONE OF THE POWERS THAT BE.

Underneath :—

THOMAS BLANCHARD BUILT A STEAM CARRIAGE 1825.

PETITION FOR A RAILROAD 1826. THE FIRST IN AMERICA.

In front of No. 69, was displayed the honored name of

LAFAYETTE.

On the end of the building at the corner of South Suffolk street, were suspended in gilt letters, in the form of an arch, the words,—

LIVERPOOL, HALIFAX, BOSTON.

Just below Suffolk street, across Dover street, were full-length portraits of President Fillmore and Lord Elgin shaking hands, and underneath, this inscription :—

"Now let us haste these bonds to knit,
And in the work be handy,
That we may blend 'God save the Queen,'
With 'Yankee Doodle Dandy!'"

On the right of the President was the American eagle surrounded by gilt stars, and surmounted by the word,—

FULTON.

And on the left of Lord Elgin, the Lion and Unicorn, surmounted with the name of,—

WATT.

The other banners across the street were as follows :—

WELCOME TO OUR GUESTS FROM THE BRITISH PROVINCES AND OUR SISTER STATES.

A chain of three links was surrounded by the words,

MONTREAL, BOSTON AND HALIFAX.

Other flags bore the mottoes :

COMMERCE.

AGRICULTURE.

MECHANIC ARTS.

CUNARD.

And on the last was a representation of the cities of Montreal and Boston, with this inscription :—

MONTREAL AND BOSTON—UNITED WE PROSPER.

Along the right side of the street, below Suffolk street, were the names of FRANKLIN and the several Mayors of the city—PHILLIPS, QUINCY, OTIS, WELLS, LYMAN, ARMSTRONG, ELIOT, CHAPMAN, BRIMMER, DAVIS, QUINCY, Jr., and BIGELOW. Across Emerald street was erected a large platform, covered with the American and British flags, and on which were thirty-three beautiful girls, thirty-one of whom were dressed in white, and had upon their heads wreaths of splendid flowers. They were intended to represent the different States, and each wore a sash with the name of the State which she represented upon it. Each bore also in her right hand a small American flag. In the centre of these young ladies was a fair daughter of our city, dressed in regal style, and wearing upon her head a golden crown, the front of which sparkled with diamonds. She was intended to personate Queen Victoria. On the extreme right of the platform was a young lady who personated Massachusetts. The whole affair was most tastefully arranged, and presented a beautiful appearance. The young ladies upon the platform were all residents of Dover street, and, most of them, pupils of the Franklin School.

As the carriages which contained the members of the Cabinet and Lord Elgin successively approached the platform, the young ladies commenced singing the beautiful song "New England," and continued to do so until the carriages were directly in front, when Miss Carey, who personated the Queen, descended from the platform, and, escorted by Mr. John D. Philbrick, the master of the Quincy School, proceeded to the carriage appropriated to the President and his Cabinet. She held in her hand a beautiful bouquet, which she had designed to present to the President,—but, in his absence, Mr. Secretary Stuart rose to receive it. She accompanied the offering of the bouquet with the following appropriate remarks: —

"Mr. President,—

"I am happy to meet you under circumstances which exhibit in so striking a manner the prosperity and happiness of your country, and the harmony and good feeling which exist among the people of the nation over whose interests you preside."

To this Mr. Secretary Stuart replied: —

"I am very happy to receive this beautiful bouquet in the name of the President. We regret exceedingly that he is not here in person to receive it."

The "Queen" returned to her place, and then Miss Paxton, representing Massachusetts, was escorted to the carriage containing Lord Elgin, to whom she presented a fine bouquet, with this address: —

"Massachusetts welcomes to the hospitality of her metropolis, with cordial salutation, the distinguished Chief Magistrate of Her Majesty's Provinces in North America."

To this his Lordship replied in substance as follows: —

"I shall preserve this as a token of the kindness and hospitality of the State of Massachusetts and the city of Boston."

Loud cheers were then given for Queen Victoria, for Lord Elgin, and for the Canadas. In response, the Viceroy called for cheers for the President and for Massachusetts. Other cheers followed for Mr. Webster and others. A little further on, Lord Elgin, holding up his beautiful bouquet to the crowd around him, said :—

"I received this from a fair representative of the State of Massachusetts, and shall keep it as a memorial of her."

This pleasing incident of the procession will not soon be forgotten by those who witnessed it.

In front of No. 33 was the inscription:—

Bless the Power that has made and preserved us a Nation.

A very neat steel engraving of Lord Elgin was suspended over the entrance to this building. Over the entrance to No. 26, was a banner with the inscription:—

"Knowledge is Power."

In front of No. 23, was the motto:—

"The Schoolmaster is Abroad."

The brick block Nos. 6, 8, 10 and 12, looked very finely. Along the balustrade in front were the words:—

Britannia and Columbia.

Perhaps no part of the city presented at any time a more beautiful and animating sight than that which delighted the eye, as the procession was moving through Dover street; nor was the hospitality of the inhabitants of the street, so far as there was opportunity of exercising it, less striking.

TREMONT STREET.

From the corner of Dover street to the Johnson School House there were no very conspicuous decorations, though there was the usual number and variety of flags. At the Johnson School House, however, a very attractive scene was presented.

In consequence of the tender age of the pupils belonging to the Primary Schools, they took no public part in the celebration. But the public spirit of Dr. J. Odin, the Chairman of District No. 13, had caused a platform to be erected over the area in front of the above named school house, upon which were arrayed two or three hundred of the Primary School children of that District, from four to eight years of age, accompanied by their teachers. The platform was handsomely ornamented, and directly behind the children was a line of flags, bearing the words:—

WELCOME! OUR PRESIDENT!

Along the front of the fence was the inscription, in large letters:—

PRIMARY SCHOOLS.

On the right,

NO. OF SCHOOLS, 189.

On the left,

NO. OF PUPILS, 12,110.

And over the children,

HERE ARE OUR JEWELS.

One of the boys held a banner, on which was inscribed:—

"TALL OAKS FROM LITTLE ACORNS GROW."

When the carriage which contained Secretaries Stewart and Conrad came opposite this point, a little girl was carried to it in the arms of a gentleman, and presented to Secretary Stewart a beautiful bouquet, saying to him:—

"Will you, Sir, request the President to accept this bouquet from the Primary School children of Boston?"

The Secretary, in the kindest manner, and with that benignity which won all hearts while he was here, assured her that he would.

As the carriage of the Earl passed this point, the same little girl, with childlike courtesy, presented him, too, with a bouquet, as an offering from her little companions. His Lordship received the blushing child with a fatherly kindness which it is hoped she may long live to remember.

In front of the Winthrop House, and overhanging the street, was a large map of the United States and the Canadas, in the upper corners of which were interwoven the Union Jack and the Stars and Stripes. On the map were these inscriptions :—

THE CANADAS.

(A pair of hands interlocked.)

And,

THE UNITED STATES OF AMERICA,
FROM OCEAN'S WAVE TO OCEAN'S WAVE.

PERPETUAL PEACE AND FRIENDSHIP.

This was almost the last of the prominent decorations with which the buildings along the whole route of the procession had been so liberally provided, and which contributed so materially to throw over the whole scene an air of gaiety and beauty, constituting its peculiar attraction.

On reaching the foot of Park street, the procession turned into the Mall, and passed through the long files of children extending the whole length of the Malls on Park, Beacon and Charles streets, to the Boylston street gate, where it passed out and was dismissed.

Through the efficient and cheerful co-operation of the masters and pupils of the schools, the arrangements of the Committee of the School Board were carried out with eminent success; and a delegation of about five thousand pupils of both sexes were presented to the view of the guests of the city, as the representatives of nearly twenty-five thousand in the Public Schools of Boston.

The appearance of this array of intelligent and happy boys and girls, extending more than a mile, could not fail to make, upon every reflecting mind, a deep and most delightful impression. Here, by the pupils of her Free Schools, was represented the chief glory of the city. Here were some of the fruits of that system which, from the earliest period of her settlement, has ever been, as now, the chief object of her fostering care; which has given to her enterprise and industry, success and prosperity, and crowned her with a name, of which she may well be proud. So long as this name shall continue to be deserved, and this glory rightly claimed,—so long may her sons repeat, in faith and hope, the prayer engraved on the City's seal—" SICUT PATRIBUS SIT DEUS NOBIS."

The enthusiasm with which the distinguished guests of the city were received by this portion of the "Standing Army" of New England, excited, in a high degree, their surprise and wonder, and called from them frequent and strong expressions of gratification at this peculiar and beautiful feature in their reception.

To Lord Elgin and his Suite, and to the members of the United States' Government, as they passed through the line, offerings of flowers were made by the young misses representing the first classes of many of the schools; while the boys, by their animated looks and hearty cheers, gave abundant testimony of the warmth of their feelings, and of the pleasure they took in uniting their voices to the general welcome, and in offering their tokens of honor and respect to those whom their fathers had so cordially received.

As her system of public instruction has ever been considered as the foundation of the prosperity of the city, and as giving life, energy and direction to all the industrial pursuits of her people, there would seem to be a peculiar appropriateness in introducing, in this connection, some account of the exhibition, made by her artizans, of the products of their labor and skill,—an exhibition which constituted the most prominent, as well as the most attractive, feature of the procession. But of the character of the display mention has already been made, though no notice was taken of the fact, which should not be overlooked, that only about ten days had elapsed from the time when it was decided that such a display should be made, and the preparations for it were begun, to the day when all things were in readiness for the procession. Had more time been taken, the beauty and variety of the exhibition—beautiful and varied as it was—would, probably, have been greatly increased.

It will readily be conceived that any account which

should be drawn up during the march of the procession, must be exceedingly imperfect; and yet, upon such, chiefly, is the following description based. In the hurry and confusion incident to such an occasion, many exhibitions were but slightly noticed, and some not even mentioned. To supply these deficiencies, and to ensure, if possible, a full and accurate description, notice was given, through the public papers, of the desire of the City Government that, in the official account of the Celebration, this feature of it should be prominently noticed, and inviting those interested to furnish all such information as they might possess which would conduce to this end. In consequence of this call, several valuable communications were received, which have aided much in giving fulness to the description; yet, with all these aids, and with all the effort that has been made to render it in some measure worthy of the reality, it is still by no means such as the beauty and magnitude of the display—so honorable alike to the mechanics and the city—justly demanded.

To those who were the delighted spectators of the "Procession of Trades," the inadequacy of the following account will be readily apparent; to others, it may serve to convey some, though at best but a faint, idea of its most striking features.

This Division of the procession consisted of about fifty Sections, each representing some particular branch of industry. The position of each Section in the line was determined by lot, and many of them were under the direction of marshals of their own choice. The whole Division was under the direction of

GRANVILLE MEARS, ESQ., Chief Marshal.

Aids,	Aids.
Joseph M. Wightman,	H. J. Richardson,
Frederic W. Lincoln, Jr.,	F. W. Winship,
J. W. Leavitt,	J. W. Bradford.
John P. Ober, Jr.,	

At the head of the "exposition" of the Trades was a fine model, in plaster, of Stephenson's "Wounded Indian," borne on an appropriately decorated platform; after which followed, in the order of the programme, as established by lot, manufacturers of the following articles:

STEEL TRAPS AND WROUGHT IRON HINGES.

Fifteen different patterns of steel traps, and as many varieties of wrought iron hinges, were shown by Mr. J. Watkins, of Roxbury.

TRUNKS, HARNESSES AND SADDLERY.

Mr. H. Cross, of this city, had a wagon filled with fine specimens of saddlery. Heavy festoons of white and red, from the top of his vehicle, had a pleasing effect. Mr. E. A. G. Roulstone had a similar display. His wagon was draped with the American colors. A display from Mr. Baker's saddlery store, in Court street, was noticed as exceedingly neat and tasteful.

BRONZE AND ORNAMENTAL IRON WORK.

In bronze and ornamental iron work, the specimens of Chase Brothers & Co. attracted particular attention. In the front, the bronzed sleeping lions, which were most admirably designed, were much admired. Between and over these stood a silver eagle, with extended wings, grasping a golden globe in his talons. A rich and heavy roll of evergreens, with flowers interwreathed, was suspended over them; and, on an arch above, were the words—

WE ARE NEIGHBORS AND FRIENDS.

Our national banner, and the red cross of St. George, floated above the whole. Amongst the various objects of interest, was a metallic cast of a Newfoundland dog. On the end of the wagon, was the motto—

"PAX ET AMICITIA IN PERPETUO!"

HATTERS.

The journeymen hatters made a fine display in a large wagon, (furnished by Gilson & Evans,) which bore a neat shop, in full operation, and presenting a busy appearance—several girls taking a prominent part in the work. The procession which followed was a very full one, and bore a banner, inscribed with the words—

THE HATTERS.
BOSTON, SEPTEMBER 19TH, 1851.

On the reverse—

WE CROWN THE HEADS OF THE SOVEREIGN PEOPLE.

TURNERS.

Messrs. Coolidge & Moore, No. 15 Hawley street, furnished a car, containing a turning lathe and fret sawing machine in operation. The car was inclosed by a turned railing, and otherwise decorated with many handsome articles peculiar to the craft.

INDIA RUBBER GOODS.

George H. Hale & Co., of Bromfield street, exhibited specimens of the almost endless variety of rubber goods manufactured by them; among which were machine banding, every description of water-proof clothing, air pillows, life preservers, sub-marine dresses, gun cases, and drinking cups. Their articles were well arranged, and showed to much advantage; giving new evidence, if that were wanted, of the numberless uses to which india rubber is now applied.

EXPRESS MEN.

The exhibition made by the Express men was as attractive as it was unexpected, and furnished a striking illustration of the extent to which their business is carried. Their substantial but handsome wagons were drawn by noble looking horses in elegant harnesses, and were filled with boxes, bales and parcels, so arranged as to indicate, by their conspicuously written directions, the prominent places in the route of each Express. The Expresses represented were Adams & Co.'s, with boxes marked "San Francisco, California," "Philadelphia," &c.; Harnden's; Kinsley & Co.'s; Thompson & Co.'s Western Express, with boxes and bundles marked "Albany," "Buffalo," &c.; Leonard's Worcester Express;

Longley & Co.'s Eastern Express, with packages marked "Portland;" and Carpenter & Co.'s, and Hodgman & Co.'s, with wagons filled with freight for places on the Kennebec and Penobscot rivers. Harnden's Express displayed a banner, with the words—

THE FIRST EXPRESS IN AMERICA;

it having been established, in 1834, by the late William H. Harnden, Esq., the enterprising pioneer of the present system of Expresses.

IRON PIPES.

The iron pipes, though not so attractive as the other parts of the array, were felt to represent no unimportant part of our industrial interests.

CARRIAGE MAKERS.

The carriage-makers of the city proper avoided a competition with their neighbors, the craft being entirely represented by Messrs. Frye, Brainard and Rowell, of South Boston. The work exhibited was of a high order of excellence, and a band of hardy workmen spoke well for that part of the city.

RIGGERS.

The riggers were preceded by an open carriage, bearing Mr. Edward Carnes, the oldest master rigger in Boston. He bore a flag which was unfurled when Washington visited the city in 1789. Mr. James A. White, who has long been favorably known wherever Boston canvas is spread to the wind, acted as marshal to the procession of athletic men which followed, assisted by Joseph I. McClennan and Robert Smith, as aids. A fine model of a man-of-war, commanded by A. K. Bryer as Captain, aided by John Hammond, Samuel Myrick and Henry Lewis, as first, second and third mates, and drawn by five horses, accompanied them.

MUSEUM.

The Boston Museum gave the long line of people a chance "to see the elephant," attended by Malays. But as "good wine needs no bush," the managers of the institution probably thought it unnecessary to show what they could do "upon a pinch."

BAKERS.

Two most substantial loads of flour from the East Boston Steam Mills followed, affording a striking illustration of the benefits to be derived from the completion of the lines of road on account of which the celebration was instituted.

The first was a plain express wagon, with ten barrels of flour, and supporting a staff twelve feet long, surmounted with a plain gilt eagle and a white and buff banner, bearing the following inscription:—

WESTERN VIRGINIA FLOUR, VIA
OHIO RIVER, GREAT LAKES, OGDENSBURG AND VERMONT RAILROADS.
772 BARRELS FROM ONE MILL—CONSIGNED TO
LYMAN REED & CO., BOSTON.
DISTANCE OF TRANSPORTATION, - - 1000 MILES.
TIME OF TRANSPORTATION, - - - 12 DAYS.
FREIGHT PER BARREL $1.05 FROM THE OHIO RIVER TO BOSTON.

On the reverse side was the following:

"Extract from the First Report in relation to a Railroad from Boston to Ogdensburg, dated February 9, 1830:—

'We consider Works of Internal Improvement of the utmost importance to the prosperity and permanency of the UNION.

We deem the subject of Railroads of vital importance.

The Committee are of opinion that a Railroad to connect the Western Lakes with the Atlantic cannot be constructed on any location where it will afford more advantages to the inhabitants of New England and the Nation generally, than from Boston, Mass., to Ogdensburg, New York. Therefore,

Resolved, That the public good requires vigorous and persevering efforts on the part of all intelligent and public-spirited individuals, until by the enterprise of individuals, the co-operation of State Legislatures, or the aid of the General Government, the survey and completion of a route is established for a National Railroad from the seaboard at Boston, through Lowell, Mass., Concord, in New Hampshire, and thence by the most convenient route through the valley of Onion River to Lake Champlain, and thence to the waters of Lake Ontario at Ogdensburg, New York.

LYMAN REED,
E. P. WALTON, } Committee.'"
S. BALDWIN,

Following this banner was a "Boston Truck," containing the usual load of twenty barrels of the same article, drawn by two horses, and with a white banner attached to it, on which was inscribed—

BUCHANAN'S EXTRA FLOUR,
FROM
WELLSBURG, WESTERN VIRGINIA.

The above was brought into the procession at the particular request of the Railroad Committee of the City Government, with a view to show some of the fruits already resulting from the *new* railroad communications with the Great West, to produce some evidence and some facts on the subject of *transportation* entirely unknown to many persons here and at the West, and to show in some degree what may be expected hereafter.

Closely following were machines for making crackers, which were in successful operation, and very pleasantly astonished the crowd by the neatness and expedition with which they performed their work.

MASONS, CARPENTERS AND HOUSE PAINTERS.

The only display under this head was that made by Messrs. Baker, Perry & Co., No. 613 Washington street, who exhibited numerous specimens of their work, arranged on a platform, in the form of a building, 12 feet by 7, at each gable of which was a staff bearing the American flag.

The roof of the house was formed of blinds; the sides were made of doors, blinds and sashes, of various forms, and of the finest workmanship and materials. Inside were seen bundles of stair balusters, a glazier's easel, and other like articles—while two men were actively at work, glazing sashes.

The sashes, glazed with plate glass, were of cherry wood; the doors and other articles of Eastern pine; and all were admirable specimens of the perfection to which American machine work has been brought.

BELLOWS MAKERS.

Messrs. Holden & Barnum placed in the procession a mammoth pair of Lillie's patent double-acting Bellows, so constructed that, at every stroke of the handle, it fills and discharges itself twice, giving at the same time great uniformity of blast. Upon this was the inscription—

"A NEW WAY TO RAISE THE WIND."

CABINET MAKERS, UPHOLSTERERS, PAPIER MACHE AND SCHOOL FURNITURE.

The display in this department was really magnificent, and it is much to be regretted that no materials for a fuller description have been furnished.

E. A. & G. T. Smallwood, corner of Beach and Lincoln streets, sent from their establishment beautiful specimens of Sofas and Chairs, some of which were finished and some unfinished. An arch, erected in the front part of the platform, was surmounted by a gilt eagle resting upon a globe. The carriage was drawn by four horses.

Stephen Smith, No. 49 Cornhill, exhibited three splendid desks for offices. Clerks were sitting at them, and were busily engaged with day-book and ledger.

John Putnam, No. 404 Washington street, exhibited one of his best black walnut spiral spring bedsteads.

Bowler & Co., papier mache manufacturers, No. 8 Somerset street, had in the procession a finely carved and highly finished book-case. The carriage on which it was borne had the motto,

"PROTECTION TO MANUFACTURERS."

J. J. Haley, Fulton street, exhibited a complete set of ornamental chamber furniture, adorned with flower work, and representations of fountains and birds.

This chamber set has been pronounced by good judges to be as beautiful as any ever exhibited in Boston. The carriage was tastefully trimmed with drapery and festoons of evergreen, and bore on the banner in front the motto—

"THERE'S NO SUCH WORD AS CAN'T."

A. H. Allen, No. 2 Dock square, had specimens of his parlor furniture, which made a most beautiful appearance.

In front was a set of windows, hung with the richest window drapery.

A number of settees were exhibited from the establishment of W. O. Haskell, No. 66 Commercial street. The carriage on which they were borne had the motto,

SIT AT EASE.

There was a fine show of school furniture from the establishment of J. L. Ross. The desks were arranged as nicely as though they were in the school-room, and were occupied by twelve scholars and two teachers of the Hancock School. This carriage attracted great attention, and bore for a motto,

"FREE SCHOOLS—THE HOPE OF A FREE PEOPLE."

COPPER PLATE PRINTERS.

Messrs. E. H. Ball, No. 116, and Luther Stevens, No. 186 Washington street, placed in the procession a copperplate press, upon one side of which was a beautiful engraving of female figures, while above was inscribed the motto, "The Union, the Philadelphia Art-Union, and all Unions which promote the success of the Arts blending the Ornamental with the Useful." Upon the opposite side was one of the recently issued copperplate engravings of Daniel Webster, over which was inscribed his memorable expression, "Liberty and Union, now and forever, one and inseparable." A wagon accompanied the above, with a press in working order, from which was struck off some specimens of their work. The banner over this press bore the motto,

"THE ILLUSTRATION OF ALL THE ARTS."

FIRE ENGINES.

A finely finished and beautifully decorated fire engine from the celebrated establishment of Hunneman & Co., was placed in the procession, and attracted much attention.

PRINTERS.

C. C. P. Moody, of the old Dickinson establishment, had a printing press arranged on a large wagon, drawn by four horses, and with workmen upon it, busily engaged in striking off hand-bills of the Oak Hall clothing warehouse.

George K. Snow, of the Pathfinder printing establishment, No. 5 Washington street, exhibited two Book and Newspaper Folding Machines, a new and very ingenious invention of his own.

About ten thousand copies of a paper prepared for the occasion, called the "Jubilee Pathfinder," were distributed on the route.

The "Carpet-Bag" was visible in the procession, and did its part to amuse the spectators. An immense picture, designed expressly for the occasion, by Mr. Sheutz, and painted on canvas, was borne in front of the wagon, and elicited much commendation. In the upper part of the picture, and crowned by the Eagle and the Lion, was a medallion, illustrative of the belligerant feelings of England and the United States towards each other thirty years ago. Upon the right side of this, was seen a stage coach crowded to suffocation, and a heavily loaded baggage wagon, both fast in the mud; on the left, a stage ascending a New Hampshire or Vermont *hillock*, the passengers all on foot toiling up the steep ascent; and in pleasant proximity, a break-down, with an intimation, per guide-board, that Worcester was ten miles distant.

The lower division of the picture embraced a distant view of Quebec on the right, with a formidable array of the "wooden walls" of old England before the city, and on the left our own capitol at Washington, occupied the corresponding position, while the two were connected by a long railway train, speeding on amid throngs of happy people, who were giving vent to their joy by cheers. Steamships, flags and guns, made up the rest of this display of joy, while on the medallion in the centre was represented John Bull and his reconciled relative, rushing to embrace each other. Behind the picture was a frame, on one side of which was this inscription:—

OUR AIM—TO AMUSE OUR READERS.

On the other side:

OUR HOPE—TO MAKE IT PAY.

Running across the wagon, behind, was painted:

PUNCH, PARTINGTON, & CO.

On either side, a handsome and well-filled carpet-bag was suspended from the railing, and in the wagon, sufficiently elevated to be observed, and distinctly labelled, was the "Subscription Book of the Carpet-Bag," which, from its unusual size, was expected to furnish an idea of the vast extent of the paper's circulation. "Ike" rode in the wagon, and distributed copies of its prospectus. Everywhere, the Carpet-Bag was greeted cordially, and at several points, hearty cheers were given for it.

Next came the exhibition of White & Potter—a large carriage, with a house built upon it, drawn by four horses. The house was decorated with banners, and on its top, over the names of the firm, were these mottoes:

"THE PRESS—THE LIFE OF TRADE."

"THE BOND OF BROTHERHOOD."

On the reverse:

"THE PRESS—THE ENGINE OF INTELLIGENCE."

On the car were two printing presses, in full operation—a card cutter and a paper cutter. On one of the presses was printed a small paper, called the "Jubilee," nearly ten thousand copies of which were distributed while the procession was moving. The other press was also in operation, printing cards.

GRANITE CUTTERS.

Here came ponderous trucks, heavily laden with specimens of worked granite, as follows:

No. 1 was a fine specimen of rough granite from the quarry of Richards, Munn & Co., of Quincy, drawn by three horses, and surmounted by the American flag. Upon the sides of the carriage was written,

"Upwards of 200,000 tons of Granite are annually quarried within the borders of Massachusetts."

No. 2. Upon a wagon drawn by five fine horses, the "Quincy Railway Company" exhibited some beautiful and massive capitals, of the Corinthian order, upon one of which, not wholly finished, workmen were busily engaged. Over the whole, a canopy was erected, highly decorated with flags, and producing a fine effect.

No. 3 was a massive column, weighing, by computation, fourteen tons, and intended for the Custom House at New Orleans. This stone, taken from the same quarry with that of No. 1, was drawn by fourteen large horses, and was exhibited, mainly, to show how easily stones of such size are transported.

No. 4 was the Granite Block to be presented by the City of Boston to the Washington Monument, now building at the seat of the National Government. The block is four feet six inches long, three feet six inches wide, and one foot six inches thick. Within an elliptical panel, three and a half feet by two and a half, and sunk two and a half inches, was a transcript of the motto of the Seal of the City, in raised letters; the whole encircled by a moulding of great beauty. The face and letters of the stone were polished, whilst the surface of the panel was finely picked, producing a marked contrast.

This stone was of Rockport Granite, and was furnished by J. Wetherbee & Co., Boston. The decorations over it were tastefully arranged, and added much to the interest of this part of the procession.

No. 5 was a portion of a Granite door-way, wrought by A. C. Sanborn & Co., and drawn by their team.

SILVER SMITHS AND JEWELLERS.

The manufacturers of "barbaric pearl and gold" made an imposing show. They numbered about one hundred and fifty, and carried a splendid banner, bearing a silver star in the centre, and adorned with pearls, coral, gold chains, and other costly trinkets. The flag was of satin,—one side white, and the other crimson. Next followed a car, of pyramidal shape, borne upon the shoulders of four colored men rejoicing in the gorgeous oriental costume, and loaded with specimens of gold and silver ware—consisting of pitchers, vases, tea sets, goblets, card receivers, spoons, ladles, butter knives, fish knives, festoons of gold chains, and other jewelry. At the top was a silver vase, in which was deposited a beautiful bouquet. Next was borne the ancient flag used at the turnout of the trade on the visit of General Washington to this city, Oct. 28th, 1789. On each side, two lads bore waiters, on which was exhibited a variety of manufactures of the precious metals, exquisitely wrought. Next came a shop upon wheels, drawn by four gray horses. In the shop were the various implements used by the trade, and some twenty members at work, Mr. Newell Harding acting as "boss." The shop was profusely decorated with flags, evergreen and bouquets. Then came a banner, on which were the stars and stripes, and a display of silver spoons and knives. The members of the trade marched in sections, which were separated from each other by these elegant symbols of their art. Each man in the procession, with the genuine taste which belongs to their calling, instead of wearing an artificial rosette on his breast, wore a natural dahlia, to which was attached gold and silver ribbon; and each member carried in hand a baton mounted with silver.

The exhibition of Levi Willcutt, the gold pen manufacturer, followed, with a prodigious "gold" pen, borne upon a car, whose motto was—

"THE PEN IS MIGHTIER THAN THE SWORD."

SAFES AND LOCKS.

Specimens of Edwards, Holman & Co.'s Improved Salamander Safes were drawn, on a heavy truck, by four large horses in uniform caparisons. Over the top was an arch, on which was inscribed,

"OUR COUNTRY'S SAFE."

This was surmounted with a golden eagle.

Then came a car of Jones & Farwell, lock and knob manufacturers. Upon it was a great display of specimens of their manufacture, and workmen engaged at their trade.

THE NEWTON BRASS BAND.

Next came a heavy truck, drawn by four "spanking grays," and loaded with safes from Wm. Adams & Co., bearing the motto,

TO KEEP ROGUES OUT;

and also some iron grating, purporting

TO KEEP ROGUES IN.

Specimens of iron safes from John E. Wilder followed.

Samples of cell doors and locks, furnished for the new jail, were exhibited by Denio & Roberts; also, a Salamander Safe, on which was inscribed—"I defy the elements. Fire is no enemy to me. I have been tested, and came out of the great fire at Concord. $175,000 property saved in this safe."

George W. Smith showed a bank vault and safe, drawn by five large horses.

BLANK-BOOK PAGERS AND RULERS.

In this Section was a car, mounted with McAdams "Paging and Heading" apparatus, on which two young women and a man were actively at work.

IRON RAILING.

Several handsome specimens of wire work and railing, manufactured by the New England Wire-Railing Company, were appropriately arranged upon a car.

Wm. E. Weeman, of No. 19 Sudbury street, exhibited numerous specimens of ornamental wrought and cast iron railing, for cemeteries, buildings, and gardens.

FURNACE, RANGE, AND STOVE DEALERS. TIN WARE AND SHEET IRON MANUFACTURERS.

A large car of samples of tin and sheet iron ware, with manufacturers at work, attracted much attention.

A decorated car, filled with furnaces and grates, was exhibited by Pond & Co.

Among the useful articles, set out in this section, was an assortment of Emerson's Ventilators, including those adapted to ships, school-houses and railroad cars, arranged on a handsome car, drawn by four gray horses, and furnished by Jones & Son, Union street. The same firm had another car following, on which workmen were engaged in manufacturing their wares.

The magnificent display of articles in the department of stoves, ranges and furnaces, from the well known and extensive establishment of Messrs. Chilson, Richardson & Co.,

Nos. 51 and 53 Blackstone street, attracted universal attention. Their car was drawn by four large black horses, gaily caparisoned. On its front was placed one of Chilson's Air-Warming and Ventilating Furnaces, and on either side was arrayed a beautiful display of hot-air grates and registers, of or-molu and bronze. In the centre of the car was erected a pyramid of silver registers, resting in a frame, covered with black velvet; on either side of which was a specimen of the newly invented mirror-marble chimney-piece, of the most elaborate finish, with grate and fender attached. On the back of the car was another chimney-piece, inlaid with pearl, and also a large gilded ornamental centre-piece. Seldom, if ever, has so splendid a display been made, with nothing to give it beauty but the articles themselves. It fully sustained the high standing and character of the firm which made the contribution.

Messrs. Bulkley & Low, Nos. 33 and 35 Blackstone street, made a beautiful display of Waring's celebrated Air-Tight Parlor Stoves; large Pyramid Stoves for halls; the Constitution-Hot-Air-Ventilated-Oven-Cooking Stove, and others of various and novel patterns. Their exposition was highly commended for its neatness, and for the ingenuity and good taste of its mottoes and decorations.

Similar exhibitions were made by Pond & Duncklee, Winchester, Knight & Co., Gould & Pratt, Stephen Kimball, Robert Webb, S. M. Folsom & Co., J. Hayes, and J. W. T. Stodder.

SEWING MACHINES.

Sewing machines were exhibited by Grover & Baker, No. 71 Milk street, on a car, very appropriately and handsomely decorated with the American and British flags intermingled. It was drawn by handsome silver-gray horses, to whose heads blue, red and white streamers were attached, and whence they were gathered in the talons and beak of a very large eagle, with expanded wings, which was suspended some twelve feet above the car. Extending the whole length of the car, was the sign, "Grover & Baker's Patent Sewing Machines," painted in blue letters on a white ground with a border of red stripes — thus blending the colors of the American flag. Below, upon a platform, were displayed the machines, stitching on leather and other fabrics, and managed by young women, whose dresses emblematically combined the national colors of England and America.

FIRE WORKS.

One of the most novel and imposing spectacles in the procession was the Fire Work car, from the Pyrotechnical Laboratory of James G. Hovey, Esq. It consisted of a gorgeous temple, formed by two arches, in front of which was the Fire King, in appropriate paraphernalia, and behind, an attendant Fiend; the whole decorated with fire works of every description, and drawn by six large gray horses.

Messrs. Sanderson and Lanergan, Pyrotechnists, of East Cambridge, exhibited a large car, the body of which formed a highly ornamental base, supporting a design representing "ETNA" in eruption, and emitting volumes of perfumed smoke. The American flag, falling from the talons of a golden eagle, hung in festoons over the front and sides of the car, the top of which was decorated with fire works of various kinds. The base, supporting the volcano, was white, ornamented and lettered with gold. The cornice was composed of rockets, of every size and description; and a group of the same, in the back panel, supported a golden Phoenix. Similar groups occupied the front and top. The American shield, in silver, scarlet and blue, crested with cross rockets, wreathed with flowers, and bearing, in silver letters, the names of the proprietors, occupied the central base on each side, from which depended heavy double folds of drapery of crimson, powdered with gilt leaves and stars, and bound and fringed with pendants of the same. The car was drawn by six gray horses, with riders in uniform, and attended by guards in black and red costume, armed with torches.

WOODEN WARE.

A great variety of specimens of wooden ware, from the establishments of P. Dickinson & Co., D. Cummings & Co., and R. Warner & Co., were skilfully arranged on a car, and afforded an excellent illustration of this branch of business; tubs, pails, trays, measures, brooms, boxes, baskets, buckets, and an almost numberless variety of other like articles, made up this truly "Yankee" and very pleasing exhibition.

CAR MAKERS.

A splendid railroad car, from the establishment of Davenport & Bridges, in Cambridge, drawn by a long line of fine-looking horses, and followed by a large body of the mechanics in their employ, occupied a large space in the procession, and was an object of general remark.

FOUNDERS.

Seth Wilmarth, the proprietor of the Union Iron Works of South Boston, placed in the procession a drilling machine and two engine lathes. An accident prevented him from exhibiting an engine, which he had intended. About a hundred workmen joined in the procession, bearing banners with the name of their company, and with representations of their works. Following this, was the

NORTH BRIDGEWATER BAND.

From the Globe Works of John Souther was exhibited a powerful and finely finished locomotive, of seventeen tons weight, built for the Richmond and Danville Railroad in Virginia, and called the "Potomac." It was drawn by twelve noble horses. There was a deputation of 150 men from this establishment.

The Boston Locomotive Works were represented by a deputation of about 350 men, bearing banners denoting their respective employments—as blacksmiths, iron founders, boiler makers, and machinists. A locomotive was exhibited from these works, named the "Elvira," of about the same power as that of the "Potomac," from the Globe Works.

The Fulton Works were represented by 100 workmen, accompanied by an engine frame in a rough state, just as it was taken from the foundery. Then followed the

FOXBOROUGH BRASS BAND.

From the South Boston Iron Co., Alger's Works, there were about 120 workmen. As specimens of the work of this company, there were one large cannon, of eleven inch bore, and weighing nearly eight tons, two brass six pounders, a locomotive crank, a patent railroad frog, and an iron shaving thirty feet in length.

"The Glendon Rolling Mill," of East Boston, exhibited a car, drawn by twelve gray horses, handsomely adorned, and containing specimens of their manufacture, in all its various processes, from the iron ore, as dug from the bowels of the earth, to the finished bar; also, locomotive and car tires, and axles, and various other articles, arranged in a pyramidal form around a heavy forged central shaft, upwards of 30 feet high, surmounted by the American flag, and otherwise handsomely decorated.

This corporation turned out 360 men in the procession, and exhibited several banners, the principal of which had for its motto a quotation from Ovid—"De duro est ultima ferro" —[*Aetas understood*]—*The last Age is of Iron.*

LEATHER BELTING.

Ample specimens of leather belting, from the establishment of N. Hunt & Co., were exhibited on a car, highly decorated; following which was a display of leather belting, engine hose, saddlery and trunks, from the establishment of Shelton & Cheever.

LAST MAKERS.

Blanchard's patent self-directing machine, for manufacturing boot-trees and lasts, was a very interesting object, from the great ingenuity of its construction. It was kept in operation by attendant workmen.

PLUMBERS.

A fine exhibition, on a car, of manufactures from the establishment of Lockwood, Zane & Lumb, was followed by the

ROXBURY BRASS BAND.

CARPET MAKERS.

A great display was made, by from three to four hundred

operatives from Henry Pettes & Co.'s carpet factories in Roxbury, headed by the Roxbury Band; immediately after which followed a superb banner-car, covered with paintings, representing their different factory buildings. Next came a detachment of weavers, with sashes of parti-colored yarns, bearing a banner with the following inscription—"Every carpet we display is the work of our own hands, in Henry Pettes & Co.'s Roxbury carpet factories." Then came a triumphal car, drawn by four horses, exhibiting a beautiful variety of tapestry carpeting. Next came a tapestry-carpet-loom, in full operation, surrounded by weavers and all the implements of the craft. The boys bore a banner, with the motto—"We learn to work, while young, in Henry Pettes & Co.'s Roxbury carpet factories." This section was closed by a chariot, drawn by four horses, and followed by a large number of the young men of the establishment, gaily dressed, and bearing banners, with the motto—"We spin and weave in Henry Pettes & Co.'s Roxbury carpet factories. Honor and protect our industry."

The Boston Dye House placed in the procession a carriage, exhibiting specimens of their work; there were yarns, ribbons, bonnets, shawls and cloths of all kinds, and colored with all the hues of the rainbow.

OCCUPANTS OF FANEUIL HALL MARKET.

The occupants of Faneuil Hall Market—a fine looking body of men—made a very creditable appearance. They were preceded by Dodsworth's (New York) famous band of music, and attracted much attention. One of their banners exhibited a bullock's head in front; on the reverse—"We feed the hungry." Another banner was inscribed—"Our railroad and steamboat communications; may they extend to the ends of the earth. A third bore the inscription—"England and America; a worthy son of a noble sire." A car, thirty feet in length, contained a tempting variety of "vivers"—fish, flesh, fowl and vegetables, of the best quality. A few live pigs, geese and fowls, animated the picture, and occasionally contributed "rural sounds," to "exhilarate the spirits" of the hearers; and on the top of the car was perched a live rooster, who did not appear to enjoy the scene much. The car was handsomely decorated with American, English and French flags, flying from its top. Three carriages, and a procession, numbering more than 150 men, followed on foot.

PAPER HANGINGS.

This trade was represented by the Boston and Chelsea Paper Hangings Manufacturing Company, alone, but very efficiently. Upon different constructions were represented the different branches of their business.

Upon the first, drawn by four horses, were print cutters, with stock and tools, engaged in their work, and a printing machine, with men and boys in the act of printing paper, which, as soon as dry, was rolled up by another machine, managed by women. Specimens of the printing were distributed along the route of the procession.

Next followed a load of manufactured paper, drawn by two horses.

Then came a model of a parlor, drawn by one horse, with a paper hanger and his apprentice engaged in decorating it in various styles. Attached to the outside were sample cards of paper hangings and borders.

LAMPS AND GAS FIXTURES.

Andrew J. Gavit exhibited a great variety of handsome lamp and gas fixtures, tastefully arranged upon a carriage, and drawn by two horses.

INTELLIGENCE OFFICES.

A representation of Porter's Intelligence Office was transported by six horses—some twenty men and women being seated in a car covered with handbills specifying the various classes of persons wishing situations, (*not* including political offices,) and of those whose services were wanted.

PIANO FORTE MAKERS.

The piano forte makers of the city, (with the exception of Chickering's establishment,) marshaled by Russell Hallet, numbered about 200, and were accompanied by the Lowell Brass Band. On a large car, temple-formed, drawn by four black horses, were three beautiful pianos, from Lemuel Gilbert, T. Gilbert, and D. B. Newhall; one of them exhibiting carvings of most exquisite skill. From the beak of an eagle, in front, the car was handsomely draped, and from the corners waved two American, one English, and a French flag. Two banners were borne—one with the inscription, "Nothing is denied to well deserved labor;" the other having on the obverse a Harp, and on the reverse, "Harmony."

The operatives in Chickering's piano forte establishment, numbering more than 100, with a band belonging to the establishment—the "Excelsior Band"—made a fine appearance. A two horse car, handsomely "decored," (to use the language of old Caleb Balderstone,) carried one of Chickering's grand pianos, with an inscription on either side—

> "There's sure no passion of the human soul
> But finds its food in music."

GILDERS.

The gilders, on a car drawn by four white horses, exhibited a variety of mirrors, picture frames, and other ornamental work, handsomely arranged, with two flags draped from the top.

BOOK BINDERS.

The artists of Gleason's Pictorial Companion rode in two barouches, with banners, and the motto —

"HONOR ALIT ARTES."

The bookbinders made a good appearance, and numbered about one hundred, George A. Fields as Marshal, and were accompanied by the "Holliston Band." A beautiful banner, with a large open book upon it, and having a book upon its staff, contained the inscription—"We bind and preserve the knowledge of the past for the benefit of the future." A four-horse car contained an embossing machine, cutting press, forwarding press, and other appropriate machines, in operation, with girls folding and stitching books. Another large car contained a cutting machine, standing press, and ruling machine, in operation. Several carriages contained some of the leading men engaged in the business.

AGRICULTURAL WARES.

Prouty & Mears had two teams; one with two horses, containing several varieties of their famous plough, including the kind which obtained a premium at the World's Fair. A six horse team, with a car, contained twelve men at work, plough making; and portions of work, in its several stages, were exhibited.

Blodgett, Clark & Brown, on a six horse car, exhibited agricultural implements, and a great variety of hardware, very well arranged. On the tines of two pitch-forks were suspended small flags.

Ruggles, Nourse & Mason, with a four horse car, exhibited the various articles of their manufacture, contrasted with an old plough used by Roger Sherman in 1742. A rooster, acting the part of a weather-cock, surmounted the vehicle.

From the Agricultural Ware-House and Seed Store of Messrs. Parker & White, Nos. 8 and 10 Gerrish Block, was a car, (drawn by four large gray horses, belonging to Mr. Bailey, of South Weymouth,) and filled with every variety of implements of their manufacture and trade, comprising ploughs, harrows, hay cutters, shovels, hoes, spades, hay and manure forks, handcarts, wheelbarrows, fanning mills, corn shellers, chains, and, in fine, tools of every description used by the agriculturist, or the cultivator of flowers.

Their banner, of wide canvas, extending the whole width of the street, bore the picture of a plough, with the old but not worn-out motto—

"SPEED THE PLOUGH."

BRUSHES.

Adams' Brush Manufactory was represented by a Russian boar, mounted on a light vehicle, drawn by the celebrated mare "Jane Eyre." Attached to the car were a mammoth brush and other emblems of the trade, the whole being in excellent taste and appropriate to the business. Upwards of thirty workmen, employed in this establishment, followed, having a banner inscribed—"From Adams' Brush Factory;" and on the reverse, the motto—"A new broom sweeps clean."

BOAT CLUBS.

The Franklin Boat Club, whose head quarters are near Braman's Baths, rode in their boat, thirty-eight feet in length, drawn by two horses.

CARVERS.

A two horse car, containing some beautiful specimens of ship carving by Gleason, on Commercial street, was gaily trimmed with flags.

Besides the above, there were several excellent "expositions" not included under either of the specific sections, but not the less worthy of special notice.

Blodget, Clarke & Brown, of Pearl street, furnished a car, drawn by six horses, and covered with specimens of American hardware, from all parts of New England, but chiefly from Connecticut. Among the articles exhibited were Ames' Shovels, Clarke's Knives, Douglass' Pumps, Blake's Latches, and Holley & Co.'s Pocket Cutlery. On the platform, in the rear, was a model of the celebrated "Chain Pump," which drew much attention.

An elegant omnibus of Hobbs & Prescott's line contained, on one side, "The way to the Railroad;" on the other, "We come at your call," and behind, the standing joke, "Room for one more,"—although it appeared to be full, or as nearly so as a vehicle, proverbially unsusceptible of repletion, can be. The carriage was neatly decorated, and drawn by four superb horses.

A wagon, containing a display of spices, with the words, "The Colonies and the States—Reciprocity of Trade, and more Spice in our Commerce," was from the City Coffee and Spice Mills of Stiles, Hurbs & Hasselberg, No. 4 Liberty square, Boston. On the same wagon, a banner bore the inscription—"Hon. Joseph Howe and the Colonial Railways,"—in honor of the labors of Mr. Howe in furtherance of the great scheme by which the Colonies are to be united by a railroad from Canada, through New Brunswick, into Nova Scotia.

Jonathan Pierce exhibited, on a one horse car, various articles of pumps, blocks, and the like.

A carriage, covered with millinery goods, and containing several girls at work, was furnished by L. S. Driggs, and was quite attractive in its appearance, though it may be doubted whether the inanimate portion of the lading received its due attention.

In another carriage were exhibited numerous specimens of "Southern brogans," with several men at work making the like.

J. Russell Spalding, Perfumer, Tremont row, exhibited a mammoth oval bottle, fourteen feet high, five feet broad, and three feet wide,—set off with a showy label.

The clothes-drying machine of J. H. Evans, of Cambridgeport, as it moved along the line, attracted much notice. The last article in the Seventh Division was followed by a cavalcade.

On reaching Charles street from the Common, the procession was dismissed, and the guests of the City assembled at the State House, to move thence to the dinner, which had been spread under an extensive Pavilion.

The Pavilion was erected on a level spot of the Common, nearly opposite West street, and immediately adjoining the Tremont street Mall, and its appearance, as it burst into view from this point, was peculiarly striking, and attracted great admiration. On a line extending from one end of the first, or original tent, to the other, were fastened a large number of small ensigns, signals, flags, and streamers, handsomely and appropriately arranged. Conspicuous among the whole, were the Stars and Stripes of our own Flag, while the Cross of St. George, in honor of the occasion, was also spread to the breeze.

On the three masts which supported the tent, were flying the respective flags of Great Britain and America. Of the second tent, or that which was subsequently added to the original, each corner was decorated with a handsome American flag. In the centre of the pavilion was flying a faded and ancient-looking standard, which fluttered proudly in the breeze, as if in contempt of its fresh but untried companions.

At the northern end, facing Park street, over the entrance, through which the procession passed to partake of the civic dinner, an arch was erected on which was the following motto :

LITERATURE, SCIENCE, AND THE ARTS ; ENCOURAGEMENT TO ALL.

In the centre was represented an engine and cars in motion. Two handsome gilt stars decorated each side.

After the erection of the first division of the tent, it had been ascertained that it was insufficient to accommodate the vast crowd which would be assembled. It was therefore enlarged by the addition of ninety feet each way, making the whole dimensions of the tent 250 feet in length, and 90 in breadth. This latter erection had more the appearance of a canvas building—the canvas being fastened on frame work,—than the former, and was not so fully decorated on the exterior. This defect of uniformity could not be remedied on account of the want of time. The whole, however, presented a most beautiful appearance, and from all quarters, the snow white canvas of the immense pavilion contrasted strongly with the hundred gaily-colored banners which fluttered in the breeze.

The interior of the pavilion was profusely decorated with flags and many-colored bunting. From the immense roof hung the flags of all nations, appropriately interspersed and arranged. Large maps of Boston and of the different railroad routes were also fastened so that they were flat, or nearly so, upon the roof. The flags were so arranged, that, for the whole length of the tent, upon each side of the beams which supported the centre of the canvas, there was a row of the largest, while immediately behind were displayed smaller ensigns. The insignia of nearly every nation in the world were seen in the vast array of gay pennants which lined the roof of the pavilion. Among them, from their size and beauty, were particularly noticeable the banners of Sweden, China, Belgium, Poland, Mexico and France, while the "Meteor Flag of England" was visible in the most prominent and honorable positions. Between the beams which supported the centre of the canvas, the whole length of the tent was hung in festoons, alternating in colors of red, white and blue streamers, pennants and ensigns of all descriptions.

The head of the tables was situated at the south end of the Pavilion, towards the Public Garden, and not at the north as was at first intended. Immediately over the seat of the President great taste was displayed in the designs and decorations which were put up. On the canvas roof above his head, were two very large flags of England and the United States, the former on the right. On an arch behind his seat was the motto:

ENGLAND AND AMERICA—PERPETUAL PEACE; THE QUEEN AND THE PRESIDENT.

From the base of the arch were draped in a beautiful manner, the flags of the two nations, while the back ground was formed of an American ensign. Immediately between the first two flags was a golden eagle, with wings outspread, in a protecting attitude, supporting in his talons the palladium of liberty, and an olive branch, the emblem of peace. The whole was very prettily decorated with evergreens.

On each side of the centre of the tables, small evergreen trees were fastened to every post, between which were paintings, lithographs, and engravings of all descriptions, and of various qualities, representing marine views, railway views, maps, charts, and the like. Prominent among others, was noticed a fine lithograph print of the S. S. Lewis.

Opposite the arch over the seat of the President, in the middle of tent, was another arch with the following motto:

THOU SHALT LOVE THY NEIGHBOR AS THYSELF:
TORONTO, COBOURG.
MONTREAL, HAMILTON, QUEBEC, BOSTON.
HONOR TO THOSE WHO HAVE BROUGHT US TOGETHER.

In the centre of this was a design representing the telegraph wires, and a train of cars in motion. Below, was a maritime view, representing a ship under full sail. The whole was handsomely trimmed with evergreen. At the entrance of the tent on the inside, on a direct line with the others, was an arch with the following inscription:

THE UNITED STATES AND THE CANADAS: HARMONY, PROSPERITY, AND RECIPROCITY.

In the centre of this were the American and British flags crossed, with two clasped hands—emblematic of the above motto,—decorated with evergreen. Farther down was an arch, with the following motto:

AGRICULTURE, COMMERCE, AND MANUFACTURES—THE TRUE SOURCES OF OUR NATIONAL WEALTH.

In the centre of this was a marine view, with vessels under full sail; a city in the distance; in the foreground a steamship in the process of erection. On the arch, on the opposite side, was the following motto and design:

RAILROAD JUBILEE, SEPT. 17TH, 18TH, 19TH, 1851.

In the centre, a representation of a train of cars in full career, and a steamship ploughing the water.

At the lower end of the tent was an arch, with this motto:

COLUMBIA, THE LAND OF LIBERTY, THE HOME OF ALL NATIONS.

In the centre, were the British and American flags, crossed; clasped hands beneath; a lion on one side, and a shield on the other.

On the opposite side was an arch, with the following inscription:

MERCANTILE ENTERPRISE; RAILROADS AND TELEGRAPHS.
BOSTON FROM 1630 TO 1851.

In the centre and in the back-ground, a representation of a steamer advancing; the old pine tree on the left, and a train of cars in motion on the right.

The whole of these arches were very prettily decorated with evergreen, or festooned with streamers and flags, and added much to the beauty of the scene.

The arrangement of the tables was most excellent. Extending entirely around the tent, with spaces at the two entrances, was a table for the more distinguished guests, on a raised dais, handsomely carpeted. Directly opposite the main entrance, and at the other (the south-westerly) end of the pavilion, was the head of the table, running perpendicularly to which were ten tables, extending through the whole length of the tent. In the centre of the side next West street, was another entrance, opening into a broad passageway running at right angles with the aisles which separated the tables. The effect of this very convenient arrangement, as the main entrance was reached, was extremely fine, as, at a glance, the plan of the whole was obvious.

The tables were capable of comfortably accommodating thirty-six hundred persons, and, as well as the seats, were covered with white linen and supplied with the best of refreshments and eatables, in abundance. The viands consisted of cold roasted and boiled fowls, cold roast beef, ham, tongues, oyster pie, lobster salad, and the like, very neatly served, and garnished with pastry, fruit, and flowers, arrayed most invitingly. A fragrant little bouquet graced each tumbler, and larger ones, in elegant vases, adorned the tables at regular intervals.

The tent was erected under the supervision of Col. N. A. Thompson, of the City Committee, and was decorated by Mr. William Beals. The dinner was under the immediate direction of Mr. J. B. Smith, and did him much credit.

At about half past three, the procession reached the tent, and, with great quietness and order, the whole immense area was filled in less than twenty minutes.

Mr. Mayor Bigelow took his seat in the centre of the dais; on his right sat Mr. President Fillmore, and on his left Lord Elgin. On the right of the President, were seated the Hon. Messrs. Stuart and Conrad, of his Cabinet; and on the left of Lord Elgin, sat the Hon. Mr. Crampton, the British Chargé de' Affaires at Washington, in the absence of Sir Henry L. Bulwer. Taking the platform westward, were noticed Mr. Brinley, President of the Council; the Hon. Colonel Bruce, the Hon. Francis Hincks, Inspector-General of the Canadas; Lord Mark Kerr, the Hon. Mr. Waldegrave, the Hon. Mr. Price, Commissioner of Crown Lands; the Hon. Mr. Taché, Receiver General; the Hon Mr. Bourret, Chief Commissioner of Public Works; Sir Allan N. McNab, M. P. P.; the Hon. W. B. Robinson, M. P. P.; Mr. Solicitor General McDonald, of Canada; Ex-Governor Paine, of Vermont; the Hon. H. H. Killaly, Assistant Commissioner of Public Works, of Canada; the Hon. Edward Everett, the Hon. Josiah Quincy, Sen.; His Honor John G. Bowes, Mayor of Toronto; G. Duggan, Jr., Esq., Recorder of Toronto; Rev. E. Ryerson, D. D., Chief Superintendent of Education in Canada West; Capt. Robinson, R. N.; Rear Admiral Owen, R. N.; Col. Hemery, Jersey, England; the Hon. Josiah Quincy, Jr.; Major General Edmands and Staff; Stuart Chisholm, M. D., Senior Surgeon of the Royal Regiment of Artillery; Lieut. Archibald Chisholm, 42d Royal Highlanders; the Rev. A. Digby Campbell, of Trinity Church, Montreal; Capt. Harding, Capt. Webber and Capt. Newman; Lieut. W. A. Bartlett, U. S. N.; Capt. Nye, of the 20th Reg. of the British Army; Mr. Wm. G. Thompson, 54th Reg.; Mr. Hughes, of the Q. M. Department; Drs. Rutherford and Barrett, of the Medical Staff; Dr. Lowber, of the U. S. Navy; Capt. Marjory, of the 54th Reg.; Dr. Wright, of the U. S. Navy; Capt. Jones, of the 54th Reg.; Dep. Asst. Com. Gen. Webb; Capt. Stevens, 20th Reg.; Mr. J. R. Pilkinton, Royal Engineers; Capts. Sweedenham and Swan, of the 54th Reg.; John Egan, Esq., M. P. P.; Mr. John Ferrie, Hamilton, C. W.; Mr. W. Gillespie, Capt. Percival, U. S. N.; Mr. Robert Maitland, of Toronto; Mr. Thomas Davidson, of Toronto; Edmund A. Grattan, Esq., H. B. M. Consul for Massachusetts, and S. S. Lewis, Esq., of this City.

On the eastern wing of the platform, on the right of the members of the U. S. Cabinet, were seen His Excellency,

Gov. Boutwell; Lieut. Col. H. A. Williams, Governor's Aid; Maj. Sherman, U. S. A., of Fort Adams; Hon. William B. Lawrence, Acting Governor of Rhode Island; Gen. Pitman, of Rhode Island; Messrs. Aldermen Rogers, Briggs, Holbrook, Grant, Kimball, Munroe, Clark and Smith; Rev. Dr. Bigelow, of Boston; the Hon. John P. Hale, Senator in Congress from New Hampshire; the Hon. Joseph Grinnell; the Hon. Alexander Stewart, Master of the Rolls of Nova Scotia; the Hon. J. H. Duncan, and the Hon. Benj. Thompson, Reps. in Congress from Massachusetts; the Hon. Joseph Howe, Provincial Sec. of Nova Scotia; the Hon. P. H. Moore, member of the Legislative Council of the Canadas; the Hon. William Young, Speaker of the N. S. House of Assembly; the Hon. Col. Gugy, M. P. P.; Oliver Berthelot, Esq., of Montreal; Mr. Sheriff Thomas, of the counties of Wentworth and Halton; Mr. Sheriff Smith, of the county of Simcoe, on Lake Huron; and James Stewart, Esq., of Halifax.

The aspect of the vast assembly, when the tables were filled, was beyond description striking. There was a vast sea of human brotherhood under a firmament of flags; and in that, were many distinguished personages of both hemispheres.

The assembled thousands having at last been seated, which, though not a thing to be accomplished at once, was done in a most orderly manner;

The Rev. ANDREW BIGELOW, D.D., (Chaplain of the Day,) rose and, in the following words, invoked the Divine blessing:

O God our Father; Giver of life, and Parent of all good! Thou hast nourished and brought us up — hast fed us with thy bountiful hand—and vouchsafed to us all our capacities for improvement and happiness.

Great has been thy favor to the people of this land. Peace and plenty, the sources of personal and national prosperity, civil liberty, the lights of knowledge, the means of moral and religious instruction thou hast abundantly provided and opened up. Blessings in profusion thou hast showered upon us; blessings in the city and in the field; blessings in our basket and in our store; blessings in the fruits of the ground, and the treasures drawn from the sea and the sands. These thy mercies proportionably enhance our responsibilities. May they be duly pondered and weighed. Let not our hearts be lifted up to a forgetfulness of Thee. But where success follows upon the work of our hands, on the sweat of our brows, or the travail of our souls, may the praise and honor be rendered to Thee who giveth life and health and breath and all things—the strength to toil, the skill to plan, and means to execute.

Continue to us, we entreat thee, thy benignant smiles. Sanctify our privileges. Bless every useful industrial pursuit prosecuted among us. Multiply the commercial, and strengthen the friendly and social ties which knit us to our fellow kind. And do thou, O Father, who hast made of one blood all the nations of the earth, unite them in one great family. Teach them to be lovers of concord. May they drink of the spirit of a common Lord and Saviour. May rulers and people, princes and subjects alike bow to the sceptre of his grace. May they learn from him, along with the truth which sanctifies, the arts which conduce to humanity, to civilization and peace. May wars and fightings, cruelty and injustice, the lust of aggression and conquest, and every species of iron despotism over the bodies, the consciences and the souls of men, come to a speedy end. May the sons of violence and strife beat their swords into ploughshares, and their spears into pruning hooks. May animosities amongst nations, uncharitableness betwixt sects, bitterness between man and man, every where cease. And may the wise and equitable, the benign and merciful principles of the gospel of grace and truth, obtain an universal and perpetual prevalence.

And now, O Father, look down, we beseech thee, with special favor upon us thy children, on the present occasion. Smile upon this vast assemblage,—and the purposes, so bright in promise, for which it has been gathered here, and within our city walls, at this season jubilant. May they be crowned with joyful issues. Bless them who exercise rule—the Executive Head of our country, and other distinguished functionaries of this Nation, its several States, and our City. Bless the Governor in chief and others in authority, with the many associated guests, here welcomed from neighboring Provinces; and all of every rank and class brought together, in this auspicious hour, around this festive board.

Bless, Father, the fruits of thy bounty spread before us. May thy hand be seen in them all. Help us to connect a sense of thy goodness with every comfort we receive. Whilst we partake and are made glad, may we rejoice in the LORD. And now as at all times, whether we eat or drink or whatever we do, may we do all to Thy glory, through Jesus Christ. Amen.

In about fifteen minutes after the commencement of the repast, His Honor the Mayor rose and said—

I deeply regret to announce, that the President feels obliged to leave us, thus early in the feast, on his return to Washington,—the hour for the departure of the train having arrived. Let not, however, the misfortune of his withdrawal befal our assemblage before we proffer him our respects in the usual manner: [Applause.]

I propose—

"The Health of the President of the United States."

When the enthusiastic cheers, which this sentiment called forth, had subsided, the President rose and responded to the compliment as follows—

MR. MAYOR AND FELLOW CITIZENS:

In acknowledging the compliment which you have paid to the high office which it is my fortune to hold, I rise rather for the purpose of excusing myself than to make an address.

You have been pleased to drink my health. I would that it were as perfect on this occasion as it usually is; but unfortunately for me, a slight indisposition within the last twenty-four hours has deprived me of the pleasure I should have enjoyed this day in participating in your exercises; and I am now incapable of partaking of the tempting viands under which your miles of table groan. Indeed I am scarcely able to enjoy "the feast of reason and the flow of soul." And more than all this, I am compelled by imperious circumstances to leave you thus early in the banquet, because I feel that my public duties require that I should be at Washington with the utmost possible despatch. I have stolen from the hours that were, perhaps, due to the Nation a brief space to meet my fellow citizens of Boston. [Applause.] I meet you as *citizens* of Boston. On this festive occasion we know no party distinction. [Applause.] Nay, more, we scarcely know a national distinction. [Great applause and cheering.] There are gathered at this board the Briton and the American, living under different laws, but, thank God, representing two of the freest nations under the sun. [Cheering.] The asperity that was engendered by the revolution which separated us from our mother country, I am happy to say, has long since disappeared, and we meet like brethren of the same family. Speaking the same language, and enjoying the same religion—are we not one? [Applause.]

I trust, Fellow Citizens, that the unfortunate necessity which compels me to leave you thus early on this occasion, will induce no one to leave the table on my account. I trust particularly that his Lordship, the Governor General of Canada, will remain with you. [Applause.] I know that he, and those with whom he is associated, will receive from you, as they have already received, a most cordial greeting. [Applause.]

Fellow Citizens;—I cannot say more, but my heart is full. I had no conception of what I have witnessed to-day from my window. I thought, when I entered your city, that I saw Boston in all its glory. I knew that it had its "merchant princes," but I did not know until to-day, that it had its mechanic noblemen of nature. [Great applause and cheering.]

But, Fellow Citizens, pardon me, and permit me to bid you adieu. I can assure you that this joyous occasion will be remembered by me, and that, to the latest hour of my life, I shall look back upon it with delight. May our glorious Union, which sheds its inestimable blessings over twenty-five millions of happy people, continue until time shall be no more. [Nine cheers.]

As soon as silence was restored, Lord Elgin rose and said—

One single word. [Three cheers.] I should have felt it my bounden duty to follow the President of the United States out of this room, if he had not interposed to prevent me from doing so. But I do not forget that while I am on the territory of the United States, I am under his authority. [Applause.] As, therefore, he has imposed upon me his commands to remain with you, most certainly I shall remain. [Applause.] And I must say that I never received an order, which more completely jumped with my own wishes. [Laughter and applause.]

The President, after having cordially shaken hands with Lord Elgin,* the Mayor and others, left the Pavilion; when the Hon. A. H. H. Stewart, having been called upon, replied briefly as follows—

GENTLEMEN,—

I have no time to respond to your flattering call for a speech. The President has told you that the hour for our departure has come. I can only speak with the manly frankness of a true Virginian, and say, God bless Massachusetts! God bless New England! God bless you all! [Applause.]

* As the President held Lord Elgin's hand for a considerable time, across the breast of the mayor (whose position intervened,) the cheers of the company were deafening and prolonged,—seemingly ratifying the cordial relations, so indicated, as existing between the kindred nations, and recognizing Boston as furnishing a new bond of mutual good-will.

A like call was made upon the Hon. Charles M. Conrad, to which he responded as follows—

Gentlemen,—

I am summoned to depart, otherwise I should have taken great pleasure in addressing a few remarks to you, on this, one of the most agreeable moments of my life. I go away from Boston with the frank declaration—although I said a few days ago that I was not a stranger upon your soil—with the frank declaration that I have never before known what Boston was. [Applause.] I have never before known the heartiness, the cordiality, the warmth, of the true New England character. But the acquaintance, I have now had the happiness to make with it, satisfies me that it has not degenerated from that of the forefathers of the country. I regret exceedingly that I am compelled to take this unceremonious and abrupt departure, and to interrupt the flow of your festivity by so sudden a retreat; but you know the necessity for it. The President awaits me, and I bid you farewell—I hope a short farewell, and that it will not be long before I shall have an opportunity to revisit Boston, and to pay my respects to her citizens, and especially to friends with whose public life I have long been acquainted, but whose acquaintance I have now formed in their private capacity, and at home. Gentlemen, I bid you farewell, and wish to all of you, all possible prosperity and happiness. [Applause.]

Messrs. **Stuart** and **Conrad**, then having taken a courteous leave of Lord Elgin, the Mayor and others, left the pavilion.

The Mayor,—Lord Elgin says he is not afraid to shake hands even with our Secretary of War. [Laughter.]

Due attention was then given to the more commonplace but equally obvious duties of the occasion, which had been entirely neglected during this episode, and a sufficient time was allowed to do justice to the really excellent repast which had been provided.

The **Mayor** then arose, and introduced the more attractive and important part of the banquet as follows—

Gentlemen,—

This is a proud and memorable day for Boston. We commemorate the completion of works that cannot fail to enhance her wealth and greatness; and the celebration is honored by an assemblage as truly noble as was ever convened for similar purposes, in this or any other country. It is a vast gathering of the Anglo-Saxons (and those of other races who have united with them) of North America. The Chief Magistrate of the American branch of that great family has come to the feast, and saluted his children,—while the Governor General of Canada is here to speak for our kindred under British rule. The elder and the younger brothers are sitting at one common table.

The meeting being thus held, under the apparent auspices of two mighty nations, with the ceremonies appropriate to their object, calls to mind, not unnaturally, the celebrated meeting of Henry of England and Francis of France, with their followers, upon the "Field of the Cloth of Gold." Splendid as was that pageant, the lustre of which is unsurpassed in the annals of pomp, yet in moral grandeur it does not compare with this less ambitious gathering. *That* meeting was arranged for the purpose of consolidating alliances, and planning wars, for the personal aggrandizement of the high contracting parties,—"to shut the gates of mercy on mankind." *This* meeting is held to celebrate the triumphs of the arts of Peace; to rejoice in the result of enterprises which tend to cultivate good will among men, to promote their material interests, and augment the sum of human happiness.

Boston takes occasion, in this presence, to acknowledge, with honest pride, that her founders were Britons. We claim, as New Englanders, that the history of the British people, until a comparatively recent period, is *our* history,—that the poets, statesmen, philosophers, patriots, and warriors,—in a word, the myriads of the good and great, who for many centuries contributed to the happiness and glory of the British Isles, were the brethren, the fellow-countrymen of our ancestors. Indeed, when we hear it said that "the sun never sets upon the dominions of Great Britain," we think of it with kindred interest,—principally, however, in reference to a great moral fact, rather than the question of her mere territorial greatness. That colossal empire may crumble and fall in pieces: but the sun will never cease to shine upon regions, all round the globe, where principles or institutions derived from Britons or their American brethren, will exist and flourish for the enlightenment and happiness of mankind.

These views, of the progress and position of our common race, lead to the consideration of the special purpose, for which this goodly company is now convened. It is, that we may rejoice together upon the accomplishment of gigantic enterprises, uniting this city with Canada and the Great West, in social and business relations of the most auspicious character to all parties concerned. The pledge that Boston gives that she has the spirit and ability to improve these new advantages, is a reference to the fact that she became a large and an important city, long before she possessed any facilities of intercourse with the interior, other than our common roads. The sterile soil, the rugged surface, the stern climate, and deficiency of navigable streams in New England, would have seemed to render it improbable that it would ever be considerably peopled, or that any great commercial mart would arise within its borders. But the principles of civil and religious freedom, established by the Pilgrims and their successors, aided by the universal diffusion of education, gave rise to a spirit of intelligent industry, which overcame every obstacle to prosperity and wealth. The region sneeringly stigmatized as having "no natural productions but granite and ice," now teems with three millions of the children of freedom, and its metropolis has long since ranked with the prominent cities of the globe. Recently, science and art, backed by the accumulated wealth of two centuries of industrious thrift, have come to our aid, to relieve us from the natural isolation of our position. Hills have been cut in sunder, vallies have been filled up, and running waters have been spanned, to facilitate our communication with every section of the land. Our iron pathways are our rivers, and they more than compensate for deficiency of natural channels. They follow the routes, and terminate at the exact points, indicated by our judgment or wishes. They allow of velocity of transit, of which no water courses admit; they are never frozen by the winter's blast, nor is their passage dangerous in autumnal storms. And now, from the North and the South, from the East and the West, they roll down to us their precious argosies, laden with the products of a continent. A people who could achieve a distinguished mercantile position under most discouraging and repelling circumstances, may be depended upon to avail themselves, to the full, of these, their new and extraordinary advantages.

I have alluded to our Puritan forefathers, and I should be unworthy of the trust which their descendants have committed to my hands, if I did not pay an affectionate tribute to their memory, on an occasion like this. Boston owes to them not only her existence, but the principles and institutions which have illustrated her history, and given her a name and an eminent rank among the cities of the earth. Pioneers of modern emigration—virtual founders of an empire,—they sleep in their humble graves, by the hill-side or in the valley, with rarely a stone to mark their dwellings of rest. But Boston is their especial monument, and the influence of their lives and actions pervades the world. It is true that the Pilgrims had errors of judgment and practice, which I will neither palliate nor deny; but these were as spots on the sun, compared with their substantial virtues. It is true that they not unfrequently manifested an exclusive spirit, and exercised that persecuting intolerance in the wilderness, which they had denounced, and fled from, in Europe. But even their most repelling and objectionable points of character had, under God, a manifest influence in fulfilling his great designs. They prevented the presence, or interference, of meddlesome adventurers, who had little sympathy for the cause of civil and religious liberty, or impracticable enthusiasts, whose teachings and conduct practically tended to retard the growth and prosperity of "the Christian Commonwealth." In this connection, my Lord, [here the Mayor turned to the Earl of Elgin,] permit me to borrow an illustration from the thistle, which is the national emblem of your own glorious old Scotland. Its flower opens to the light amidst thorns and briery foliage. But these are its safeguards; they repel the intrusive hand of the spoiler, and enable it to bloom in beauty and in peace.

But I will no longer postpone the salutations, which Boston respectfully tenders, on this joyous occasion. To-morrow our festival will have terminated; our tents of jubilee will be struck, and many of you will be far away on your return to your pleasant homes. But to-day you are our honored guests. I bid you welcome, rulers and ruled; statesmen, scholars, soldiers, farmers, mechanics and merchants. Welcome! ye from the banks of the Ottawa, the Chaudière, the St. Lawrence, the Niagara, and the St. John. Welcome from the shores of Erie, Ontario, Huron, Michigan and Superior. Welcome, from the borders of the Penobscot, Kennebec, Connecticut, Hudson, Delaware, Susquehannah and Potomac,—the waters of the sunny South, and of the Valley of the Mississippi and her tributaries. Welcome from every city, town and hamlet which is here represented. Welcome! Englishmen, Scotchmen, Irishmen, Frenchmen, Germans and Americans. Welcome! thrice welcome! are you all, to the Pilgrim City, and the Pilgrim Feast!

This address was listened to with marked attention, and repeated bursts of applause. The allusion to the Thistle of Scotland was particularly well received. After a brief pause, the Mayor again arose and proposed the following sentiment:

"The health of her Majesty, the Queen of the United Kingdom of Great Britain and Ireland."

This toast was received with nine such cheers as would have made her Majesty, had she been present, forget that she was beyond the limits of her own dominions; and the band struck up the tune "God save the Queen," as if to complete the illusion.

Lord Elgin, in rising to respond to the sentiment, was most cordially greeted, and spoke as follows:

MR. MAYOR AND GENTLEMEN,—

It is not very customary, with us, for any individual to take it upon himself to return thanks for the toast which you have just now so cordially, so enthusiastically drank. I feel an additional difficulty in rising to discharge that duty at this time, because I have at my left hand a gentleman who fills an important diplomatic situation in this country, [alluding to the Hon. Mr. Crampton] and from whom a response to this toast would come, perhaps, more appropriately than from myself. In obedience, however, to the call of His Honor, the Mayor, and in compliance, I believe, with the wishes of my friend on the left, I rise to express, in the name of all British subjects here present—for I feel that every one of them has an equal right with myself to answer this toast—Canadians, Englishmen, Scotchmen and Irishmen,—on behalf of all I beg leave to express our cordial and hearty thanks for the manner in which this toast has been received by you.

Gentlemen, as I have the honor to address a company which consists, in the greater part, of persons who live under different institutions from myself, perhaps I may be permitted to observe that we British subjects honor and respect our Queen, not only because of her exemplary character, her many public and private virtues, and the singular tact and firmness which has enabled her to secure the well-being of her own people, and to promote cordiality and good will among the nations of the earth, but also because we recognize, in the constitutional and hereditary throne upon which she is seated, the symbol of our national unity, and the type of the continuity of our existence as a people. [Applause.]

Allow me, Gentlemen, as there seems to be in America some little misconception on these points, to observe, that we, monarchists though we be, enjoy the advantages of self-government, of popular elections, of deliberative assemblies, with their attendant blessings of caucuses, stump orators, lobbyings and log-rollings—[Laughter]—and I am not sure but we sometimes have a little pipe-laying—[Renewed laughter]—almost, if not altogether, in equal perfection with yourselves. I must own, Gentlemen, that I was exceedingly amused the other day, when one of the gentlemen who did me the honor to visit me at Toronto, bearing the invitation of the Common Council and the Corporation of the City of Boston, observed to me, with the utmost gravity, that he had been delighted to find, upon entering our Legislative Assembly at Toronto, that there was quite as much liberty of speech there as in any body of the kind he had ever visited. [Laughter.] I could not help thinking that if my kind friend would only favor us with his company in Canada for a few weeks, we should be able to demonstrate, to his entire satisfaction, that the tongue is quite as "unruly" a "member" on the north side of the line as on this side. [Renewed laughter.]

Now, Gentlemen, you must not expect it, for I have not the voice for it, and I cannot pretend to undertake to make a regular speech to you. I belong to a people who are notoriously slow of speech. [Laughter.] If any doubt ever existed on this point, it must have been set at rest by the verdict which a high authority has recently pronounced. A distinguished American—a member of the Senate of the United States, who has lately been in England, informs his countrymen, on his return, that sadly backward as poor John Bull is in many things, in no one particular does he make so lamentable a failure as when he tries his hand at public speaking. [Laughter.] Now, Gentlemen, deferring, as I feel bound to do, to that high authority, and conscious that in no particular do I more faithfully represent my countrymen than in my stammering tongue and embarrassed utterance, [continued laughter,] you may judge what my feelings are when I am asked to address an assembly like this, convened under the hospitable auspices of the Corporation of Boston, I believe to the tune of some four thousand, in this State of Massachusetts, a State which is so famous for its orators and its statesmen, a State that can boast of Franklins, and Adamses, and Everetts, and Winthrops and Lawrences, and Sumners and Bigelows, and a host of other distinguished men; a State, moreover, which is the chosen home, if not the birthplace of the illustrious Secretary of State of the American Union. [Applause.]

But, Gentlemen, although I cannot make a speech to you, I must tell you, in the plain and homely way in which John Bull tries to express his feelings when his heart is full—that is to say, when they do not choke him and prevent his utterance altogether [sensation]—in that homely way I must express to you how deeply grateful I and all who are with me [hear, hear,] feel for the kind and gratifying reception we have met with in the city of Boston. For myself, I may say that the citizens of Boston could not have conferred upon me a greater favor than that which they have conferred, in inviting me to this festival, and in thus enabling me not only to receive the hand of kindness which has been extended to me by the authorities of the city and of the State, but also giving me the opportunity, which I never had before, and perhaps may never have again, of paying my respects to the President of the United States. [Applause.] And although it would ill become me, a stranger, to presume to eulogise the conduct or the services of President Fillmore, yet as a bystander, as an observer, and by no means an indifferent or careless observer, of your progress and prosperity, I think I may venture to affirm that it is the opinion of all impartial men that President Fillmore will occupy an honorable place on the roll of illustrious men on whom the mantle of Washington has fallen. [Applause and cheers.]

Somebody must write to the President, and tell him how that remark about him was received. [Laughter.]

Gentlemen: I have always felt a very deep interest in the progress of the lines of railway communication, of which we are now assembled to celebrate the completion. The first railway that I ever travelled upon in North America forms part of the iron band which now unites Montreal to Boston. I had the pleasure, about five years ago, of travelling with a friend of mine, whom I see now present—Governor Paine—I think as far as Concord, upon that line.

Ex-Gov. Paine, of Vermont—It was Franklin.

Lord Elgin—He contradicts me; he says it was not Concord, but Franklin; but I will make a statement which I am sure he will not contradict; it is this—that although we travelled together two or three days—after leaving the cars, over bad roads, and in all sorts of queer conveyances, we never reached a place which we could with any propriety have christened Discord. [Laughter and applause.]

But, Gentlemen, although I take a deep interest in these lines, I must tell you, because I never wish to sail under false colors, that the interest which I take in them is not exclusive: for I am free to confess that there are other lines, some in progress and some prospective, which are destined to connect Canada with the Ocean, in which I feel an interest not less lively. But I come here to express my sense of the great obligation which the trading interests of America generally, those of Canada included, owe to the citizens of Boston, for their liberality and enterprise, not only because they have opened new channels of trade, but also because by their great outlay in these works, as stated by the Mayor, and by the satisfactory results of these outlays, they have shown how materially the settlement of a new country may be advanced, how greatly the value of property may be increased, and how largely the aggregate wealth of the community may be augmented by expenditures of this kind, when judiciously conducted. I think that from your example we Canadians will return home, certainly not "sadder," but "wiser" men than we came here. [Applause.]

There was, also, allow me to say it, another reason for my coming here at this time. I wanted to show by my presence here, that I appreciate and value the moral and social, as well as the economical effects of these increased facilities of intercourse. By coming here over your lines, to tender to you the hand of good fellowship, I wanted to show that I was aware that your lines are made for the transport of men and women, as well as for the carriage of bales of goods and barrels of flour; nor can I forget that the year in which I thus come to tender to you the hand of good fellowship, is likely to be a memorable year in the history of our species;—that it is a year in which a new planet has been added to our solar system; a planet, which has been, with singular felicity and singular appropriateness, christened Irene, the planet of Peace. [Applause.]

And as I have touched upon this point, allow me to add, that I have felt most deeply the kind terms in which England has been alluded to by all whom I have met since I entered the territory of the United States. [Applause, and cries of hear, hear.] I cannot say that I feel surprised when I hear Americans speak in the way in which his Honor the Mayor has spoken of England; but I own that I am surprised, that I am grieved, that I am, if you will allow the expression, shocked, when I hear, as I sometimes do, though much more rarely now than was the case some years ago, language of a very different kind employed by Americans when speaking of England. I remember that the code of an illustrious law-giver of an ancient Grecian Republic was famous, because, although it contained a vast number of special provisions and details, relating to all sorts of crimes, it affixed no specific penalty to the crime of parricide. It was perfectly well known however, that the omission did not arise from any doubt as to whether or not parricide was a crime. And in the same way, although perchance it may be a *casus omissus* in the criminal codes of your great Republic, I trust that no true hearted American thinks that he can, without being sadly wanting in self-respect, speak ungenerously or disparagingly of his old grandmother on the other side of the Atlantic. [Applause.]

Sir, it is impossible to live as long as I have done in America, without entering very keenly into the feelings of pride and gratification with which Americans, and Canadians too, talk of their country. It is wonderfully progressing, and has wonderful resources. But when I hear these blessings referred to in language which is somewhat disparaging, as respects other countries less advantageously situated, I am reminded of an eloquent passage in the writings of an eloquent friend of mine now no more, the late Dr. Chalmers, in which he refers to the simultaneous discovery of the telescope and the microscope—and, in his gorgeous and emphatic language, dilates upon the light shed by each in its respective sphere upon the beneficence, the wisdom, and the power of the Almighty. I am tempted, I say, to address a speaker who indulges in the language I have described in some such terms as these:

" Sir, when you have satisfied your gaze by contemplating the magnificent scene spread out before you; when, with the aid of the telescope, you have scanned those mighty prairies which the ploughshare has not yet broken; when you have cast your eye over those boundless forests which the axe has not yet touched; when you have surveyed those extensive territories underlain by valuable mineral fields, which the cupidity of man has not yet rifled; when you have done all this to your heart's content, just lay your telescope aside, and take this little microscope from me. I will show you a little Island far hidden behind that eastern wave; an island so diminutive that you might take it up bodily, and toss it into the lakes which lie between the Canadas and the United States, without filling them up; but which, nevertheless, as my friend, the Mayor, has pointed out, was the source from whence came forth the valor and the might which laid on this continent the foundations of Empire,—[Applause,]—from whence came also the wisdom and moderation, the happy combination of a love of liberty with a respect for order and law, in the absence of which, permit me to say it, you can have no sufficient security that Empire will prove enduring.

Now, gentlemen, before I take my seat,—permit me to close,—[Cries of "go on."] why, Gentlemen, it must be the air of Boston, for I never made so long a speech before in my life. [Laughter.] I will now offer you as a sentiment—

"Prosperity to the trade and the city of Boston."

No one, I am sure, will question the sincerity with which I propose this toast; for most assuredly, if I did not wish well to the trade and the city of Boston, I should not be here now. It may be, that some of those western towns, which spring up in a night, and pass in the twinkling of an eye from small villages to mighty cities, may, as respects population merely, have advanced more rapidly than Boston; but there is a stability and a solidity about Boston, which I must say is agreeable to an old countryman like myself.

I see buildings in Boston, which look as if intended not only for the owners, but for their sons, and their sons' sons to live in, after they are dead and gone. I know it has been the practice to say, that a Yankee would not be satisfied with Paradise, if there was any place farther west to which he could go. [Laughter.] But I think it is very clear, that a good many genuine Yankees have found Boston an exceedingly proper place for a permanent location, although it happens to be one of the most easterly points of the continent.

As to the citizens of Boston, I shall not attempt to detail their merits, for their name is Legion; but there is one merit, which I do not like to pass unnoticed, because they always seem to have possessed it in the highest perfection. It is the virtue of courage. Upon looking very accurately into history, I find one occasion, and one only upon which it appears to me that their courage entirely failed them. I see a great many military men present, and I am afraid that they will call me to account for this observation; [laughter.]—and what do you think that occasion was? I find, from the most authentic records, that the citizens of Boston were altogether carried away by panic when it was first proposed to build a railroad from Boston to Providence, under the apprehension that they themselves, their wives and their children, their stores and their goods, and all they possessed, would be swallowed up bodily by New York. [Laughter.]

I hope that Boston has wholly recovered from that panic. I think it is some evidence of it, that she has laid out fifty millions in railways since that time. I beg leave to offer the sentiment I proposed a few minutes ago, and to express my earnest hope that the city of Boston may pass equally unscathed through all the difficulties she may have to encounter in her path of onward progress. I give you, Gentlemen,

Prosperity to the trade and the City of Boston.

The toast was received with cheers, in which Lord Elgin took the lead; after which three tremendous cheers were spontaneously given by all the vast assembly for his lordship himself.

The Mayor then rose and said:—Gentlemen, I give you as the next sentiment,

"The Commonwealth of Massachusetts,"

and I have the honor to present to you His Excellency Governor Boutwell.

The Governor was received with cheers, and replied as follows:

Mr. Mayor and Gentlemen,—

In what language shall I speak for Massachusetts? How, on an occasion like this, can I utter with distinctness and power, as I desire to do, the sentiments which I feel when a name so dear to all her sons is received with such ardor and enthusiasm, and by so large an assemblage of men; some of whom owe nothing to her except the satisfaction of observing in her annals some resemblance to the country to which they belong.

Massachusetts is not here to-day to speak for herself. You have taken by the hand the citizens of her metropolis; but her yeomen—from her hills, her mountains, and her valleys—are not here to speak to you.

Her citizens upon the coast—those who "go down to the sea in ships,"—are not here to reply to you. Her mechanics you have seen to-day collected together in the streets of the city, and you have witnessed specimens of their handiwork. I am sure, they desire that the kindness which has beamed from the faces of those you have seen, and the cordial sentiments of regard which have been expressed by those whom you have met, may be taken as expressive of the sentiments of the State, and of the feelings which exist in every breast, among her citizens. They all desire to give a hearty welcome to our brethren from the other side of the line.

Massachusetts welcomes you, Gentlemen. PEACE is her motto, to-day, henceforth and forever. Why should we be jealous of our ancient enemy? You will pardon me for alluding to the fact that our countries have at times been enemies. Is it not true that we have a similar history, similar political principles, and a similar destiny? Do we not begin to date the liberty of both countries from the year 1215 of our common era?

It has been well observed that no man could be an American statesman who did not thoroughly understand the history of Great Britain. He who fails to understand the history of Britain, fails to understand the history of this country, or the character of this people. We are a reproduction of the mother country—but on a large scale. We have a more extensive territory. We have boundless prairies and far reaching views, which are strangers to her land.

But there is here no cause for jealousy. Peace is the necessity of the age. Great Britain and America have together six millions of tons of shipping, and war is too expensive an amusement for either nation, and can be resorted to only in defence of valued rights or great principles. You will allow me to express the sentiment of a modern English historian, who said;—"In two centuries the name of England may be unknown, or exist only in the shadow of ancient renown; but three hundred millions of people in North America will be speaking its language, reading its authors, glorying in its descent."

I have alluded to our indebtedness to Great Britain for that history and literature which are the basis of our own; and we are continually receiving additions to our population, of men who will materially aid in the development of the physical, intellectual and moral character of the American Republic.

The name and history of Great Britain deserve to be cherished next—pardon me if I say *next*—to the name and fame of America, by every American citizen. [Cheers.]

When the Governor had taken his seat, and the applause had subsided, the Mayor said:—

The remarks, Gentlemen, which you have listened to with pleasure and respect from His Excellency, the Governor, call to mind the extent and the amount of the influence exerted in contriving, carrying out and perfecting the railroad system of Massachusetts, by those able men who have preceded him in the high office which he adorns. No one, perhaps, has exerted more of that influence than the illustrious individual who sits near me on my right, and whom I take pleasure in introducing to you. I present to you, Gentlemen, the Hon. Edward Everett.

Mr. Everett then arose, amid long continued cheering, and, after a sportive allusion to his being called an Ex-Governor, spoke as follows:

May it Please your Honor,—

It is not easy for me to express to you the admiration with which I have listened to the very beautiful and appropriate speech with which his Excellency, the Governor General of Canada, has just delighted us. You know, Sir, that the truest and highest art is to conceal art; and I could not but be reminded of that maxim, when I heard that gentleman, after beginning with disabling himself, and cautioning us at the onset that he was slow of speech, proceed to make one of the happiest, most appropriate and eloquent speeches ever uttered. If I were travelling with his lordship in his native mountains of Gael, I should say to him, in the language of the natives of those regions, *sma sheen*—very well, my lord. But in plain English, Sir, that which has fallen from his lordship has given me indeed new cause to rejoice that "Chatham's language is my mother tongue." [Great cheering.]

I do not rise, Sir, to make a long speech. I think it would be rather out of taste, for any one who is at home in Boston or vicinity, unless in the performance of official duty, to make anything which could be called a long speech on this occasion. All the crowded hours of this busy day belong to our much honored guests—to those distinguished visitors who adorn the occasion with their presence. From them, indeed, Sir, the company cannot hear enough, to gratify the earnest desire which is felt to listen to their voices, and to catch their words of encouragement and congratulation.

Besides, Sir, there never was an occasion which stood less in need of a laborious commentary to set forth its importance. If ever there was anything which might be left to speak for itself*—

* At this moment the stentorian steam-whistle of the Providence cars, which were then just entering the depot, blew a blast so "loud and shrill," as to startle the vast assemblage, and furnish a convincing proof of the truth of the orator's remark. It is hardly necessary to say that the incident was greeted with tremendous cheers.

it is this mighty and all but animated system of railroads, that now embraces New England and the neighboring States and Provinces, and which, more than realising the accounts of those enormous sea monsters of which we read in northern legends, winds its sinuous way through the gorges of the hills—leaps across the rivers—stretches over the plains—clings with one of its Briarean arms to Boston Bay—grapples to Diamond Rock with another—seizes with the right upon Providence and New York, and Albany, and Buffalo, and the farthest South, and the farthest West; while on the left, he is already stretching forth his iron feelers upon New Brunswick, Nova Scotia, and Newfoundland. In the presence of this miracle of science, and art, and capital, I feel, Sir, that we have no need of flowers of rhetoric or figures of speech.

We have, Sir, in this part of the country long been convinced of the importance of this system of communication; although it may be doubted whether the most sagacious and sanguine have even yet fully comprehended its manifold influences. We have, however, felt them on the sea-board and in the interior. We have felt them in the growth of our manufactures, in the extension of our commerce, in the growing demand for the products of agriculture, in the increase of our population. We have felt them prodigiously in transportation and travel. The inhabitant of the country has felt them in the ease with which he resorts to the city markets, whether as a seller or a purchaser. The inhabitant of the city has felt them in the facility with which he can get to a sister city, or to the country; with which he can get back to his native village;—to see the old folks, aye, Sir, and some of the young folks—with which he can get a mouthful of pure mountain air—or run down in dog days to Gloucester, or Phillips' beach, or Plymouth, or Cohassett, or New Bedford.

I say, Sir, we have felt the benefit of our railway system in these and a hundred other forms, in which, penetrating far beyond material interests, it intertwines itself with all the concerns and relations of life and society; but I have never had its benefits brought home to me so sensibly as on the present occasion. Think, Sir, how it has annihilated time and space, in reference to this festival, and how greatly to our advantage and delight! When Dr. Franklin, in 1754, projected a plan of union for these colonies, with Philadelphia as the metropolis, he gave as a reason for this part of the plan, that Philadelphia was situated about half way between the extremes, and could be conveniently reached even from Portsmouth, New Hampshire, in eighteen days! I believe the President of the United States, who has honored us with his company at this joyous festival, was not more than twenty-four hours actually on the road from Washington to Boston; two to Baltimore, seven more to Philadelphia, five more to New York, and ten more to Boston.

And then Canada, Sir, once remote, inaccessible region—but now brought to our very door. If a journey had been contemplated in that direction in Dr. Franklin's time, it would have been with such feelings as a man would have now-a-days, who was going to start for the mouth of Copper Mine River and the shores of the Arctic Sea. But no, Sir; such a thing was never thought of—never dreamed of. A horrible wilderness, rivers and lakes unspanned by human art, pathless swamps, dismal forests that it made the flesh creep to enter, threaded by nothing more practicable than the Indian's trail, echoing with no sound more inviting than the yell of the wolf and the warwhoop of the savage; these it was that filled the space between us and Canada. The inhabitants of the British Colonies never entered Canada in those days but as provincial troops or Indian captives; and lucky he that got back with his scalp on. [Laughter.] This state of things existed less than one hundred years ago; there are men living in Massachusetts who were born before the last party of hostile Indians made an incursion to the banks of the Connecticut river.

As lately as when I had the honor to be the Governor of the Commonwealth, I signed the pension warrant of a man who lost his arm in the year 1757, in a conflict with the Indians and French in one of the border wars, in those dreary Canadian forests. His Honor the Mayor will recollect it, for he countersigned the warrant as Secretary of State. Now, Sir, by the magic power of these modern works of art, the forest is thrown open—the rivers and the lakes are bridged—the valleys rise, the mountains bow their everlasting heads; and the Governor-General of Canada takes his breakfast in Montreal, and his dinner in Boston;—reading a newspaper leisurely by the way which was printed a fortnight ago in London. [Great applause.] In the excavations made in the construction of the Vermont railroads, the skeletons of fossil whales and palœozoic elephants have been brought to light. I believe, Sir, if a live spermaceti whale had been seen spouting in Lake Champlain, or a native elephant had walked leisurely into Burlington from the neighboring woods, of a summer's morning, it would not be thought more wonderful than our fathers would have regarded Lord Elgin's journey to us this week, could it have been foretold to them a century ago, with all the circumstances of despatch, convenience and safety. [Applause.]

But, Sir, as I have already said, it is not the material results of this railroad system in which its happiest influences are seen. I recollect that seven or eight years ago there was a project to carry a railroad into the lake country in England—into the heart of Westmorland and Cumberland. Mr. Wordsworth, the lately deceased poet, a resident in the centre of this region, opposed the project. He thought that the retirement and seclusion of this delightful region would be disturbed by the panting of the locomotive, and the cry of the steam whistle. If I am not mistaken, he published one or two sonnets in deprecation of the enterprise.* Mr. Wordsworth was a kind-hearted man, as well as a most distinguished poet, but he was entirely mistaken, as it seems to me, in this matter. The quiet of a few spots may be disturbed; but a hundred quiet spots are rendered accessible. The bustle of the station house may take the place of the Druidical silence of some shady dell; but, Gracious Heavens! Sir, how many of those verdant cathedral arches, entwined by the hand of God in our pathless woods, are opened to the grateful worship of man by these means of communication! [Cheers.]

How little of rural beauty you lose, even in a country of comparatively narrow dimensions like England—how less than little in a country so vast as this—by works of this description. You lose a little strip along the line of the road, which partially

* The following are the Sonnets alluded to by Mr. Everett:—

On the Projected Kendal and Windermere Railway.

Is there no nook of English ground secure
From rash assault? Schemes of retirement sown
In youth, and mid the busy world kept pure
As when their earliest flowers of hope were blown,
Must perish;—how can they this blight endure?
And must he, too, the ruthless change bemoan,
Who scorns a false utilitarian lure
Mid his paternal fields at random thrown?
Baffle the threat, bright scene from Orrest-head
Given to the pausing traveller's rapturous glance:
Plead for thy peace, thou beautiful romance
Of nature; and, if human hearts be dead,
Speak, passing Winds; ye Torrents, with your strong
And constant voice, protest against the wrong.

October 12th, 1844.

Proud were ye, Mountains! when, in times of old,
Your patriot sons, to stem invasive war,
Intrenched your brows; ye gloried in each scar;
Now, for your shame, a power, the thirst of gold,
That rules o'er Britain like a baneful star,
Wills that your peace, your beauty, shall be sold,
And clear way made for her triumphant car
Through the beloved retreats your arms enfold!
Heard YE that whistle? As her long-linked train
Swept onwards, did the vision cross your view?
Yes, ye were startled;—and, in balance true,
Weighing the mischief with the promised gain,
Mountains, and Vales, and Floods! I call on you
To share the passion of a just disdain!

changes its character; while, as the compensation, you bring all this rural beauty,—

> "The warbling woodland, the resounding shore,
> The pomp of groves, the garniture of fields,"

within the reach, not of a score of luxurious, sauntering tourists, but of the great mass of the population, who have senses and tastes as keen as the keenest. You throw it open, with all its soothing and humanizing influences, to thousands who, but for your railways and steamers, would have lived and died without ever having breathed the life-giving air of the mountains;—yes, Sir, to tens of thousands, who would have gone to their graves, and the sooner for the privation, without ever having caught a glimpse of the most magnificent and beautiful spectacle which nature presents to the eye of man—that of a glorious combing wave, a quarter of a mile long, as it comes swelling and breasting toward the shore, till its soft green ridge bursts into a crest of snow, and settles and dies along the whispering sands! [Immense cheering.]

But even this is nothing compared with the great social and moral effects of this system, a subject admirably treated, in many of its aspects, in a sermon by Dr. Gannett, which has been kindly given to the public. All important also are its political effects in binding the States together as one family, and uniting us to our neighbors as brethren and kinsfolk. I do not know, Sir, [turning to Lord Elgin,] but in this way, from the kindly seeds which have been sown this week, in your visit to Boston, and that of the distinguished gentlemen who have preceded and accompanied you, our children and grandchildren, as long as this great Anglo Saxon race shall occupy the continent, may reap a harvest worth all the cost which has devolved on this generation. [Cheers.]

Mr. Everett having resumed his seat, the Mayor remarked, that—

As the mind reverts to the infancy of the settlement of Boston, a wish is rationally felt to know what our stern progenitors would say, if permitted to witness the moral and physical changes, which have come over the scenes of their trials and triumphs. What, in special, would they think of such a festival as this, held within their sacred borders, where are gathered, at the same table, Catholics and Protestants of every sect; monarchists and republicans; nobles and commoners of the mother country, with representatives of every section of a continent, of which they knew nothing but a narrow margin? The wish is vain,—but, next to its gratification, we have the comfort to know, that the Pilgrims are represented at this board, by a proxy, who is preeminently able to speak for them, in the person of a lineal descendant of their great leader,—the Moses, who led them, across the wilderness of waters, to this home of their refuge. I present to you the Honorable Robert Charles Winthrop, late Speaker of the House of Representatives of the United States.

Mr. Winthrop was most cordially received, and spoke as follows—

I am deeply sensible, Mr. Mayor, that the honors and compliments of this occasion belong to others. They belong, in the first place, as my friend, Mr. Everett, has just suggested, to the distinguished and illustrious strangers of our own country and of other countries, who have adorned our festival with their presence. [Warm applause.] And they belong, in the next place, to those of our own fellow citizens, of whom I see not a few around me, to whose far-seeing sagacity and persevering efforts and personal labors we owe the great works whose completion we celebrate. [Cheers.] For myself, Sir, I have no pretension of either sort; but I am all the more grateful for the opportunity you have afforded me of saying a few words, and for the kind and cordial manner in which you have presented me to this assembly. Most heartily do I wish that I could say anything worthy of such a scene. Most heartily do I wish that I could find expressions and illustrations in any degree commensurate to the vast and varied theme which such an occasion suggests. And still more do I wish that I could find a voice capable of conveying, even to one-half of this countless and crowded audience, such poor phrases as I may be able to command. But voice, language and imagination seem to falter and fail alike in any attempt to do justice to circumstances like the present. [Loud cheers.]

Mr. Mayor, the very dates which you have selected for your three days' jubilee, would furnish material for a discourse which would occupy far more than all the daylight which is left us. The 17th, 18th and 19th days of September! How many of the most memorable events in our local, colonial and national history, are included in this brief period!

It was on one of these days, in the year 1620, that the Pilgrim Fathers of New England took their final departure from the mother country, their last and tearful leave of Old England, and entered on that perilous ocean voyage, of more than three months' duration, which terminated at Plymouth rock!

It was on one of these days, ten years later, in 1630, that the Puritan Fathers of Massachusetts, with one of whom you have done me the honor to associate me, first gave the name of Boston to the few tents and huts and log cabins which then made up our embryo city!

It was on one of these same days, too, in 1787, that the Patriot Fathers of America set their hands and seals, at Philadelphia, to that matchless instrument of government—*the Constitution of the United States*—which has bound this nation together for better or worse—let me not say for better or worse, but for the best and highest interests of our country and mankind—[Cheers]—in one inseparable and ever-blessed Union forever! [Renewed cheers.]

Nor, Mr. Mayor, is this eventful period in the calendar without associations and reminiscences of pride and glory, for our brethren whom we have welcomed from over the borders. It was, if I mistake not, on one of these same three September days, in the year 1759, that the proud fortress of Quebec was finally surrendered to the British forces—surrendered as the result of that memorable conflict on the heights of Abraham, five or six days before, in which the gallant Wolfe had expired in the blaze of his fame, happy, (as he said,) to have seen his country's arms victorious—and in which the not less gallant Montcalm had lain down in the dust beside him, happy, too, (as he also said,) not to have seen the downfall of this last stronghold of the French power on the North American continent.

Nor is this a reminiscence, Sir, in which we of New England, and of Massachusetts particularly, have no part or heritage; for, let it not be forgotten, that Massachusetts, during that year, besides furnishing to the British army her prescribed quota of six or seven thousand men to fight the battles of a common Crown, at Louisburg, in Nova Scotia, and elsewhere, actually raised three hundred additional men, at the request of General Wolfe himself, who served as the very pioneers of that seemingly desperate assault upon Quebec. [Cheers.] Let it not be forgotten, either, that the Colonial Assembly of Massachusetts testified their admiration of Wolfe, and their sorrow for his loss, by voting a marble monument to his memory.

But all these, I am aware, are but the accidental coincidences of this occasion. We have assembled not to recall the past, but to rejoice in the present; not to commemorate the early trials and exploits of our fathers, but the mature achievements and proud successes of their sons. We come not to celebrate the triumphs of the forum or the battle-field, but the peaceful victories of science, of invention, and of those mechanic arts, so many of whose noble products, and nobler producers, we have seen in the splendid pageant of the day. [Loud applause.]

And in whatever aspect we contemplate these great highways of intercommunication, in whose construction and completion we this day exult, we find it difficult to express, and impossible to exaggerate, our sense of their magnitude and importance. It is for others, and upon other occasions, to speak of their influence on our material interests, our commercial prosperity, and our local advantages.

Your own intelligent and accomplished Committee of Arrangements, indeed, have anticipated all that could be said by any one, on any occasion, on this part of the subject. They have prepared a tabular representation (which I am glad to see has been laid upon every plate) which tells in figures less deceptive or equivocal than those of rhetoric, how much has been done in this way for Boston, for Massachusetts, for New England, for the country, for the whole unbounded continent, by the enterprise, industry, capital and skill of our citizens. Here, too, is a miniature map [holding it up] which they have furnished us, exhibiting our little Commonwealth, as it really is, covered all over with railroad lines, as with the countless fibres of a spider's web. They tell us here of a hundred and twenty passenger trains, containing no less than twelve thousand persons, shooting into our city, on a single, ordinary, average summer's day, with a regularity, punctuality and precision, which make it almost as safe to set our watches by a railroad whistle, as by the old South clock! [Laughter.]

But, Sir, by what figures of rhetoric, or of arithmetic either, shall we measure the influence of those great improvements on our political condition, or on our social relations, domestic or foreign?

Consider them for an instant, in connection with the extent of our own wide-spread Republic. By what other agency than that of railroads could a Representative Government like ours be rendered practicable over so vast a territory? The necessary limits of such a Government were justly defined by one of our earliest and wisest statesmen, to be those within which the Representatives of the People could be brought together with regularity and certainty, as often as needful, to transact the public business.

And by which do you think, sir, of the old-fashioned modes of transportation or travel—the stage-coach, the pack-saddle, or the long wagon,—or by which, even, of those queer conveyances which His Excellency the Governor General of Canada tells us he once shared with my friend Governor Paine,—could Delegates from California, or Utah, or even from some of our less recent and less remote acquisitions, be brought to our sessions of Congress at Washington, and carried back at stated intervals to consult the wishes of their constituents, within any reasonable or reliable time?

Mr. Mayor, in view of this and many other considerations, to which I may not take up further time by alluding, and which, indeed, are too familiar to require any allusion, I feel that it is no exaggeration to say, that our Railroad system is an essential part of our Representative system; and that it has exerted an influence, second in importance to no other that can be named, material, political, or moral, in binding together, in one indissoluble brotherhood, this vast association of American States. It is hardly too much to add, that it seems to have been Providentially prepared, as the great centripetal enginery, which is destined to overcome and neutralise forever those deplorable centrifugal tendencies, which local differences, and peculiar institutions, and sectional jealousies, have too often engendered. [Marked applause.]

The President of the United States, in his admirable reply to your most appropriate address, Sir, welcoming him within the lines of Boston, reminded us that his illustrious predecessor, Washington, occupied eleven days in travelling by express from Philadelphia, to the neighboring city of Cambridge, in one of the most critical emergencies of our local history. Let me remind you, also, of a similar experience in the journeyings of another of his predecessors. In the recently published diary of our own John Adams, will be found the following entry, dated at Middletown, Conn., on the 8th day of June, 1771:

"Looking into the almanac I am startled. Supreme Court at Ipswich is the 18th day of June; I thought it a week later, 25th; so that I have only next week to go home, one hundred and fifty miles. I must improve every moment. It is twenty-five miles a day, if I ride every day next week."

John Adams startled,—and let me say that he was not of a complexion to be very easily startled at anything,—at having only a week for going a hundred and fifty miles! Startled at the idea of being obliged to go twenty-five miles a day every day for a week! [Laughter.] While here, but a moment since, was his illustrious successor, who, having already travelled nearly five hundred miles in twenty-four hours, and having spent three or four days in Newport and Boston, which we hope have been as delightful to him as they certainly have been to us, is now on his way back, and is about to reach Washington again before the week in which he left there is fairly at an end!

And here, Mr. Mayor, I turn, in conclusion, to what to-day, at least, in the minds and hearts of us all, is the great charm of this modern miracle of rapid intercommunication. It is that it enables us to see, to know, and to enjoy personal intercourse with the great, the good, the distinguished, the admired of our own land and of other lands. We can take them by the hand, we can see their faces, we can hear their voices, and we can form ties of mutual respect and regard, which neither time nor distance may afterwards sever.

There have been those here to-day whom none of you will soon forget; and there is at least one of them to whom I had particularly proposed to myself the pleasure of alluding. I refer to the Secretary of the Interior, the Honorable Alexander Stuart—[applause]—a noble son of old Virginia, with whom in other years

I have been associated in Congress, and whom I am always proud to call my friend. He has already taken his leave of us, Sir; but I am sure we all desire to follow him with our good wishes, and to assure him that though out of sight he is not out of mind.

But let me congratulate the company that we have another Alexander Stewart still left at the table—a distinguished son of Nova Scotia—an eminent citizen of Halifax—a high functionary of the Provincial Government—whom it has been my good fortune to have at my side during the last hour, and who is every way entitled to our highest consideration and respect. With a view of introducing him to the company, I propose, as a sentiment,—

"Prosperity to Nova Scotia and the city of Halifax, and the health of our distinguished guest, the Hon. Alexander Stewart, the Master of the Rolls." [Applause.]

To this sentiment the Hon. Mr. Stewart, having been presented by the Mayor, responded by saying that he wished the state of his health would enable him to follow the eloquent gentlemen who had preceded him in depicting the social, moral, and political results of the system of railroads, the completion of which was celebrated this day. But since, unfortunately, that was not the case, he would call upon one —an Advocate of Nova Scotia—whose voice had been heard in the Canadas, and heard in England, and whom he was happy to have at hand, to stand in his place.

This was understood to refer to the Hon. Joseph Howe, Provincial Secretary of Nova Scotia, who was immediately called on, and thus addressed the meeting:

Mr. Mayor and Gentlemen,—

At this late hour it would be unfair to trespass long upon your patience. With the voices of the eloquent speakers who have preceded me still charming the ear, how can I venture to address you at all? Though feeling the full force of the comparisons which must be drawn, and representing one of the smallest Provinces of the British Empire, I am reluctant to be altogether silent, lest it might be supposed that my countrymen do not appreciate your hospitality, or take an interest in the great works, the completion of which we have met to celebrate. To me the occasion is full of interest, for I stand here, the son of a banished Loyalist, to rejoice with you in the prosperity of the city of which my father was a native. How many stirring passages of old colonial history have the scenes presented to my eye during the past three days revived! How strangely has the past been blended with the present, as I have listened to sentiments of mutual respect and friendship breathed by the leaders of two great nations, sternly opposed in the olden time, but now rivals only in the graces which embellish life, or in the fields of profitable industry. As the son of a Bostonian, I cannot but rejoice,—whatever may be the distinctions of allegiance, the claims of country, or the high hopes of the future which we British Americans cherish,—in the permanent prosperity and advancement of this city.

Mr. Mayor: I have looked on the great pageant of the day with extreme interest and care, have marked the thronged streets in which the citizens of Boston conduct their profitable commerce, and observed the praiseworthy evidences of the skill and ingenuity of your mechanics. But the sight which challenged the highest interest and admiration—which appealed to the finest and most elevated feelings, were the lines of life and intelligence presented by the young Bostonians who represented the fostering care of the Free Schools of New England. I might have passed the other features of the celebration with comparative indifference, but when I saw those children, I was reminded of that German schoolmaster who declared that when he entered his schoolroom he always took off his hat, for there he met the future dignitaries of his land. So here, Sir, I saw the guarantee and the gage of the future prosperity of this interesting State. The sight of those children, even more forcibly than the beaming faces which smiled from your balconies and windows as we passed, naturally called to mind those upon whose knees they had been nurtured, and led me to conclude that though we had seen this proud city in its holiday attire, and might, perhaps, see it in its working dress to-morrow, we could see nothing more interesting than the Free Schools which educate its children, and the beautiful and virtuous mothers who nourish them in their bosoms.

Gentlemen: I speak to you as the descendant of a son of the old soil of Massachusetts—the representative of an offshoot which has some of the virtues of the original stock. I hope that Massachusetts men will come to the Northern Provinces and note them. We British Americans who share with you, down to a certain period, the vicissitudes of a common history, and the treasures of a literature bequeathed to us all—who have, since the revolution divided us, made for ourselves a noble country out of its wilderness, while we survey your prosperity without envy, and cherish attachment to the parent state, have not forgotten the trials or the traditions of a common ancestry. Nova Scotia has adopted the little "Mayflower" as the emblem upon her escutcheon, and those who laid the foundations of her society, and built up her towns and seaports, were as proud of their Pilgrim stock as you are here. Though Halifax dates one hundred and twenty-seven years after Boston in point of time—though all that our fathers toiled for in that century and a quarter, they left behind them at the Revolution—still we are following in your footsteps—emulous, it may be, but I think I may assure you that throughout the British Provinces on the continent there is now no feeling but that of cordial friendship towards these noble States. We desire to see you work out in peace the high destiny which your past achievements and free institutions promise. At the same time, as the territory we occupy is as broad as yours—as broad as the whole continent of Europe—watered by lakes as expansive as your own—drained by noble rivers—blessed with a healthy climate and unbounded fertility—with fisheries and commercial advantages unrivalled, we are content with our lot, and feel that the mutual prosperity and success of both nations are to be found in peace, harmony, and brotherly love. I hope, Sir, that many years will not pass away before you are invited to a railroad celebration on British soil, and this I promise you,—that when that day comes, even if our Railroads should not be as long as yours, the Festival shall be as long, and the welcome as cordial. In conclusion, Sir, permit me to make another allusion to those who, if they are not here, ought to be "freshly remembered;" for they have enlivened our visit by their marked beauty and fascinations. You have tried once or twice, I believe, to invade our frontiers. When next you make the attempt, let me advise you to put the Women of New England in front, and then you will be sure to succeed.

At the conclusion of Mr. Howe's remarks, which were received with great applause, the Hon. Francis Hincks, Inspector General of Canada, having been called upon by the Mayor, arose and addressed the assembly as follows:

Mr. Mayor, and Citizens of Boston,—

I rise to address you under great embarrassment, for I fear that the eloquent address of your illustrious guest, the Governor General of Canada, and the speech more recently delivered by my honorable friend who represents the Province of Nova Scotia on this occasion, will indispose you to listen with patience to any remarks of mine. His Excellency the Governor General has already given expression to the feelings of all your Canadian guests, who are most deeply grateful to you for your truly hospitable reception. On the part of my colleagues and myself, who have received special attention at your hands, I desire to say that we feel that those attentions have not been paid to us on account of our own deserts, but as a compliment to the Canadian people, and as the incumbents of offices which we can hold only so long as we enjoy their confidence. I can assure you, Mr. Mayor and

Gentlemen, that the moment that I heard that this celebration was contemplated, I foresaw the important results which are likely to follow it. When I had the pleasure of meeting in Toronto the deputation which you were kind enough to send to invite us, and which was accompanied by my esteemed friend, Governor Paine, I told them that if I were above ground I should be in Boston on the 17th of September. I feel, Mr. Mayor and Gentlemen, that it is good for us to be here. It is well that you, citizens of the United States, should have had an opportunity of witnessing the enthusiasm with which all classes of Her Majesty's British American subjects responded to the sentiment proposed by the Mayor, "The Health of the Queen." You must be convinced that every British subject in this vast assemblage is animated by a sentiment of devoted loyalty and attachment to the person and government of that beloved Sovereign. It is likewise well that you should have witnessed the enthusiastic reception given by all classes of the Canadian people to Her Majesty's illustrious Representative in one of the most important possessions of the Crown. You must be satisfied, Mr. Mayor and Gentlemen, that we are a happy and contented people. We enjoy the blessings of civil and religious freedom under a Constitution which, as we are proud to declare, is the very image and transcript of that glorious Constitution which our ancestors and your ancestors shed their blood on the field and on the scaffold to obtain. Differing in many important particulars from the written Constitutions of your States, there is yet this striking similarity between them. In our Provinces, as in the States of the American Union, the Government must be conducted in accordance with enlightened public opinion, which we ascertain by the votes of the representatives of the people. It is, Mr. Mayor and Gentlemen, well for us to be here, because we have much to learn from the people of New England. Their history has not been a sealed book to us. We can admire, as well as you can, the spirit which animated the Pilgrim Fathers who landed on Plymouth Rock. Whatever opinions we may entertain on political questions, we have sufficient generosity to admire the spirit displayed by the sons of New England in your great Revolutionary contest. We have likewise sufficient generosity to admire the spirit displayed at a still later period by the same race, though by another generation, in the war of 1812, in which they were frequently brought into collision with our own gallant Canadian militia, several officers of which, some of them wearing decorations conferred by their Sovereign, for their services in the field, are now listening to me. We have now, Mr. Mayor and Gentlemen, to admire the same spirit, developed in another generation in the prosecution of great enterprizes, such as those which have caused the demonstration of this evening. May we not hope, Gentlemen, that we shall be inspired with the same faith in the success of these enterprizes, which has sustained you—with the same courage in undertaking them, and the same perseverance in surmounting the obstacles which we, like you, shall have to encounter. We have much to learn from you, Citizens of Boston, but we have no cause for despondency. Like the American people, we are natives of, or descended from the natives of, Old England, Old France, Old Germany, and Old Holland; and works that you have accomplished, we ought at least to have courage to undertake.

Already we have proved what we are able to accomplish, by the completion of our line of ship canals—works so magnificent in their character as to be inferior to none on this continent. Until recently, our improvements and our trade have excited little interest in Boston. So long as the railway horizon of New England was bounded by Salem, Bradford, Nashua and Providence, the canals of Canada were of little importance to you; but now that your railways extend to Lake Ontario, you are as deeply interested in them as ourselves; and I confess that I was surprised, in reading the pamphlet which has been placed in our hands, to find in it no notice whatever of these great feeders of your railways. But for the Welland Canal, the produce of the far West would never reach the port of Ogdensburgh.

Intimately connected with this subject is one which, I have reason to believe, has hitherto attracted but little attention in New England. I allude to our commercial relations. Many of you, I am sure, are not aware that, until within a few years, heavy differential duties were imposed on American manufactures when entering our province for consumption. Without any application on the part of your government or people, we spontaneously repealed those duties, and admitted your manufactures on the same terms as those of Great Britain. Mark the consequence. Since that time, our trade with you has been steadily on the increase, and last year our imports from the United States were nearly equal to those from Great Britain. The exports of your manufactures to Canada are, if I mistake not, equal to those to any other three nations to which you trade. And in this connection allow me to mention, that one-half of the cargo of the Europa, which arrived on the day your celebration commenced, was destined for Canada, and has passed over the lines of railroad which unite us, and a portion of it is now, without doubt, on this last day of your festival, on sale in Montreal. Without entering on the subject of political economy, which it would be improper for me to do, even if time permitted, I would say that your protectionists ground their opposition to free trade with England on the fact that in that country labor is cheap, and money so plentiful as to cause a low rate of interest to rule. These objections do not apply to us; but moreover, our trade with you is of precisely that character which you profess to be most anxious to encourage. We want to furnish you with raw products, with lumber, wheat, flour, the coarser grains, and other products of our agriculturists. We wish you to give us, in exchange, your domestic manufactures, as well as teas, sugars, fruits, and other commodities obtained by you from other countries in exchange for your manufactures. We can give you an unlimited supply of such products, and the entire trade gives employment to American shipping, as well as to various classes of your operatives. You are too shrewd a people not to perceive the absurdity of extending your lines of railway to the Canadian frontier for the purpose of facilitating intercourse by means of cheap transport, while, at the same time, you keep up an army of customhouse officers to obstruct the very traffic which it is the interest of both countries to facilitate. I freely admit, Gentlemen, that our interests will be advanced by this freedom of trade, if I may be allowed to use an expression not very popular in New England; but I do not believe in the doctrine that in individual or in international exchanges it is necessary that one party must be the loser by the bargain. I have adopted the sounder opinion that in voluntary exchanges each party is well satisfied that his bargain has been good. In this assemblage you have a large representation from all classes of the Canadian people. You have members of the two Houses of Parliament, the Judges of our land, the Mayors and Corporations of our principal cities; our Ministers of the Gospel have left their flocks, Lawyers have left their clients, Doctors their patients, Agriculturists their farms, Merchants their counting-houses, Mechanics their shops. Last, though certainly not the least, the Press, the great exponent of public opinion, is represented by a numerous body of the corps editorial. I find, indeed, all classes of our people but one. There is an absence of Collectors of Customs. They are, unfortunately, kept too busy in the discharge of their duty—which is, to obstruct the trade between the two countries—to be able to assist at this splendid demonstration. All, however, that are here are of one mind. And I am sure that I give utterance to the universal feeling when I again, Mr. Mayor and Gentlemen, assure you of our deep gratitude for your hospitable reception. [Very great cheering.]

Although it had now become quite dark in the pavilion, wishes were expressed in all quarters to hear from Hon. Josiah Quincy, Jr., before adjourning. He was accordingly called upon by the Mayor to "*enlighten* the audience."

Mr. Quincy remarked,—

That he had been requested to speak on the important question of Reciprocity of Trade between Canada and the United States, but that the lateness of the hour would prevent his doing more than adding his congratulations to the shareholders and officers of the several roads whose completion was now celebrated. Their sacrifices and anxieties were forgotten in the general joy; but he believed that whatever might be the pecuniary results, such a recognition of the importance of their labors must ever be a source of satisfaction. He had devoted two years exclusively to this work, and been responsible personally for millions of dollars in order to insure its completion; and when the Head of the Nation and the Representative of the Queen met to acknowledge the national importance of the undertaking, he felt that neither his friends nor himself had labored in vain.

After some further remarks, Mr. Quincy gave, alluding to the darkness of the Pavilion,—

"*The Canadians and Bostonians*,—They may meet after sundown and without candles, but can never again be in the dark as it respects the sentiments they entertain for one another." [Cheers and laughter.]

After three cheers for the Ladies, given at the suggestion of Lord Elgin, the Mayor, intimating that, although it was dark within the pavilion, the City, without, was blazing with illuminations and fireworks, put the question, "Shall this meeting now be dissolved?" This was carried *nem. con.*, and the Mayor closed the ceremonies with these emphatic words,—

"The meeting is dissolved accordingly. God Save the Commonwealth of Massachusetts."

Immediately on leaving the Pavilion, the President and his Suite, accompanied by Alderman Rogers, the State Committee, Lieutenant Colonels Heard, Chapman and Needham, of the Governor's Staff, and Benjamin Stevens, Esq., Sergeant-at-Arms, took the cars for Fall River, where they arrived at 8 1-2 o'clock, and went on board the steamer Empire State, for Newport.

On taking leave of the President at Newport, Colonel Heard said,—

Mr. President,—

In compliance with instructions from His Excellency, the Governor of Massachusetts, his military staff will now take their leave of you. In doing so, permit me to say that the duty of the staff, in attending you to and from the capitol of the State, has been to them a most pleasant one, and they trust that the manner in which it has been discharged meets with your approval.

To which the President replied as follows,—

Colonel,—

I feel deeply grateful to the Governor of Massachusetts for the kind attention and the many tokens of respect he has been pleased to show me from the time I first entered the borders of your State.

And to you, Gentlemen, I will say, that nothing has given me greater pleasure than the personal attention and gentlemanly kindness which I have received from the Governor's Staff.

Gen. Wilson, Chairman of the Committee, then said—

Mr. President,—

Having accompanied you to the borders of the Commonwealth, we must now take our leave by bidding you farewell. In behalf of the Committee, and in the name of the Commonwealth, allow me to express to you the high gratification which your visit has conferred. I need not speak for the people; they have spoken for themselves. I hope, Sir, that you and the members of your Cabinet who have accompanied you, have received pleasure from this visit. I trust, Sir, you will return to the Capitol, with the assurance that the people of Massachusetts know no lines of latitude or of longitude, but that they embrace in their affections the whole country and all the people, of every race and condition.

The President, in reply, said that his visit had been one of unalloyed enjoyment. He had had no previous conception of what he and his associates had witnessed. He rejoiced in the evidences of prosperity which had presented themselves to him, and he felt sure that the people loved the whole country, knowing no North, no South, no East, no West. He thanked the Committee for the attention which he and his associates had received from them, and wished them prosperity and happiness.

The President, and the distinguished gentlemen who had accompanied him hither, then took leave of their escort, and proceeded on their return to Washington.

Although multitudes, in the city and its neighborhood, had been deprived, by the temporary indisposition of the President and the necessity for his early departure, of the satisfaction of seeing and welcoming him on the last day of his visit, still his presence at Boston on this occasion was the source of the highest pleasure to her citizens. The impressions which his courteous, cordial and dignified manners, his undisguised enjoyment of the scenes he witnessed, and the warm interest he manifested in the prosperity and welfare of the city, left upon the minds of her people, will not soon be effaced. Not only his eminent office entitled him to respect, but his own admirable qualities commanded the most cordial esteem. The people of Boston will long cherish the recollection of his visit, and the pleasant associations which connect his name with the festive scenes of the celebration.

As night closed over the city—the last night of the Jubilee—and while thousands thronged the streets happy in the consciousness of pleasure given and received, and rejoicing that their most sanguine anticipations had been so fully realized, and that the connection of the City to the once remote Provinces of the North and distant regions of the West had already produced a gladsome harvest of kindly social intercourse and mutual regard; the illuminations which had been prepared to illustrate this hoped for result, and as emblematic not only of present joy, but of bright hope for the future, one by one, irradiated the scene, and called forth the admiration of all.

To describe the various and brilliant exhibitions of that kind, which were witnessed in many parts of the city, is of course impossible, but such reports, as are at hand, of particular displays will however be given; though perhaps there were others, equally worthy of notice, the peculiar features of which cannot now be ascertained.

The Old State House, for many years the Capitol of the Province of Massachusetts, and now venerable for its age, was most brilliantly illuminated, as were also the buildings on each side of it, among which the "Journal" building was conspicuous; so that the head of the street was as light as day.

The City Hall was one blaze of light on both sides, and the situation of the building added greatly to the effectiveness of the display.

The Tremont House is especially worthy of notice for the extent and splendor of its illumination. The columns of the portico were like pillars of flame. Two thousand lights were placed in the windows, besides which there were dazzling rosettes of gas in front. The exhibition called forth the warmest encomiums of thousands.

The piano-forte manufactory of Hallett, Davis & Co., No. 409 Washington street, rivalled the most brilliant displays in the city. More than six hundred and thirty lights were burning, while the architecture of the building, with its dark freestone front, served as a set-off, and added much to the magnificence of the sight. A continual flight of rockets, wheels, blue lights, and other pyrotechnics, were discharged from the front of the building.

Comer's Initiatory Counting Room, at the corner of Washington and School streets, was lighted up with more than one hundred and fifty lamps, which gave it a truly resplendent appearance.

The beautiful façade of the American House, in Hanover street, was radiant with the numerous and tastefully arranged lights which blazed at every window.

Faneuil Hall, the time-honored "Cradle of Liberty," was also, on this joyous occasion, most brilliantly illuminated from its base to the cupola, and surrounded by crowds of delighted spectators, attracted thither as well by their interest in the noble old building itself, as by the beautiful spectacle it presented amid the commingled blaze of a thousand lights.

Of the numerous displays which were made by the public spirit of individuals or companies, no one, perhaps, surpassed that which was exhibited by the Boston Gas Light Co. on Washington street. In front of the office of this Company was seen the word "Union," in "letters of living light," supported by four vines, above all which blazed a single star of dazzling brilliancy. The simplicity and significance of the design, combined with the perfect success of its execution, merited and received the hearty admiration of the throngs which lingered near.

But before the eye had been wearied with the radiant, but now fading, beauty of the illuminations, it was anew delighted with the splendor of the fire works which were now blazing in all parts of the city.

These coruscations, one after another, disappeared; the multitudes reluctantly but quietly dispersed; the sounds of festivity gradually died on the ear, and soon the silence of night reigned over the City. The Jubilee was at an end.

CONCLUSION.

It only remains, in order to bring the account of the celebration to its conclusion, to notice a few of the events which occurred on the succeeding day.

And it may not be unworthy of remark that unlike the three preceding days, which were singularly beautiful, the morning of Saturday, Sept. 20th, was cloudy, and gave evident tokens of an approaching storm. "How fortunate!" was the exclamation that came unbidden from the lips of all, in view of the great disappointment so many would have felt, had the clouds gathered earlier.

> "Triste lupus stabulis, maturis frugibus imbres,
> Arboribus venti,"

but quite as sad a thing and as much to be lamented would have been an equinoctial storm in the midst of the festivities of the Jubilee. Happy, indeed, was it, and gratefully to be remembered, that no such occurrence was permitted to derange the preparations which had been made for the occasion; but that, on the contrary, even the very elements of nature seemed to combine, to throw over the festive scenes all the glories of a New England summer.

This was the day for separation, and in the course of it the greater number of those who had come from Canada, and other distant places, took their departure; though many still remained to visit the schools and other public institutions of the city and vicinity.

Very early in the morning Lord Elgin took his departure,* bearing with him an abundant harvest of golden opinions and cordial good wishes. Having declined a public escort, he was attended to the Lowell Railroad Station by Mr. Mayor Bigelow and John P. Putnam, Esq., of the Council, and was accom-

* Lord Elgin reached Montreal in sixteen hours from the time of leaving Boston, by the route of the Lowell and Vermont Central Railroads. For remarks upon his visit to Boston, see his Answer to an Address of the Corporation of Montreal, in the Appendix.

panied to his home by his Suite, Gov. Paine, of Vermont, and the Mayor and Corporation of Montreal.

In the course of the morning a large number of the guests (about two hundred) from Canada met at the Revere House, and marched thence in procession to the City Hall, where they presented to the Mayor the following address of thanks, (read by Judge Aylwin,) which had been prepared by a Committee* of their number, appointed for that purpose at a meeting held on the previous evening:—

TO THE MUNICIPAL AUTHORITIES AND CITIZENS OF BOSTON:

While we, inhabitants of Canada, congratulate you on the completion of the numerous and extended lines of Railroad in your State, and acknowledge the benefits which we, as well as yourselves, must derive from them, we cannot depart from your city without an earnest assurance of our sense of the munificent hospitality and kindness with which we have been received and entertained by you on this interesting occasion.

It would be impossible, within the compass of a hurried address, to enter at length into the feelings of gratification which the events of the last three days have left on our minds, or adequately to express the sentiments to which these events have given rise.

There are recollections connected with the relations which the Province in which we are residents bears to the great country of which your city is one of the proudest ornaments, that render the interchange of kindly feelings a matter of deeper interest than would attach to the same intercourse between the several cities of either country; and we congratulate you that, with a magnanimity worthy of the intellectual and moral culture for which your city is justly famed, you have furnished an example which has warmed into life and strength those genial impulses of mutual friendship which ought ever to exist between those who are bound together by so many ties of a common brotherhood. The passing enjoyments must yield to the stern pursuits of life; but there are impressions and sympathies which no lapse of time can efface or chill.

We shall long remember the occasion upon which we have been thus so happily drawn together—it will constitute an important era in the history of your State and of our Province. Your magnificent railroad communications with the other States of the Union and the British Provinces afford to the continent of America and the world at large a bright example of what may be achieved by the intelligence and indomitable energy of an enlightened people.

* See Appendix, for names and proceedings of the Committee.

Permit us, then, to offer to you in our own name, and we may venture to add, in the name of the Province of Canada, our heartfelt thanks for the welcome extended to us, for the courtesy with which we have been treated, and most of all, for that kindly spirit which has beamed in every face, and greeted us in every part of your prosperous city, and to add our fervent wish for your welfare, and that this great meeting may be but a beginning of those social and friendly relations which it is the duty not less of nations than of individuals to cultivate.

On behalf of the meeting,

T. C. AYLWIN, *Chairman.*
JOHN ROSE, *Secretary.*

Boston, 19th Sept. 1851.

After reading the address, and receiving the reply of the Mayor, the delegation withdrew to the square in front of the City Hall, and gave three cheers for Mr. Mayor Bigelow, and six for the city of Boston.

Subsequently, the Canadian Ministers, together with Sir Allan McNab, appeared and presented the following expression of their sentiments through the Honorable Mr. Hincks:—

TO HIS HONOR THE MAYOR AND THE CITY COUNCIL OF BOSTON:

We, the undersigned, while cordially concurring in every sentiment of the address presented to you by our fellow subjects from Canada, feel called upon to acknowledge the attentions which we have received as special guests of the city of Boston, on the interesting occasion of your great Railroad and Steamship Jubilee, and to assure you one and all that we shall long remember your hospitalities with gratitude, and that nothing will afford us greater pleasure than to have an opportunity of reciprocating them.

F. HINCKS,
Inspector General.
E. P. TACHE,
Receiver General.
JOS. BOURRET,
Chief Commissioner of Public Works.
J. H. PRICE.
Commissioner of Crown Lands.
LEWIS T. DRUMMOND,
Solicitor General for Lower Canada.
J. SANDFIELD MACDONALD,
Solicitor General for Upper Canada.
HAMILTON H. KILLALY,
Assistant Commissioner of Public Works.
ALLAN N. MCNAB.

Boston, 20th September, 1851.

A deputation, consisting of Mr. Mayor Bowes of Toronto, and several members of the Council of that city, next appeared, and read the following address:—

TO HIS HONOR THE MAYOR OF BOSTON:

Sir:—The Mayor and Corporation of Toronto, in taking leave of the Mayor and other municipal authorities of Boston, beg to express their deep sense of the unbounded hospitality shown to them during their stay in this city; and they know they can speak confidently in assuring the municipal authorities of Boston that the debt of obligation thus contracted will be gladly acknowledged by their fellow citizens of Toronto; and they trust that the kindly feelings thus created, may continue to increase, and produce its appropriate results in a frequent interchange of those courtesies which are so agreeable in themselves, and so eminently conducive to the welfare of cities, as well as of individuals.

They beg, in conclusion, to offer the expression of their sincere hope, that the most sanguine anticipations of the new lines of railroad, whose opening gave occasion to the recent truly magnificent festivities, may be amply realized in the opening up of new channels of commerce and the consequent increased prosperity of the city of Boston.

JOHN G. BOWES, *Mayor.*

Boston, September 20, 1851.

The following address was then presented by a large deputation from the *citizens* of Toronto, who were present at the celebration:—

To the Mayor and Municipal Authorities of the City of Boston:

MR. MAYOR AND GENTLEMEN:

We the undersigned, inhabitants of the city of Toronto and its vicinity, who have been partakers of the hospitality of your city during the Railroad Festival which has just been concluded, beg leave, before departing for our homes, to return to you our warmest thanks for the attention which we have received from you and your fellow citizens, and to express to you our most grateful acknowledgments for the honor and the pleasure conferred upon us in being made participators in a Jubilee, calculated, as we devoutly hope, to cement and render permanent an union, of interests as well as of affection, between the citizens of our respective countries, so happily commenced under your auspices.

Through the instrumentality of the works, the completion of which we have been invited to celebrate, we flatter ourselves that we see a tide of prosperity flowing into Canada from your shores which, in its ebb, will convey back to you the productions of a soil teeming with wealth incalculable and as yet to you unknown.

Through our Province and through our city the iron link, which is to connect your city with the "Far West," must of necessity be made; and we are not blind to the importance, to ourselves, as well as to you, that this link should be formed with as little delay as possible.

In extending these channels for commercial intercourse through our country, it will be our object to endeavor to emulate you in that spirit of enterprise and self-reliance which has not only elevated your city to its present prosperous position, but is one of the chief of your national characteristics, and to which in a great measure your country is indebted for that exalted rank among the nations of the earth which it has attained within so short a period.

We feel assured that our exertions will be attended with your hearty wishes for our speedy success.

The destinies of the world for good or for ill, for peace or for war, are suspended in the united hands of the two great nations to which we respectively belong; and we sincerely pray that the sentiments of fraternal regard with which we have felt inspired during the celebration of your great festival may be perpetual, and that peace and happiness under the joint influence of our respective Rulers may forever pervade the earth.

John Arnold,
A. M. Clark,
Edward G. O'Brien,
Wm. Rees,
John M. Gwynne,
Alex'r Dixon,
E. Bradburne,
George Ewart,
Thos. Davidson,
Robert S. Maitland,
Walter Gorham,
Alex. Manning,
John Patton,
John Watkins,
W. B. Skelton,
Richard Dempsey,
Thos. Brunskill,
Joseph Rogerson,
Gavin Russell, M.D.,
John Welsh,
Wm. Hallowell, M.D.,
Jas. Jno. Hayes, M.D.,
Edw'd Goldsmith,
Wm. Turner,
W. E. Twynam,
Russel Inglis,
Jno. C. Betteridge,
J. R. Mountjoy,
R. Pilkington Crooks,
Kivas Tully,
J. Dodsley Humphreys,
Charles L. Davies,
George Herrick, M. D.,
Jas. Reed,
John Elliott,
James Hodgert,
Robert Davis,
W. J. Fitzgerald,
J. Silverthorn,
Jas. Young,
George Cheney,
Eyre M. Shaw,
Robt. Beekman,
Frederick Perkins,
A. V. Brown,
Angus Dallas.

GEO. A. PHILLPOTTS,	CHARLES ROBERTSON,
RICE LEWIS,	EDWARD LAWSON,
JOHN HUTCHINSON,	JOHN HELLIWELL,
FRANKLIN JACKES,	JOHN M. MONRO.
JOHN COTTON,	

To each of these addresses the Mayor responded in an appropriate manner, but their presentation being wholly unexpected, no reporters were present, and no sketches of the replies have been preserved excepting a portion of the answer to the Canadian Ministry, having special reference to Lord Elgin.

In this reply, after reciprocating expressions of consideration and regard, and touching upon appropriate topics, the Mayor said that he availed himself of the occasion to speak of his own impressions, and the impresssions of those whom he represented, concerning His Excellency, the Governor General; the shortness of whose visit, was the subject of regret throughout the City. His frank and courteous bearing, his ready and generous appreciation of the character of our people and institutions, his glowing and captivating eloquence of speech, indicating a cultivated intellect of the highest order, had commanded the respect and admiration of this community for him as a MAN, no less than as the accomplished representative of his Sovereign. Although "rank" is not always like "the guinea's stamp" indicative of intrinsic worth, yet in this case none will question that the patent, emanating from royal favor, worthily graces a nobility of nature's own coining.

The Mayor then alluded to the genealogy of Lord Elgin, and spoke of the services of his ancestor, the first Lord Bruce of Kinloss, in preparing the way to a peaceful union of the Crowns of England and Scotland, on the death of Elizabeth,—a union, he said, pregnant with the most momentous consequences to the progress of the Anglo Saxon race, and which will never cease to affect the destinies of mankind. James was indeed the rightful heir, but the English aristocracy (the Commons had but little weight at that period) naturally looked with no small jealousy at the accession of a foreign monarch to the throne of the Tudors; accompanied, and doubtless to be influenced, by the nobles of his native land. Had such jealousy availed to exclude the Scottish King, a war of succession would probably have ensued, which would have wasted the resources and crippled the strength of both countries, for successive generations. At any rate, for want of Union, neither country could have kept pace with the advance of continental nations, in prosperity and power. The star of France would have culminated without a rival. England could have had neither fleets nor armies adequate to protect her own colonies, (if indeed she would ever have possessed any,) much less to wrest such from the hands of her powerful antagonist. The annals of modern warfare on this continent, as well as elsewhere, would have been far different from the existing record,—Montcalm might have lived to the natural term of an honored life, and the blood of Wolfe might not have sealed his country's triumph.

The great current of human events is often turned by seemingly inadequate causes; and it may be that the festival which has assembled in harmonious fellowship so much of the talent, wealth, and representation of power, of the British and American nations, will exercise an important influence in confirming and perpetuating amity between branches of a kindred race. Our celebration will owe much of its moral and political effect to the presence, and conciliatory bearing, of him who has represented, in chief, the MOTHER COUNTRY and her colonies, on the occasion. If, as I believe, he has contributed largely to strengthen the bonds of national brotherhood, and thereby to the diffusion of the immortal principles of "peace on earth and good will" among men, he will have added new lustre to the honors of a house, which history has adorned with the laurels of Bannockburn.

Here concludes the account of the Railroad Jubilee. The motives which led to its institution have been already stated, and the eloquent words of the deputation of the citizens of Toronto may well be used to express also the sentiments of the citizens of Boston, in regard to its moral result:

"The destinies of the world for good or for ill, for peace or for war, are in a great degree suspended in the united hands of the two great nations to which we respectively belong—and we sincerely pray, that the sentiments of fraternal regard, with which we have felt inspired during the celebration of this Festival, may be perpetual, and that peace and happiness, under the joint influence of our respective Rulers, may forever pervade the earth."

APPENDIX.

APPENDIX.

OFFICIAL CORRESPONDENCE IN RELATION TO LORD ELGIN'S VISIT TO BOSTON.

The following correspondence between the Representative of Great Britain at Washington, and the Secretary of State, grew out of the late visit of Lord Elgin to this city:

WASHINGTON, NOV. 28, 1851.

SIR:—In reference to our late conversation, I have the honor to enclose the copy of a despatch which has been addressed to me by Her Majesty's principal Secretary of State for Foreign Affairs, by which I am instructed to express the gratification felt by Her Majesty's Government on being apprized of the cordial reception which was given to the Earl of Elgin during the ceremonies which took place at Boston on the 17th, 18th, and 19th of September last, in celebration of the completion of a line of railroad connecting the Canadas with New England; and in expressing the grateful sense which Lord Elgin entertains of the courtesy and hospitality which he experienced during his visit to Boston, to convey to the President of the United States, and the citizens of Boston, the cordial thanks of Her Majesty's Government for this proof of their kindly feelings towards Her Majesty's Government and the British nation.

I avail myself of this opportunity to renew to you, Sir, the assurance of my highest consideration.

JOHN F. CRAMPTON.

The Hon. Daniel Webster, &c., &c., &c.

FOREIGN OFFICE, OCT. 31, 1851.

SIR:—With reference to your despatch, No. 23, of the 20th of September, reporting the cordial reception which was given to the Earl of Elgin during the ceremonies which took place at Boston on the 17th, 18th, and 19th of September, in celebration of the completion of the line of railroad connecting the Canadas with New England, I have to acquaint you that Her Majesty's Secretary of State for the Colonial Department has received from Lord Elgin a despatch to the same effect respecting his visit to Boston; and, in compliance with Earl Grey's request, I have to instruct you to state to the Government of the United States that Her Majesty's Government have read with great pleasure the accounts which have reached them of the distinguished reception which was given to Lord Elgin by the President of the United States, and by the citizens of Boston, on the occasion in question, and that Her Majesty's Government are more especially gratified by it, inasmuch as they look upon it as a proof of the prevalence and extension of that good and friendly feeling between the people of the two countries which Her Majesty's Government are so desirous to encourage and confirm.

You will also say that Lord Elgin entertains the most grateful sense of the courtesy and hospitality which he experienced during his visit to Boston, and that Her Majesty's Government also beg most cordially to thank the President of the United States, and the citizens of Boston, for this proof of their kindly feeling towards Her Majesty and the British nation.

I am, &c.,

PALMERSTON.

John F. Crampton, Esq., &c., &c., &c.

DEPARTMENT OF STATE,
WASHINGTON, NOVEMBER 26, 1851.

SIR:—I have the honor to acknowledge the receipt of your note of the 22d instant, accompanied by a copy of a despatch addressed to you by Her Majesty's principal Secretary of State for Foreign Affairs, directing you to express to the President of the United States, and the citizens of Boston, the cordial thanks of Her Majesty's Government for the reception given to the Earl of Elgin during the ceremonies which took place at Boston on the 17th, 18th, and 19th of September last, in celebration of the completion of a line of railroad connecting the Canadas with New England.

Your communication has been laid before the President, who has directed me to express, in reply, his gratification that Her Majesty's Government should have been favorably impressed with the reception given to Lord Elgin on the occasion referred to.

I avail myself of this opportunity, sir, to offer to you a renewed assurance of my very distinguished consideration.

DANIEL WEBSTER.

John F. Crampton, Esq., &c., &c., &c.

BOROUGH OF BOSTON, ENGLAND,

AND

CITY OF BOSTON, MASS.

The three letters, which follow, have been recently printed by order of the City Council, and although they have no reference to the celebration of September, they are inserted here, not only as historically interesting to the citizens of Boston, but as another "proof of the prevalence and extension of that good and friendly feeling between the people of the two countries," which it is so desirable to cultivate and confirm, and which, it is hoped and believed, if not one of the primary objects, will be one of the lasting results, of that celebration.

City Hall, Boston, Dec. 4, 1851.

Sir:—I transmit to the Common Council certain interesting seals and documents, which I received some time since from the Borough of Boston, in England, through the agency of John Louis Clarke, Esq., of this City. Mr. Clarke's letter, together with one from the Mayor of that Borough, which accompany this communication, will explain the circumstances which led to the transmission of these acceptable presents. The frame, in which the seals are encased, is stated to have been made out of one of the original timbers of the church in which John Cotton preached, for some years previous to his emigration to this country,—*the* Cotton, in honor of whom our City is supposed to have been named. Such a fact, in an antiquarian point of view, enhances the value of the gift.

I recommend that the seals be placed in some conspicuous position in the Council Chamber, and that the letters be printed and placed on file.

I have caused a suitable acknowledgment of the compliment, together with books and maps appertaining to our City and State, to be forwarded to the authorities of the Borough of Boston.*

Respectfully, &c.,

John P. Bigelow, Mayor.

To the Honorable

Francis Brinley,

President of the Common Council.

* Note, (*by the Mayor,*) *attached to the foregoing Message.*

Boston is a seaport, market town and borough of Lincolnshire, on the River Witham, ninety miles north of London. The name is an abridgement of "Botolph's Town." In 1630 there were probably about 600 families in the borough. In 1811 it had 1,837 houses and 8,113 inhabitants. In 1841 its population had increased to 34,680. Its principal object of curiosity is its famous church, (St. Botolph's,) the foundation of which was laid in 1309. The building, which is in the Gothic style of architecture, is considered the largest *parochial*

BOSTON, JUNE 2, 1851.

SIR:—You will receive, enclosed herewith, a copy of a letter, addressed to me by Meaburn Staniland, Esq., Mayor of Boston, Old England, dated January 13th, but only very recently received. The somewhat long interval, between its date and receipt, may be accounted for, by the fact that it accompanied the present, to which it refers.

In complying with the request of Mr. Staniland, it may not be out of place to offer a few words, explanatory of the circumstances, to which I am indebted for this pleasure. In the Spring of 1849, I went up to Boston from London, to gratify a curiosity, which had ever been strong, to see this old city, and compare it with its younger namesake on this side of the water. I had no letters of introduction, nor any other passport to such civilities as I received, and for which I have ever since been most grateful—than *my place of residence* and the object of my visit! Upon ascertaining these, Mr. Staniland at once extended the hand of friendship, offering me every possible facility to promote my wishes, and personally accompanying me to all places and objects of interest to a stranger there. He presented me to the Magistrates of the Court, over which he presides. When present he is addressed in Court, as "Your Worship." The insignia attached to the office of Mayor are two maces and an oar of silver gilt, which are borne before him by two Sergeants-at-Mace and the Marshal of the Admiralty.

I had the honor of meeting at the hospitable table of the Mayor, three Ex-Mayors of Boston and other gentlemen of the different professions, and it was peculiarly gratifying to a stranger, to hear so much interest expressed in relation to every thing connected with Boston, his home; and to realize that so much was known there of her benevolent Institutions; her Schools; the enterprising spirit of her citizens, in the construction of railroads, and in the building up of manufacturing establishments; her extensive and extending commerce; and her rapidly increasing numbers, wealth and importance. These matters were freely discussed, and let me add, all alluded to them with great satisfaction, and confessed their pride in her growing greatness, and the enviable reputation she was securing for her honored name.

The Mayor proposed as a sentiment—"The prosperity of Boston,

church in England,—its length being 245 feet in the clear, by 98 feet in width. The tower (of stone) is 300 feet high, and on its top is, or was, an octagon lantern, intended to serve as a guide to mariners entering the channels of the Deeps, (so called.) It is said that the light could be seen at a distance of 40 miles, by land or water. There was a legend among our Pilgrim Fathers, that the lamp ceased to burn, when Cotton left the place to become a shining light in the wilderness of New England. Cotton was vicar of this church 21 years. The immediate cause of his emigration was the issue of a warrant to bring him before the infamous "High Commission Court," to answer concerning his supposed heretical opinions. He concealed himself from the search, while his patron, the Earl of Dorset, interceded for him with the prelates. The intercession was ineffectual, and his Lordship wrote to Mr. Cotton, that, "if he had been guilty of drunkenness, uncleanness, or any such faults, he could have obtained his pardon; but as he was guilty of puritanism and non-conformity, the crime was unpardonable, and therefore he advised him to flee for his safety"; which he accordingly did.

New England:" expressing all kind wishes for her future greatness, &c.; and his sentiment and remarks were received with a warmth of feeling, which made me, for a time, forget that there were two Bostons.

I acknowledged the compliment, and my own gratitude as well, for such attentions as I had most unexpectedly received there; and I doubtless took no unauthorized liberty, in the assurance that such kind and friendly sentiments as had been expressed by all composing the dinner party, would be fully responded to by those not only, who held in keeping the honor and interests of the City of my residence, but also by the citizens generally.

At this dinner party, a suggestion was made in regard to the propriety of some little token from the Mother to the Daughter, to be placed in my charge for presentation, and it was arranged, before I left Boston, that the same should be sent forward to Liverpool to await my arrival there, on my return. At the time I sailed, however, it had not reached Liverpool, but the inscription on the frame is of that date.

It was a singular coincidence in the history of both cities, that an effort had been made, almost simultaneously, for a better supply of water for both, and at the time of my visit, the Mayor placed in my hands an Act of Parliament for, and other Documents relating to, the introduction of water into Boston, to be presented with the Seals. These Documents I have meantime kept, in the expectation that the token, alluded to, would in due time be forthcoming, and, as it has now been received, I avail myself of the earliest opportunity to present the same, with the Documents alluded to.

The Church, of which Mr. Staniland speaks, is without a rival, as a Parish Church, in England, and was erected about the middle of the fourteenth century, of the ornamental or middle Gothic style of architecture, having a tower three hundred feet in height. The Church has the grandeur and imposing effect, almost, of a cathedral.

Allow me to add, in conclusion, that, influenced by the peculiar and obvious delicacy of alluding to my personal experiences there, I should have remained silent, had I alone been interested, but, under the circumstances, in which this communication is written, I have thought it my duty to overrule any such scruples on my part, and to do justice to others, and to the interest and kind sentiments, which they so generally and generously expressed in behalf of Boston, the younger. And I have alluded to personal attentions there, as evincing an interest in a stranger—simply on account of his place of residence.

I am, Sir, very respectfully,

Your ob't serv't,

JOHN L. CLARKE.

Hon. John P. Bigelow, Mayor, &c. &c., Boston.

Boston, Jan. 13, 1851.

My Dear Sir :—You will, I dare say, have frequently thought I had quite forgotten my promise of sending you, for the Mayor of Boston, U. S., the impressions of our Corporate Seals. I had not, however, done so, but a variety of circumstances have delayed its fulfilment, which I now (though tardily) perform.

The Seals are in duplicate, one being the Corporate Seal, another the Admiralty Seal, (the Corporation, at one time, having had Admiralty jurisdiction along the Coast,) and the other is the Official Seal of the Mayor. All these Seals are of the period of Henry the 8th, when the Borough was incorporated.

I have had the Seals placed on parchment in an oak frame, to which, I am quite sure, considerable interest will attach from the circumstance of its having been made out of one of the original beams of our beautiful Church, under the roof of which, for several years, preached as Vicar that Cotton, in honor of whose character and exile your fair City received its name.

This small token of respect, from the Chief Magistrate of "Old" "Boston," for his official brother in "New" "Boston," though intrinsically valueless, will nevertheless, I am sure, awaken associations and feelings, which I trust, may ever prevail between our respective countrymen, and if, in the Council Chamber of the City of Boston, this little offering finds a place, it will be to me a source of great gratification.

Do me then the favor to present the same to your Mayor, with an assurance that should he ever come to the Old World and honor me with a visit, it will afford me the greatest pleasure to receive him. And believe me to be,

My dear Sir,
Yours faithfully,
M. Staniland.

John L. Clarke, Esq., Boston.

Note. Documents referred to in the correspondence.

An Act of Parliament for the Boston Water Works.
A Plan and Section of the Boston Water Works.
Engineer's Report on the Boston Water Works.
Directors' Report on the Boston Water Works.
Blank Certificates of Stock of the Boston Water Works.

CORRESPONDENCE RESPECTING THE JUBILEE.

The letters below are but a small portion of those received by the Committee of Invitation. These however have been selected as expressing the sentiments of distinguished official personages, both of our own country and the Canadas, in relation to the Railway Celebration.

[From the Hon. Daniel Webster, Secretary of State.]

BOSTON, SEPT. 9, 1851.

GENTLEMEN:—I acknowledge with all due respect the honor conferred on me, and communicated through you by the City Council of Boston, in inviting me to attend the proposed Railroad Jubilee on the 17th, 18th and 19th of this month.

I regard the occasion, Gentlemen, as one of high and peculiar interest, likely to be honored by the presence of many distinguished persons belonging to this and other States, and also to the adjacent British Provinces; and I assure you, Gentlemen, that it is with extreme regret that I feel obliged to say, that it is not in my power to accept the invitation of the City Government.

I am, Gentlemen, with sincere personal regard, your obedient servant,

DANIEL WEBSTER.

To Messrs. Francis Brinley, H. M. Holbrook, Ezra Lincoln, Albert T. Minot, N. A. Thompson, Henry J. Gardner, Otis Kimball, *Committee.*

[From the Governor of New York.]

ALBANY, SEPT. 8th, 1851.

GENTLEMEN:—I have had the honor to receive your letter, requesting me to unite with the Municipal Authorities of your City, in celebrating "the completion of the various lines of Railway which connect Canada and the Great West with the tide waters at Boston." I regret sincerely that my engagements are of such a nature as to preclude an acceptance of yoúr invitation. You must permit me, however, to congratulate you upon the success which has crowned your efforts, and to express my admiration of the wisdom and energy displayed by your citizens in the completion of a system of improvements, alike honorable to the fame of your city and conducive to its growth and prosperity.

We, the people of New York, claim to have some interest in the trade of the Great West, for which you are reaching. Yet we have desired to act the part of friendly and generous neighbors towards you. We have seen you invading our soil, filling our valleys, boring our mountains at some points, levelling them at others, and turning your steam engines loose upon us to run up and down, roaming at large throughout our borders. Indeed, it has long been evident that you intended to ride over us in your efforts to entice away our western brethren. But no voice of complaint or of resistance has been heard. We are a patient and accommodating people. Instead of employing our sovereignty to arrest your aggressions and repel your bold incursions, our Legislature has contributed largely to the success of your designs. I am somewhat curious to know at what point your next encroachments will begin. There are limits to human endurance, and I must warn you to pause and take breath before making fresh tracks upon our territory.

We have never desired to monopolize the Western trade. After yielding to you a share sufficient to satisfy any but an inordinate and grasping ambition, enough will remain for us. A fair survey of the vast and fertile region beyond the Lakes, and a just estimate of its resources, its rapid increase in population and production, and its wonderful progress in opening new communications, ought to extinguish all narrow, local jealousies among the States and cities of the seaboard. The exigencies of such a country demand a liberal and enlightened policy. Let us have ample room and free scope for all. A manly and generous competition is beneficial to every interest. The vast and swelling commerce of the Western Lakes will furnish full and profitable employment for all the artificial lines of communication that have been opened. We are willing you should share with us in advantages proceeding from a source so inexhaustible. In my contemplations of the subject, I always feel that New York can afford to be not only just but magnanimous.

With great respect,
Your obed't servant,

WASHINGTON HUNT.

Hon. John P. Bigelow, Francis Brinley, and others, *Committee.*

[From the Governor of Vermont.]

RUTLAND, SEPT. 15, 1851.

GENTLEMEN :—I have the honor to acknowledge the receipt of your invitation to attend, on the 17th inst., the commemorative festivities on the completion of the various lines of railway which connect Canada and the Great West with the tide-waters at Boston, and have to regret that my other duties forbid my acceding to your polite request.

Attached by the ties of birth to the State of Massachusetts, everything which promotes her prosperity has a deep hold upon my affections. Calling to mind that when, in early childhood, I removed from your vicinity, it required eight days to accomplish the journey which is now performed in a less number of hours, I here witness an eminent example and evidence of the industry, the perseverance, and the wealth of my native State, and of the city of Boston in particular. The benefit of this industry, enterprise, and wealth, is not confined to the city and State alone, but is equally shared by the community with whom she has any private, public, or commercial relations—among whom the State in which I reside participates largely and extensively.

With the most ardent aspirations that your prosperity may still be continued, and your enterprise be rewarded by still greater success, I have the honor to be,

Your obedient servant,

CH. K. WILLIAMS.

To the Mayor and Municipal Authorities of the City of Boston.

[From the Governor of Maine.]

HALLOWELL, ME., SEPT. 15, 1851.

GENTLEMEN:—Yours of the 3rd, extending to me an invitation to attend the railroad celebration, to be held at Boston on the 17th, reached here when I was absent for a fortnight.

I regret that an executive session, to be held at the time, will forbid my being present with you on that occasion.

Nothing could afford me greater pleasure than to join in the festivities which are to commemorate the glorious results of Boston enterprise and energy, and to mark an era in the progress of a sister Commonwealth to wealth and power.

I am, with high consideration,

Yours,

JOHN HUBBARD.

Messrs. John P. Bigelow, Mayor.

Francis Brinley, President of the Common Council.

Henry M. Holbrook, and others, of the Aldermen and Common Council, City of Boston.

[From the Governor of Connecticut.]

HARTFORD, CONN., SEPT. 16, 1851.

HON. J. P. BIGELOW, Mayor of Boston.

SIR:—I have had the honor to receive your invitation to the proposed Railway celebration, which is to take place in the City of Boston on the 17th inst. The occasion will be one of great interest to all concerned, and highly honorable to the citizens of Boston, whose enterprise has contributed so largely to produce the mighty results which it is proposed to commemorate in an appropriate manner.

I regret that it will not be in my power to participate with you in the festivities of the occasion; and more so from the fact that it will mark an important event, not only in the history of your city and State, but of New England also. Be pleased to accept, Sir, in behalf of the Municipal Authorities of Boston, my warmest acknowledgments for the honor of the invitation, and believe me to be, very respectfully,

Your obedient servant,

THOS. H. SEYMOUR.

[From Sir E. W. Head, Governor of New Brunswick.]

GOVERNMENT HOUSE,
FREDERICKTON, N. B., SEPT. 5, 1851.

His Excellency, Sir Edmund Head, desires to express to the municipal authorities of the city of Boston, his sense of the honor which they have done him by their invitation for the 17th inst.

Sir Edmund Head deeply regrets that urgent public business will prevent his acceptance of their invitation.

To Daniel N. Haskell, Esq., Secretary.

[From Hon. R. S. Baldwin, Senator in Congress, from Connecticut.]

NEW HAVEN, SEPT. 15, 1851.

GENTLEMEN:—I have the honor to acknowledge the reception of your obliging invitation, in behalf of the municipal authorities of the city of Boston, to be present at the proposed celebration of the completion of the various lines of railway which connect the Canadas and the Great West with the tide water at Boston, and the establishment of American lines of steamers between your city and Liverpool.

I regret exceedingly that my engagements are such as will not allow me to avail myself of your kindness, and that I am compelled to forego the gratification I should otherwise enjoy, of uniting in the festivities commemorative of the accomplishment of enterprises so interesting and important to your City and State, and which cannot fail to prove most auspicious in their influence on the common welfare and prosperity of the widely-extended regions they so advantageously connect.

I have the honor to be, gentlemen, with great respect, your obliged and obedient servant,

ROGER S. BALDWIN.

To Hon. John P. Bigelow, Mayor.

Francis Brinley, Esq., President of C. C., &c., Committee of the Municipal Authorities of the City of Boston.

[From Hon. C. Sawtelle, Rep. in Congress, from Maine.]

NORRIDGEWOCK, ME., SEPT. 11, 1851.

SIR:—I have the honor to acknowledge the receipt of your favor of 9th ult., inviting me, in behalf of the Municipal Authorities of the City of Boston, to attend the proposed celebration on Wednesday, the 17th inst., commemorative of the final completion of the great lines of Railroads, which connect the Canadas and the Great West with the tide water at Boston, and the establishment of American lines of steamers between that city and Liverpool.

I regret, extremely, that circumstances do not permit me to avail myself of the gratifying invitation to visit your city, and the obliging tender of hospitality that accompanied it.

The age in which we live is emphatically one of enterprise and progress; and he who does not rejoice in the consummation of these great works of improvement, is unworthy to enjoy the incalculable benefits resulting therefrom.

I am, Sir, with great respect,
Your obedient servant,
CULLEN SAWTELLE.

Hon. John P. Bigelow, Mayor of Boston.

[From the Hon. the Speaker of the Legislative Assembly, Canada.]

MONTREAL, SEPT. 10, 1851.

SIR:—It would have been a great pleasure for me to be able to partake in the proffered hospitalities of the City of Boston on the 17th instant, and following days. The fatigues of the late protracted session of our Legislature, and some unavoidable business consequent thereto, now put it out of my power to be present. In expressing to you my regret, and my high appreciation of the invitation with which I have been honored, I beg to subscribe myself, Sir,

With great respect,
Your obedient humble servant,
A. N. MORIN,

Daniel N. Haskell, Esq., Secretary, &c., &c.

[From the Hon. P. B. De Blaquiere, Member of the Legislative Council, and Chancellor of the University of Toronto.]

WOODLANDS, WOODSTOCK,
UPPER CANADA, AUG. 29, 1851.

SIR:—I beg to acknowledge the receipt of your letter, conveying an invitation from His Worship the Mayor, and citizens of Boston, to a dinner in celebration of the opening of a railway communication between that city and the British North American Provinces and Canada, and I deeply regret that bodily infirmity alone prevents my availing myself of the honor of being present, on an occasion so eminently gratifying to every one who desires the advancement of the great interests which are so well calculated to promote the prosperity of the United States and of Great Britain, in harmonious co-operation.

Be assured, Sir, that although I cannot in person attend, as I wish to do, there is not an individual amongst those who will enjoy this honor, more sincere in their expressions of cordial approbation of the auspicious event which has called forth the hospitable invitation of the Mayor and citizens of Boston.

I have the honor to be, Sir,
Your very obedient servant,
P. B. DE BLAQUIERE.

Daniel N. Haskell, Sec'y, &c.

[From the Hon. John Bazalgette, Lieut. Colonel and Administrator of the Government of Nova Scotia.]

GOVERNMENT HOUSE,
HALIFAX, N. S., SEPT. 9, 1851.

DEAR SIR:—I have the honor to acknowledge the receipt of your kind letter, conveying to me the invitation of the Municipal Authorities of Boston, to partake of the proposed commemorative festivities to take place in that city on Wednesday, the 17th instant, and have, in reply, to express my sincere and deep regret that circumstances imperatively prevent my availing myself of their kindness, and the participation in celebrating so important an undertaking.

I have the honor to be, Sir,
Your most obedient humble servant,
JOHN BAZALGETTE.

To Daniel N. Haskell, Esq.

[From the Hon. Wm. H. Draper, Judge of Court of Queen's Bench.]

TORONTO, UPPER CANADA, SEPT. 8, 1851.

SIR:—I am honored by your letter, received on Saturday last, inviting me to join in the proposed commemorative festivities in Boston, on Wednesday, the 17th of this month.

My judicial duties make my presence necessary at Goderich, on Lake Huron, on the 23rd of September, and render it therefore impossible for me to avail myself of your polite invitation. I must therefore content myself with this mode of expressing my sincere congratulations on the event which has called forth these festivities, and my very warm hopes that the fullest measure of success may follow the completion of so magnificent an undertaking as the connection of the tide water at Boston with the Canadas and the boundless West, by the means of railways now opened.

I have the honor to subscribe myself, Sir,
Your very obedient servant,
WM. H. DRAPER.

Daniel N. Haskell, Esq., &c., &c., &c.

[From the Hon. R. E. Burns, Judge of Court of Queen's Bench, C. W.]

TORONTO, SEPT. 9, 1851.

SIR:—I have duly received the kind invitation of the Municipal Authorities of the City of Boston, to be present at the festivities proposed to take place on the 17th inst., but owing to indispensable judicial duties, to be performed here on the same day, cannot avail myself of the honor intended.

I have taken a lively interest in the promotion of communication by railways, and am fully sensible of the great advantages which the completion of your roads, connecting our great waters with the seaboard, through your portion of this continent, will be, not only to you, but also to the Canadas.

My best wishes are, that the bright anticipations which your city holds out for the future trade, increasing through all this country, may be as truly realized, as I am sure your hospitalities will be, on the 17th inst.

With the greatest respect to the Mayor, and the other members of the Committee, I subscribe myself

Your obedient servant,

ROBERT E. BURNS.

D. N. Haskell, Esq., Secretary, &c., &c.

[From the Governor of the Hudson's Bay Company.]

Sir George Simpson presents his compliments to His Honor the Mayor and the Corporation of Boston, and regrets to state that severe indisposition in his family will prevent his having the honor of being present at the Railroad Festival, to be held in Boston on the 17th, 18th and 19th instant, agreeably to their kind invitation.

HUDSON BAY HOUSE,
LACHINE, CANADA EAST, SEPT. 15, 1851.

HALIFAX, N. S., SEPT. 13, 1851.

MY DEAR SIR:—I beg you will convey to His Honor the Mayor, and the City Authorities of Boston, my most grateful thanks for their polite invitation to the railroad celebration of the 17th inst., as well as the assurance of my deep regret that private arrangements will prevent my attendance on that occasion. Permit me also to add, that though unavoidably absent, my feelings and best wishes will be with you—for I fully anticipate that your celebration will be of a character corresponding to the high reputation so fairly earned by the public spirit and enterprise of the citizens of Boston.

As you will have many of my fellow-countrymen present with you on this occasion, I trust they will be so far animated and inspired by the noble example you have set before them, and the substantial proofs that will be exhibited of the universal benefit of such enterprises, as to decide them, on their return, to cast all doubts and hesitation to the winds, and apply their utmost energies towards the accomplishment of those magnificent projects which now occupy the public mind, both British and Colonial—having for their object the uniting of these Provinces by the same *iron band*, and elevating them to a higher position of national rank and influence.

I must visit Canada next month, and shall avail myself, in passing through Boston, of the pleasure of paying my personal respects both to yourself and His Honor the Mayor, with whom I have the pleasure of being acquainted.

I am, Sir, with much respect, yours very truly,

JOHN E. FAIRBANKS.

[From the Hon. P. B. de Boucherville, M. L. C.]

BOUCHERVILLE, L. C., AUG. 22, 1851.

SIR: I regret that old age and infirmities will prevent my having the honor to attend to the great commemorative festivities in Boston, on the 17th day of September next.

If the United States are yet susceptible of aggrandisement, Boston, as heretofore, will stand in the advance; and, I ask, who is the man, within the New England States, who will not be proud to be a Bostonian.

I hope that the great facility of communication between Canada and the United States, will forever cement that good understanding which should exist between neighbors, and prepare us, Canadians, for future events.

Wishing all sorts of prosperity to the Bostonians and their Municipal Authorities,

I have the honor to be, Sir,

Your very obedient servant,

PIERRE BOUCHER DE BOUCHERVILLE.

Daniel N. Haskell, Esq., Boston.

[From the Hon. Leslie Combs of Kentucky.]

ALBANY, N. Y., SEPT. 20, 1851.

MY DEAR SIR:—Hurried, as I was, from scene to scene of your magnificent *three days' festival*, I had no time to express my personal thanks to you for your kindness and attention, and therefore seize the opportunity afforded by this first resting place on my way home, to address you a note of grateful acknowledgment.

In your address to the guests assembled at the great feast yesterday afternoon, you *specially* greeted the residents upon the Ottawa, the Chaudiére and the St. John's—upon the Hudson, the Connecticut and the Potomac, as well as those hailing from the shores of the Great Lakes.

Had an occasion offered, an humble private citizen of the West—a *native son* of old Kentucky, would have told you, that the inhabitants of that mighty valley watered by the great Father of Rivers, whose hundred heads are in those same vast inland seas to which you so appropriately alluded—whose Briarean arms grasp the Alleghanies in the East, while they reach out to the far distant, cloud-capped Rocky Mountains in the West—whose rolling waters throw themselves across the continent into the Gulf of Mexico—rejoiced as heartily as did any persons present, in the enterprise, energy and success of the good city of Boston and the "Old Bay State," in commencing and completing their magnificent and costly system of Railroads.

He would, at the same time, in justice to KENTUCKY, have modestly suggested, that when, as well as he remembered, there was not a mile of Railroad on the continent of Europe, and but one great work of the kind in England, and one ill-constructed one, some four or five miles long, in all *New* England, that distant, young, interior State had chartered and commenced a Railroad from her agricultural centre to her capital, in the direction to her principal seaport; and that while Boston in Massachusetts and Montreal in Canada had become united by this magnificent mode of internal improvement, *Kentucky* and her sister States, West and South, were constructing a great trunk with many branches, to connect indissolubly the *Southern Atlantic* and *Gulf of Mexico* with the *Northern Lakes*, and at the same time were making others, hundreds of miles long, to unite the fertile, grain-growing and stock-raising States, as well as the "broad, untouched prairies and boundless forests," referred to so aptly by the eloquent Governor General of Canada, with the manufacturing and commercial States of the East; so that, hereafter, the iron bands of commerce and social intercourse might bind together more firmly those sections far distant from each other—heretofore only united by the chain of political sympathy.

These mighty works being finished, as well might we expect the solid foundations of the earth to be upturned, or its adamantine crust burst asunder, by the petty rumblings of Hecla or Vesuvius, *as that our glorious Union would be rent in twain by any sectional excitement.*

But, Sir, I pray you to pardon me for extending this note much more than I intended, and I will close it with the assurance that it will, at all times, give me great pleasure to reciprocate, in my poor way, the courtesies received at your hands.

Very truly, your most ob't serv't,
LESLIE COMBS.

To His Honor,
Mr. Bigelow, Mayor of Boston.

MEETING OF CANADIANS.

[REFERRED TO ON PAGE 192.]

At a meeting of the citizens of Canada, who have availed themselves of the invitation of the Civic Authorities of Boston to attend the Railroad Festival, which took place on the 17th, 18th, and 19th instant, held at the Revere House last evening, the Hon. Mr. Justice Aylwin was called to the chair, and John Rose, Esq., requested to act as Secretary.

It was then moved by the Hon. W. B. Robinson, M. P. P., of Toronto, and seconded by the Hon. John Molson, of Montreal, and resolved unanimously, that a Committee be named to draft an address expressive of our gratitude, and the high estimation entertained by this meeting, and the inhabitants of Canada, of the kind and generous hospitalities extended to them by the Municipal Authorities and citizens of Boston; and that the following gentlemen be named a Committee forthwith to prepare such address:—

The Hon. Mr. Justice Aylwin, the Hon. Mr. Justice Day, and the Hon. Mr. Justice Mondelet, of Montreal; Sir Allan N. McNab, M. P. P.; T. Kirkpatrick, Esq., of Kingston; the Hon. Samuel Crane, and A. Jones, Esq., of Prescott; Capt. Wainwright, of Carillon; John Rose, Esq., of Montreal; N. F. Belleau, Esq., of Quebec; P. Leclerc, Esq., of St. Hyacinthe; A Leframboise, Esq., of Hecaluly; Col. Gugy, M. P. P.; W. A. Chaffers, Esq., of St. Cesaire; N. Dumas, Esq., M. P. P., and Benj. Holmes, Esq., M. P. P., of Montreal; A. Merrick, Esq., of Merrickville; Jos. Aumond, Esq., of Bytown; John Bruneau, Esq., B. Brewster, Esq., and Harrison Stephens, Esq., of Montreal; Hon. J. Æ. Irving, of Toronto; James Coleman, Esq., of Dundas; George Rykert, Esq., and W. Merritt, Esq., of St. Catherine's; Captain C. Sweeney, of Montreal; James Little, Esq., of Caledonia; James Hodgert Guelph, Esq., and the Hon. P. H. Moore, of Stanstead; George Crawford, Esq., of Brockville; Mr. Sheriff Corbett, of Kingston; Mr. Sheriff Boston, of Montreal; Mr. Sheriff Smith, of Barrie; Mr. Sheriff Thomas, of Hamilton; J. B. Ewart, Esq., of Dundas; F. M. Hill, Esq., Mayor of Kingston; J. G. Bowes, Esq., Mayor of Toronto; F. R. Angers, Esq., of Quebec; James M. Ferris, Esq., of Montreal; the Hon. W. H. Boulton, M. P. P., of Toronto; Dunbar Ross, Esq., M. P. P., of Quebec; John Egan, Esq., M. P. P., of Aylmer; D. E. Boulton, Esq., of Cobourg; Judge Boswell, of Cobourg; Wm. Weller, Esq., Mayor of Cobourg; J. C. Morrison, Esq., M. P. P., of Toronto; James Shaw, Esq., of Smiths' Falls; Alexander McLean, Esq., M. P. P., of Cornwall; James Cotton, Esq., of Toronto; Henry Smith, Esq., M. P. P., of Kingston; Allan McLean, Esq., of Kingston; R. R. Strowbridge, Esq., of Brantford; Col. Horn, 20th Reg.; Capt. Radcliffe, do.; Capt. Marjory, 54th Reg.; Capt. Conner, 66th Reg.; C. S. Monck, Esq., of Montreal; Capt. the Hon H. F. Kean, Royal

Engineers; Capt. Newton, Royal Artillery; Dr. Maitland, Royal Canadian Rifles; Robert Spence, Esq., Warden of Wentworth and Halton; S. Morrill, Esq., Mayor of London, C. W.; F. C. Lemeux, Esq., M. P. P., Capt. Alleyn, R. N., H. J. Noad, Esq., and Thomas C. Lee, Esq., of Quebec; Duncan McFarland, Esq., M. P. P. for the County of Welland; Augustus Howard, Esq., of Montreal.

It was then moved by W. K. McCord, Esq., of Quebec, seconded by Captain Wainwright, of Carillon, that this meeting do adjourn, for the space of one hour, to enable the Committee to prepare the draft of an address, and again meet at the same place.

The meeting having re-assembled, the following address* was reported by the Hon. W. B. Robinson, on the part of the Committee; and, on motion of Joseph Alfred O. Turgeon, Esq., seconded by John Yule, Esq., of Chambly, was unanimously adopted.

It was then moved by Benjamin Holmes, Esq., M. P. P., seconded by William H. Boulton, Esq., M. P. P., that the address now adopted be signed by the Chairman and Secretary, on behalf of the meeting; and that the same be presented by Sir Allan McNab, the Hon. Mr. Justice Aylwin, B. Holmes, Esq., M. P. P., the Hon. W. B. Robinson, the Hon. Mr. Justice Day, Dunbar Ross, Esq., M. P. P., William H. Boulton, Esq., M. P. P., and such other inhabitants of Canada as may remain in this City,—and that public notice of the same be given.

It was then moved by the Hon. W. B. Robinson, and seconded by George Crawford, Esq., of Brockville, that the Chairman do leave the Chair, and that W. H. Boulton, Esq. be called thereto: which being carried, it was moved by Benj. Brewster, Esq., and seconded by W. B. Robinson, Esq., that the thanks of the meeting are due to the Hon. Mr. Justice Aylwin, as Chairman, and to John Rose, Esq., as Secretary, for their able and efficient conduct.

* For the address, see page 192.

PROCEEDINGS OF THE CITY OF MONTREAL.

The following are extracts from an address of the Corporation of Montreal, delivered in that city to the Governor General, Sept. 22, 1851, and from his answer, referred to at page 191.

From the address:—"We witnessed with feelings of proud and grateful satisfaction, the dignified and able bearing of your Excellency at the late immense assemblage in Boston of the most distinguished statesmen of the American Union and adjoining Provinces. And we beg to offer to your Excellency our acknowledgments and thanks for your effective and eloquent representation of our country on that interesting occasion. We beg leave, also, to express our sense of the deep obligations we owe to the authorities and citizens of Boston for their cordial reception and most hospitable entertainment of your Excellency, and the citizens of Canada, and the gratification afforded us by their enthusiastic manifestations of respect for your Excellency, as Governor General of British North America."

From Lord Elgin's answer:—"It has greatly enhanced the pleasure which I have derived from my visit to our hospitable neighbors, that I should have been able, on my return, in compliance with your invitation, to accompany you to this place. I think, indeed, that we should be justly chargeable with ingratitude, if we were not prepared to acknowledge, most warmly, our sense of the kindness which we experienced while in Boston. In parting from the Mayor of that city on Saturday morning, in the railway cars, to which he had obligingly conducted me, I made an observation to him which I fear he hardly caught, and which I am glad to have an opportunity of repeating now, as I am confident it will meet your approval. I begged him to remember for himself, and to remind his fellow-citizens, that the admirable railways which had brought Canada so near to Boston, and rendered it so easy for Canadians to go thither, had had a like effect in bringing Boston near to Canada, and making it easy for Bostonians to come to us; and I ventured to express the hope, that if he and his friends made the trial, they would find the excellent virtue of hospitality included among the many virtues, practised by the citizens of Boston, which we are glad to imitate."

THE GOLDEN RING.

In the Boston Daily Advertiser of November 29, 1851, appeared under the above head, an interesting communication, from which the following passages are extracted:—

The historical allusion to the espousal of Venice to the sea, introduced by His Honor, the Mayor, in his speech at the reception of Lord Elgin, seems not to be generally understood. An intelligent old gentleman, formerly one of the City Fathers, but now living in the quiet retirement of the country, writes thus to a friend now residing in the City. "I have read with great interest the minute descriptions, given in the newspapers of your Railroad Celebration. It was, indeed, a proud display for old Boston, and will be handed down to posterity, side by side, with the Boston Tea Party.

* * * * * * *

I have been much puzzled to find out what he [the Mayor] meant by his allusion to 'the Golden Ring.' Will you be so kind as to favor me with some explanation of this at your earliest leisure?"

It is presumed that the old gentleman, who wrote this letter, is not the only one, who has been somewhat "puzzled" to understand fully the allusion to a festival, whose origin belongs rather to the romance, than to the realities of history.

The story is thus told, with various embellishments, by the historians of the twelfth century.

In 1159, Alexander III., was called to the papal chair. He reigned till 1181, struggling with various fortune and undaunted courage against the antipopes, Victor III., Paschal III., and Calixtus III., who were contending for the pontifical throne, and against his more formidable enemy, the powerful Frederic I., Emperor of Germany.

About 1177, when the anathemas of Frederic were law throughout all Italy, as well as Germany, the persecuted Pope, "interdicted from fire and water," was obliged to flee from the continent. To Venice alone could he look for a refuge; and thither he secretly turned his steps. Ziani was then Doge, the chief officer of Venice. He received the exiled Pope with the profoundest respect and tenderest sympathy, and immediately demanded of Frederic an acknowledgment of his claims to the papal throne. Frederic hurried the Venetian messenger home with the haughty reply, "Tell your master to deliver to me the miserable Alexander, in chains, or I will plant my eagles on the gates of St. Marks, and leave but a pile of ruins, where now stands the proud city of the presumptuous Ziani!" The trump of war was sounded at once. Although the Venetian fleet numbered only half as many vessels as that of Frederic, Ziani boldly set sail, trusting in the virtue of the pontifical blessing, and not less, perhaps, in the good sword, with which the vicegerent of God condescended to gird him.

Heaven seemed propitious to the cause of the holy father, for it sent favoring winds to Ziani. Nerved by the consciousness that not only the fate of the venerated Pope, but also that of their wives and children, their homes, their beloved city was at stake, the Venetians impatiently awaited the signal for attack. It was given. Speeding along on the wings of the wind they rushed upon their astounded foes with resistless power, and, after a short but desperate conflict, the commander, Frederic's son Otho, was glad to sue for peace by the surrender of himself, his men, and the remnants of his shattered fleet. Ziani turned towards home with his prisoners. As he proudly swept up the Adriatic, the captive fleet following sadly in his train, the strains of triumphal music, and the prolonged and hearty shouts of his victorious sailors, rising over the waters, the whole city, old and young with throbbing hearts, crowded through the gates to the shore at Lido, to welcome home with tears of joy and heartfelt thanksgivings the noble defenders of Venice. Alexander, too, hastened to acknowledge his obligations to Ziani, and to render the grateful homage of an overflowing heart to Him, whose blessing he had invoked in the enterprise. As Ziani stepped from his boat, the Pope presented him with a golden ring, saying, "Take this ring, and with it take, on my authority, the sea as your subject. Every year, on the return of this happy day, you and your successors shall make known to all posterity, that the right of conquest has subjugated the Adriatic to Venice, as a spouse to her husband!"

The defeated and mortified Frederic was glad to accede to any terms, which the Pope and Ziani might be pleased to dictate. He was summoned before the man, the soles of whose weary feet he had suffered to find no resting place for many a sorrowful year in all the length and breadth of Italy. The hour of revenge had come. Arrayed in his pontifical robes, Alexander sat on his lofty throne. All the bitter recollections of the years, that were past, were rankling in his breast. Sternly he gazed on his conquered foe for a moment; and then, with a contemptuous air, pointed to his footstool. There was no alternative. The proud emperor bowed himself down; and, placing his neck beneath the foot of his hated conqueror, swore allegiance to Alexander III., as the rightful possessor of the triple crown.

For the long course of more than six hundred years, every fresh return of the Feast of Ascension witnessed the renewal of the joyous nuptials. This was the great gala-day of Venice. The man forgot his toil, the woman her household, the child his sports, and all, with one accord, joined in celebrating the marriage of the city to the peerless bride. Mass having been solemnized in the old church of San Nicolo, the Doge and his nobles, arrayed in their gorgeous robes of state, embarked in the Bucentaur, the splendid state galley, resplendent with ornaments of gold, and decked with the richest paintings, commemorative of the triumph of Ziani, and the first nuptial ceremony. As they glided along the spacious canal, they were everywhere greeted with waving of banners, strains of music, and deafening shouts from the crowded windows and piazzas and roofs, and from the thousands of richly decorated gondolas, that emulated the splendor of the Bucentaur itself. Amidst these universal demonstrations of rejoicing, they proceeded to Lido, to meet the waiting bride. The thousands of voices were hushed. The noble bridegroom arose, and dropping a golden ring into the waters, wedded the sea with this beautiful greeting, "We wed thee with this ring, in token of our true and perpetual sovereignty!"

Such was the pageant, and such its origin. It was well for the people of Venice on every returning year with festivities and rejoicing to celebrate and renew the union of the city to the munificent Bride, who had won for it its richest treasures and its highest glory—had poured into its lap the choicest luxuries of Oriental wealth, and the countless hoards of "barbaric pearl and gold," and encircled its brow with the proud diadem of "Queen of the Seas."

It was well, too, for us and our welcome guests to assemble together to celebrate the completion of those bonds, which, though of iron, shall join us in the indissoluble union of friendship and love—a union more auspicious of glorious results than that of Venice and her cherished Sea,—a union, which shall not only advance the highest commercial interests of the parties, but which shall heal the bleeding wounds so long kept open by narrow distrust and sectional jealousies, those fruits of mutual misapprehension, and shall make the two peoples, who are kindred in race and in feeling, forsake and forget the animosities of the past, and cleave to each other forever. The significance of the allusion is apparent.

* * * * * * *

OCEAN STEAM SHIP COMPANY OF NEW ENGLAND.

The following interesting article was prepared for the Boston Courier by a gentleman who has had occasion, from time to time, for several years, to devote no inconsiderable attention to the rise, progress and effects of railways, and of steam navigation in various portions of the country, where either or both of these great modes of conveyance and transportation, have been established.

THE FIRST AMERICAN LINES OF STEAMERS FROM BOSTON TO THE OLD WORLD. Five and twenty years have elapsed since that eminent merchant, the Hon. THOMAS H. PERKINS, founded in New England, the first railroad ever built in the United States. During that term of time, our capitalists, enterprising and leading men, have devoted large portions of their attention and means to the construction of railways, and the completion of the railway system among us; their expenditures upon and in connection with these public works, amounting within Massachusetts alone, to millions of dollars per annum. Indeed, so deeply and constantly have not only the principal parties, but the community at large, been absorbed in promoting the extension and success of this great and growing, though comparatively new mode for the transportation of passengers and merchandise, that they appear almost to have forgotten another means of transit and conveyance of the very first magnitude, and without the promotion and advancement of which, it can hardly be possible ultimately to maintain *in full action and prosperity* the railroads themselves or their dependencies. We refer especially to the establishment of lines of American Steamers between Boston and foreign nations. The steamship, as we all know, is five and twenty years older than the railway. For half a century or more, it has been undergoing a series of trials and progressive improvements, until human ingenuity has rendered it so extraordinary in size, proportions, accommodations, power and speed, that it no longer looks upon the common sailing ship as its competitor; and, although old-fashioned vessels will probably always be used more or less in certain voyages and in certain places; yet "for despatch and quick returns"—for all great commercial purposes and public enterprises over the sea, the time is at hand when these old-fashioned vessels must inevitably yield to the steamship the mastery of the ocean.

These "writings upon the wall" have not escaped the observation of men of intelligence and forecast; yet with these things staring in their faces, and pressing every day more and more closely upon them, what has been done in Boston or all Massachusetts for steam navigation? We have built railways, vast in extent, cost and number. We have sent forth trunks and branches in all directions. We have penetrated the interior with them—far off, and on every side:—piercing even the wilds of the wilderness with the scream of the locomotive. We have connected and bound them together, and concentrated all the principal lines within our own metropolis, and made the city of Boston the focus, the grand centre of all the principal radii of these immense net-works of iron. But what has been done to transport over the Atlantic, the merchandise and people which these roads are pouring in upon us, or are about to bring into this city from the towns on their borders from distant places, from the Canadas and the far West? what to convey to these our great depots, trunks and branches, thence to be disseminated inland, the goods and passengers, waiting and urgent to be brought from foreign climes? We have done nothing. We have attempted nothing. We have been depending upon common sailing vessels to perform the whole work of the water-carrying-trade and business; to bear hither and thither, on the main, if not coastwise, the entire mass of our freights—all our interchangeable commodities—imports and exports, grown and manufactured—of every size, quality, price and description. We are relying upon the very same vessels now; although we are well aware that they are but the *mere stage coaches of the ocean*—bearing no more relation to that magnificent mechanism, which Fulton created to be *a thing of life* upon the waves, than the most ordinary one-horse-vehicle does to the swift and powerful locomotive which Evans invented for the land.

We have not constructed within our own borders even a single sea going steamer. True, our English friends have boldly come forward, established, and maintained, a noble line of steamers between Liverpool and Boston. But this has not been followed up by lines on the part of our own citizens; and all the merchants in the capital of New England have not, up to this hour, even a solitary sea-going steamer of their own *on the route* between the new world and the old. Not one! And how is it, that among the people of Massachusetts, so renowned for their enterprise, industry, and ingenuity, perseverance, activity, adventurousness and thrift,—how is it, that in Boston, where there are so much wealth and energy, skill and traffic, so many rich-growing traders, manufacturers and mechanics; where the leading bankers, capitalists, real-estate owners, railway proprietors, ship-builders, and others, are so numerous and prosperous; having their substantial, elegant, and costly residences in the city, and their extensive, and not less costly and beautiful villas, cottages, summer-houses, and gardens, planted in every watering-place, and dotting all the country around; where there are to be found the owners of some of the finest farms and other landed estates, factories and other works, and some of the best dividend-paying railroad and other stocks, in *almost every State* of the Union; where the inhabitants possess so many, and such commodious piers, wharves, shipyards, and warehouses, and one of the broadest and most secure harbors in North America;—how is it, that among such a money-seeking and money-making race, holding commercial intercourse, year in and year out, with nearly every nation under the sun, and ever on the alert for new things, new undertakings and expenditures, as well as new gains and acquisitions—none are to be found engaged in steam navigation upon the high seas,—that Bostonians have not, to this day, one line of steamers, of their own, from their own port to any other beyond the ocean? Is it because they are ignorant of the potency of steam? of the superior capacity or powers of the steamboat? or of the progress, the beneficial effects of steamboat building, or steam navigation, in a hundred different ways, in every place where either is carried on? Are they unapprised of the fact, that in these stirring times of competition all along the coast, as well as inland, no merchant can, in the *long run*, prosecute his business to a great extent, *with the utmost facility and success*, without pressing into his service the swiftest means of conveyance and intercommunication known to man—upon the water and the land, by railway, telegraph, and steamer? Is it because they must consume half their lives in thinking and talking, debating, considering, and reconsidering, before they can make up their minds how and when to *act?* No! It is because they have been brought up to do *one* thing at a time. It is because of their determination all along—their predetermination to finish the railways in the first place; to apply all their ability and energies to the completion of the railway system; well knowing from the outset, that this done, they could, with their superabundant resources, summon at any moment the steamboat to their aid, and all other essential helps and appliances of the kind. And this object they have at length accomplished. All their main railroads are now completed, and each one is in full and successful operation.

This broad and permanent railway basis, so indispensable to our people for new and momentous operations and adventures, being thus erected, now it is that they are about to commence steam navigation. This great and wonderful race over the seas, they will now and henceforth enter upon, and they will triumph in it as certainly and signally as they have in clipper ships and internal improvements. Nor could they begin more opportunely, or under circumstances more auspicious —never, perhaps, at a better time. For they have no long and tedious trials to encounter, no doubtful or expensive experiments to go through with, in order to invent, improve, or render more perfect, the machinery, form, or structure of the steamship. All these things have been done in other parts of the country, and by other persons, who have been incessantly engaged upon "engine boilers and hull, paddles, screw-wheels, furnaces and propellers," for the last fifty years, at their *own* risk, and with their *own* money. The results of the experience and ingenuity of this half century have now become not only manifest, but public property; and Bostonians have nothing to do but avail themselves of, and, in common with others, convert the whole to their own use and benefit, at the most gainful rates, with the least procrastination, and in the best possible way. The finest steam marine models in existence are ready made to their hands, and the most accomplished naval constructors and practical and scientific engineers and naval commanders are as ready to enter into their service. They have already secured all that is necessary to make a suitable, if not an imposing beginning, and as soon as they get fairly under way, will employ, one after another, just as many ocean steam lines as the mercantile marine shall require to make their depots in Boston harbor.

The first line of these new steam packets will, we understand, consist of four vessels, and occupy the route between Boston and Liverpool. The first one will take her departure about the first of August ensuing. She is named the "S. S. Lewis," and is one of the most splendid vessels of her class ever seen. She is of not less than 1800 tons burthen, and altogether the most costly ship ever owned in Boston. She belongs to "the Ocean Steamship Company of New England," incorporated by the State of Massachusetts, with an authorized capital to an immense amount—larger, it is believed, than that of any other similar incorporated company in the United States. In a few days, then, the "S. S. Lewis" will come from the hands of the constructors, and take her berth at the wharves of the Grand Junction Railroad and Depot Company, and thence leave on her first voyage over the Atlantic. The day of her departure will be the dawn of a new era in this section of the country; for she will be the American file-leader of a new means of transportation and transit between New England and the Old World; the Yankee pioneer of a change in our commercial intercourse and relations both at home and abroad—a change, destined to be as impulsive, eventful and lasting; as marked and beneficial in its results,—so far as the traffic of our citizens with foreign climes is concerned,—as has been effected among us, in the way of internal improvements, intercommunication and internal trade by the iron horse upon the land; a change, it may be added, which as it goes on from year to year, involving, as sooner or later it must, steamboat building among us, and all matters connected with it, will create more and more activity in every branch of business among the people, to an extent, indeed, that it were vain to expect to see realized in any other way.

This new and superior line of steamers has been founded by Messrs. HARNDEN & COMPANY, of this city, in conjunction with a number of wealthy and powerful parties—not less eminent for their foresight and energy in commercial matters, than for their resources and influence in the community. The originator of this House, it will be recollected, was the person who established or led to the establishment of all the expresses upon the railroads in the United States. Leaving some time ago this particular branch of business to their successors in it, they have since been engaged as merchants and bankers, and now the public are again indebted to them for being among the first to lead in the establishment of American steamships from Boston to the ports of other nations; an undertaking, by far the most important for New England, that has been projected since the introduction of railways and locomotives among us—the most momentous and promising, in fact, that now remains to be carried on in this quarter of the country.

In this connection the following paragraphs, extracted from the Boston Journal of a late date, are not without interest.

Time was when the capacity of Boston to sustain *one* single ship in the London or Liverpool regular trade, was questioned, and many of our merchants remember with what doubtful shakes of the head the report that Messrs. Train & Co. were about to establish a line of packets, was greeted. In this connection our readers will probably be as much interested as we have been by a perusal of the following letter, which was found among the papers of an eminent merchant, recently deceased, and which forcibly illustrates, by comparison with the merchant service of the present time, the growth of the commerce of Boston:

LONDON, MARCH 1, 1804.

DEAR H.: Mrs. L. will most likely inform you of a conversation between us respecting a vessel for the Boston trade. I have thought much on the subject, and consulted with the most respectable shippers, the result of which is, a full conviction that there never was a better opening. You may rely on it that a good vessel of from 220 to 250 tons, fixed as a *regular trader* between us and Boston, would pay the owner handsomely. Now should you feel inclined to avail yourself of this opportunity, it may be the means of fixing D. in a respectable employ, and at the same time serve your interest. There are various articles, which, if attended to, will always pay a handsome freight from America. Of these I can keep you regularly informed, and I presume there are likewise articles from hence, which will, if necessary to purchase, then produce at least a freight in Boston. All kinds of Lumber have for some time past brought a handsome price, and you will observe, by the enclosed price current, that West India Produce is very high, and as the Spring trade opens on the continent, it may be expected to advance. Think of this as early as possible, and on all occasions command me when I can render you any services.

Yours sincerely.

THE STEAMER S. S. LEWIS.

This fine ocean steamer arrived at Boston, at 10 o'clock, Wednesday evening, Sept. 17th, with a large party of gentlemen from New York, Philadelphia, and Boston, on board, by invitation of Messrs. Harnden & Co., and Capt. Loper. She left Philadelphia on Saturday, the 13th, about 10 o'clock, and with colors flying, guns firing, and amid the cheers of the people, steamed it down the river in fine style. The day was beautiful, the weather warm and calm, and everything betokened a speedy and right pleasant trip to Boston; but after making about 75 miles east from Cape Henlopen, at a quarter before 3 o'clock, A. M., she was put back on account of a severe gale which she encountered, and which was so threatening in its appearance as to make such a course advisable, although a great disappointment to all on board. She reached the Delaware Breakwater at 9 o'clock, Sunday morning, and lay at anchor there till 10 o'clock, Monday night, the wind all the while blowing very hard, when she weighed anchor and stood out to sea on her course for Boston. Her behavior during the passage—standing up gallantly to the work right in the teeth of a strong head wind and in a rough sea—thoroughly tested her capabilities, and proved her to be a first rate sea boat. The passengers expressed themselves highly pleased with the performance of the ship, and with the attentions which they received on board, as will be seen by the following resolutions, passed by the passengers, just before their arrival here.

Resolved, That the manner in which the steamer S. S. Lewis performed during the gale of the 13th inst., making seven and a half knots per hour, in the very teeth of a heavy northeaster, under circumstances calculated to test severely the sea-going qualities of any vessel, have given her a title to rank in the first class of ocean steamers.

Resolved, That the arrangements of the S. S. Lewis for the accommodation of passengers, are elegant and tasteful, and as well calculated to ensure the comfort and convenience of passengers, as those of any other steamer afloat.

Resolved, That in her late passage the ship S. S. Lewis has evinced a capacity for speed which proves satisfactorily the superiority of her machinery over that of any Propeller yet constructed, the distance accomplished being 487 miles in the short space of 47 hours, against a strong north-east wind. She has also proved herself an easy sea boat, her motion being almost imperceptible to the passengers, although the voyage was made under such adverse circumstances.

Resolved, That our thanks are specially due to Capt. Cole, and the officers of the ship generally, for the kindness and courtesy they have manifested on the passage. From our knowledge of the gentlemen on this and other occasions, we have entire confidence in their capacity to fulfil the duties of their respective stations, and heartily recommend them to the travelling public.

Resolved, That the above resolutions be signed by the passengers, and published in the newspapers of Boston, New York and Philadelphia.

These resolutions were signed by the following passengers:

J. H. Vanderbilt, Charles L. Dimon, F. L. Andrews, Henry G. Clark, Samuel Hall, James Spencer, Michael V. Baker, J. W. Mc Lean, Lovell Purdy, W. J. Graham, H. D. Huston, Chas. M Simonson, C. Vanderbilt, Jr., William Flowers, Walter M. Stewart, William Gulager, J. DeForest, William H. Vanderbilt, Frank Munroe, E. H. Cob, William E. Sibell, William Guier, Samuel R. Glen, H. R. Tracy, R. B. Fitts, C. O. Rogers, William R. Pidgear, John W. Mills, Geo. W. Wheeler, Stephen M. Mitchell, David Barnet, Lewis S. Corvell, William T. Mackrell, William C. Tripler, James H. Lander, Richard Haiger, J. W. Frye, Thomas Tileston, Jr.

The meeting was then dissolved.

J. H. VANDERBILT, President.

F. L. ANDREWS,
CHAS. L. DIMON, } Secretaries.

The S. S. Lewis is a noble looking ship. Her length on deck is 225 feet, her breadth 32 feet, and her depth 26 feet. She registers 1103 tons, but measures 1850 tons, cubic capacity. Her frame is white oak, trussed together with diagonal iron bands, and most of her planking and ceiling is of the same material. She will be coppered up 18 feet forward, and 19 aft, and is painted black. She has a carved and gilded billet head, and gilded carved work along her trail boards and around her hawse-holes. The ends of her cat-heads are also ornamented, and her name is engraved in gilded letters on her head boards. Her stern is square, and is ornamented with a gilded spread-eagle and other devices handsomely arranged.

On deck she has a house 180 feet in length, 15 feet wide, and 6 1-2 feet high. The top of this house is railed in with brass, and forms an excellent promenade for her cabin passengers. The after division of this house extends across the deck, and is raised into a wheel-house. Next to the wheel-house are three water closets, before these a smoking room and a passage way, in the centre of which is a beautiful capstan, brass mounted and made of mahogany and locust. Next, forward, are five lengths of state-rooms, then the captain's cabin, before that a saloon twenty feet long, and next the staircase which leads to the cabin below. Farther forward is the hatchway which leads to the engine-room, next the galleys—then the officers' mess-room, on the starboard side, and a skylight in the middle, and a pastry room on the opposite side; next an ice house, and forward of all a tier of state-rooms, Most of these rooms are designed for the ship's officers, such as mates, engineers, surgeon, &c. The accommodations for her crew are below on the main deck forward. The house is panelled, has a projecting roof or top, and is grained in imitation of polished oak, and her bulwarks are painted fawn color. She has a spacious forecastle abaft the windlass, and a small topgallant forecastle before it.

Her main cabin is aft on the main deck, and contains 30 state-rooms with two berths in each. It is finished in a neat but not gaudy manner, with panel work, set off with pilasters and cornices, all of which are edged with tasteful carving, fringed with gold and silver. The cabin is lighted by four stern lights and a skylight. The state rooms are spacious, and well lighted and ventilated.

The space before the cabin is designed for second class passengers, and is lighted in the same way as the deck abaft. The forward and after parts of the lower deck, clear of the engine room, can be rendered available for steerage passengers or the stowage of cargo.

The motive power of the S. S. Lewis consists of two engines, with 60 inch cylinders, and 40 inches stroke, applied to one of Loper's propellers, which is of iron 14 feet in diameter, with 4 fans, formed at angles of 50 degrees, and their greatest width or face is 3 feet 6 inches. The engines were made by James T. Sutton & Co., of Philadelphia, and are compact, massive and powerful. They are capable of working 1180 horse power, but in the trip from the Breakwater to Boston, they were only worked up to 600 horse power. She is rigged similar to the Cunard steamers, and her rigging is of the best Russia hemp. Her sails are also of Russia canvas.

It is estimated that the S. S. Lewis will make seven voyages a year between this and Liverpool, will carry 300 tons of dead weight, 1000 tons of measurement goods, and accommodate 100 cabin passengers—and all this exclusive of fuel and stores. With only her lower holds full of cargo, it is estimated that she can accommodate nearly 900 passengers, including those in the steerage.

The S. S. Lewis is owned by the Ocean Steamship Company of New England. Her commander, Capt. Cole, formerly of the ship Orpheus, and late of the Steamship Tennessee, is well known as an accomplished gentleman and a thorough sailor. Messrs. Harnden & Co. are the agents, both at this port and at Liverpool for the company, and under their management its affairs will be conducted in a wise and judicious manner.

THE MASSACHUSETTS RAILROAD SYSTEM.

The following article, copied from the editorial columns of the Boston Daily Advertiser of 17th, 18th and 19th of September, last, though short, is an extremely comprehensive and interesting history of the Railroad System of Massachusetts. It is presumed to be from the pen of the editor of that Journal, the Hon. Nathan Hale, long distinguished as one of the earliest, most persevering, and enlightened advocates of the introduction of that system into our State, and to whose efforts for its establishment and extension, are due, as much perhaps as to those of any one person, its ultimate development and success:—

The city government having appointed the three ensuing days, to be observed as an occasion of public jubilee, in commemoration of the success of the works of internal improvement which have laid open to our metropolis channels of easy intercourse with distant parts of the country, in all directions, it may be incumbent on the public press to present a brief synopsis of the nature and extent of these improvements. A short description of the works which constitute the various routes of communication, imperfect as it must be, to be embraced within the compass of two or three columns of a newspaper, may serve to give some idea of their extent and varied ramifications. Such a synopsis may be even more acceptable to the strangers who have visited us on the invitation of our municipal authorities, for the purpose of participating in the jubilee, than a more detailed description.

To enable the reader to form any just idea of the importance of this system of improvements to our city and State (if system it may be called, which consists of an aggregate of independent works, constructed by private enterprise, by a great number of independent associations, and with very little formal concert with one another) it will be necessary to advert to the means of communication which existed in the Commonwealth twenty years ago, when the first shovel-full of earth had not been moved on either of the public railroads now in existence. Although seated upon the sea, and furnished with a great number of excellent harbors, which laid the State open to a ready intercourse with foreign countries, and with distant parts of our own country, Massachusetts was almost destitute of the facilities of internal navigation. Large sums of money had indeed been expended in the construction of the Middlesex Canal, leading from Boston harbor in a northerly direction, nearly to the border of the State of New Hampshire; and in the construction of locks for fostering a very limited traffic by flat boats, on the Connecticut and Merrimack rivers. The lines of boat navigation thus established extended some distance into New Hampshire. But these modest improvements disappointed public expectation, in the moderate degree of accommodation which they afforded, as well as the public spirited proprietors, in the hope of an income on their investments in them.

In the meantime improvements of another character, adverse to the commercial interests of Massachusetts, were curtailing her internal trade, and as a necessary consequence, depriving her of the means of sustaining advantageously her extensive foreign commerce. The ports of Massachusetts are situated upon bays so deeply indented along the coast, that steam navigation could be used to little advantage, as a means of intercourse between one port and another, or with the ports of distant States. At the same time the steamers of New York, by their daily and regular voyages to Providence,—to the Connecticut river,—to New Haven—and to those ports of the Hudson river which lie near the Western border of the State, united half the State at least, more intimately with that city, through her greater facilities of commercial intercourse, than with Boston. This intercourse with the great commercial emporium of the country, at the expense of our own metropolis, was further aided by the construction of the Blackstone canal, leading from Worcester to Providence, by which a water communication was opened between New York and the heart of the Commonwealth, while between Worcester and Boston, no such communication existed. A similar diversion of the trade of the Connecticut river valley was effected, by the opening of a Canal from Northampton to New Haven, and by improvements in the navigation of that river. The Western part of the State had become so estranged from Eastern Massachusetts, for all commercial objects, that no trader from Berkshire county had visited Boston for many years. The same causes were every year extending the commercial relations of New York with Vermont and New Hampshire, and consequently contracting those which had long subsisted between those states and Boston.

Under these circumstances, some of our citizens saw the necessity of effective efforts to arrest, if possible, the destiny which plainly awaited the city of Boston, if left to the undisturbed operation of these causes, upon her commercial position. Fortunately, while a portion of the ardent friends of internal improvement were endeavoring to excite the public, to the Herculean effort of establishing a canal from Boston to Worcester, for the purpose of counteracting the effects of the Blackstone, already leading to Providence, and to the still more difficult task of opening a line of navigation, by way of Millar's river to the Connecticut, and thence, by tunnelling the Hoosac mountain to the Hudson, a new light broke upon those whose eyes were open to behold it, in the discovery which was at that time made in England, of the adaptation of the *railroad*, to the purposes of public travel, and to the transportation of merchandise on public routes, as entitled to take precedence of canal transportation, which had been carried to a great extent in fostering trade and facilitating intercourse in that country.

The first clear comprehension, of the nature of this great improvement, afforded full conviction of its exact adaptation to the wants of Massachusetts. Destitute of the advantages of internal navigation—

imminently exposed to the loss of her existing trade, from the competition of the City of New York, which by the advantages of her position, with the addition of her canals, and steam navigation, was unrivalled in the facilities of water communication—without any large staples of trade, which could give effective occupation to canals, had there been far less obstacles than actually existed, to their construction—and needing not so much the means of transport for large masses of produce and merchandize, as for the speedy conveyance of comparatively light and miscellaneous articles, and for persons—the City of Boston required precisely the facilities which the railroad was capable of affording. Her chief system of internal communication then consisted of numerous lines of stage coaches, and baggage wagons, employing some thousands of fine horses. The former were capable of performing a journey of one hundred miles per day, by the fatigue of eighteen hours' travel, and the latter of performing the round trip of a hundred miles and back, with four or five tons of merchandise, once in a fortnight. These were the *rapid* modes of travel and transportation. All other modes were less efficient, and more dilatory, and for either of these a canal, if practicable, would have been an ineffective substitute.

But the railroad, imperfect as the conception of it then was, (and as it was in fact some years later even in England, compared with its present efficiency,) promised to be a substitute for all these methods of transportation, far superior to any other then known. This conviction, founded on the progress which had already been made in this improvement in England, and a faith in its further advancement, was confirmed by the successful experiment of the Quincy Railroad—a private work—three miles in length, established in 1836 for the transport of stone from the granite quarries to the place of shipment, and which fully accomplished the purpose for which it was established.

It is due to truth to say, that the announcement of this improvement as adapted to meet the wants of this community, was received by a great portion of the public, with surprising incredulity, and the efforts of its advocates to produce a general conviction of its practicability, were resisted with a pertinacity worthy of a better cause. There were, indeed, many early converts to the belief of its efficacy; but the belief was slowly embraced by the class of persons who were possessed of the means of testing their convictions by actual experiment, on a scale broad enough to give it general confidence, and to introduce it into practical use.

After much discussion of the subject in the public journals, and in pamphlets, the Massachusetts Legislature, as early as the year 1827, authorized the appointment of a Board of Commissioners, to cause surveys to be made, of the most practicable routes for a railroad from Boston to the Hudson River, at or near Albany. The Commissioners appointed under this authority made an exploration of the most difficult parts of the prominent routes, and a large part of the route deemed most eligible was surveyed. The next Legislature authorized the appointment of a Board of Directors of Internal Improvement, consisting of twelve members, and appropriated a fund to pay the expenses of surveys and plans. Under the direction of this Board, the surveys deemed necessary for the selection of the most eligible route for a railroad from Boston to the Hudson River, and three entire routes from Boston to Providence, were thoroughly surveyed, and reports thereon were submitted to the Legislature, and published in the winter of 1829, accompanied with a recommendation to make a commencement of railroads on both these routes at the charge of the Commonwealth.

The Legislature however declined to make any appropriation of public money, on the recommendation of this board, or on resolutions offered by committees in the succeeding sessions, either for undertaking the construction of railroads on the public account, or for co-operating with private corporations, to be established for the purpose. Several private charters were granted, without the subscription of any stock on public account, or other pecuniary aid, which failed for want of the necessary confidence for raising subscriptions to the stock.

At length in the summer session of 1831, the Boston and Providence, and the Boston and Worcester Railroad Corporations were established, and the charter of the Boston and Lowell granted the preceding year, being amended, these companies were organized by the subscription of the required amount of capital—the Worcester conditionally, with the reservation of the right of the subscribers to withdraw, on receiving the report of definitive surveys and estimates —and the surveys of the three roads were vigorously prosecuted during the season. The charter of the Boston and Worcester road was the first, which contained the express grant of authority to transport persons and merchandise on account of the corporation, and to purchase and hold locomotive engines and cars.

In 1832 the work of construction was actively prosecuted on these three roads, the report to the subscribers in the Boston and Worcester, having been accepted, and the conditional subscriptions to the stock made absolute. A great part of the stock in the Boston and Providence company was taken originally by New York capitalists, and much of that of the Boston and Lowell, by proprietors in the manufacturing establishments at Lowell. The stock of the Boston and Worcester was taken chiefly not by capitalists, but by men of business, desirous of promoting the establishment of a Western Railroad, which should extend ultimately through the State to the Hudson River. They deemed such an improvement essential to the welfare of the State, and they proceeded under the conviction that if their subscriptions should prove unproductive as investments of capital, they would, as members of the community, be indemnified for the loss, by their share in the public benefit of the enterprise.

The Boston and Worcester road was partially opened to public travel in April, 1834. On this occasion the use of locomotive engines was introduced for the first time in New England. This road was opened throughout, from Boston to Worcester, July 4, 1835. The Boston and Providence road was opened in part in June, 1834, and throughout in June, 1835. The Boston and Lowell was opened throughout in June, 1835.

This was the commencement of the Massachusetts system of railroads. These three works were thus the pioneer railroads in New

England. No other works of the kind were attempted in the New England States, until the success of these had been tested by their actual use, with the exception of the Norwich and Worcester, which was begun in 1835. These railroads were built by engineers who had never seen the English works, and although they adopted for the most part the general principles on which those roads were constructed, they did not blindly copy from them, but modified their respective works in many particulars, to adapt them to their difference of situation, arising from differences of locality, as well as of the amount of population and business. Several of these differences of plan consisted in the adoption of a single track in the first instance, and in retaining it in all cases so long as the traffic should be insufficient to pay a fair income on the cost of a double one—the avoidance of Tunnels, and very expensive cutting, except in cases of necessity, by admitting of higher grades—and the adoption of cross tiers of wood in lieu of stone blocks. The wooden cross tiers are now, we believe, generally adopted in England, as preferable to stone, without reference to the difference of cost. The rails have been for the most part imported from England, but they have been in most cases rolled to a pattern prescribed from this country, often deviating from the form in general use in England. The locomotives first used were for the most part imported from England, but for some years past they have been almost exclusively manufactured in this country. Their form of construction has been based in general upon English patterns, but often with considerable modifications, partly for adapting them to working on higher grades. One of the locomotives introduced upon the Boston and Worcester road within the first year from its opening, was built in Boston, and it proved to be a valuable engine. Those manufactured in this country are believed to be fully equal to those which have been imported, and there is no deficiency of engines of superior workmanship.

We cannot attempt here either to trace the history of the railroads now in operation in the State, or to give a particular description of any of them. All we can do is to present an enumeration of the different works, classified in such manner as to show the several routes of communication of which they constitute the parts. This enumeration is accompanied with a statement of the length and the cost of each road, and the amount of income derived from each, during the year 1850, together with the aggregate extent, cost and income of them all. We subjoin also a statement of the works of a similar character beyond the limits of the State constructed for the purpose of extending the several lines of communication, in various directions, where there has appeared to be such a demand for them as to encourage parties to undertake them.

There are at this time seven distinct railroads, which take their departure from different points within the City of Boston, all established by private corporations, and entirely independent of one another, and diverging irregularly to all the points of the compass, except on that side which fronts on the ocean. These seven roads are the main trunks on which are engrafted all the railroads in the State. The supplementary roads are in part extensions of the main trunks, and in part lateral branches, designed for extending the benefits of the improvement over a wider space. All these roads are constructed upon a uniform gauge of four feet ten and a half inches, and consequently carriages, entered upon any part of either of the lines, may be transmitted thereon to Boston, or to the farthest extremity of the line, or of either of its branches.

Each of the seven lines extends to the limits of the State, and with the exception of one, which terminates by branches at several points on the sea, they all connect with other railroads, held under charters from the adjoining States, by which they are extended through those States, and in several instances through the next adjoining States. We enumerate them in their order, beginning at the southeastern part of the city.

1st. OLD COLONY LINE.

This line departs from the station at the corner of Kneeland and South streets, and proceeds through South Boston, and through some of the principal manufacturing towns of Norfolk and Plymouth counties, to Plymouth. By the South Shore Road, branching on the left, it visits the seaport towns of Weymouth, Hingham and Cohasset, and by the Fall River Road, diverging on the right, it proceeds through Bridgewater to Fall River, where it connects with a daily line of steamers by way of Newport to New York. An express train runs in connexion with the steamboat line. By the Cape Cod Branch diverging again on the left from the Fall River Road, the line proceeds to Sandwich, in Barnstable County, whence it is likely to be shortly extended to the south side of the Cape, at Hyannis, where it will be the nearest point on the continent, from which a communication can be maintained with Nantucket. The line consists of the following works:

Name of Company.	*Miles.*	*Cost.*	*Rev.* 1850.
Old Colony, - - - - -	37½	$2,293,535	$296,171
Dorchester and Milton Branch, -	2¾	132,172	
South Shore, - - - - -	10¼	420,438	
Bridgewater Branch, - - -	7¼		
Fall River, - - - - -	42¼	1,068,167	210,081
Cape Cod Branch, - - - -	27¾	626,543	56,556
Total, - - - -	127¾	$4,540,270	$563,108

All the branches of this line terminate within the State. The Bridgewater Branch belongs to the Old Colony Company, and its cost is embraced in that of the main road. The revenue of roads not separately stated in the table, is included in that of the Old Colony, to which Company these roads are leased. Eleven and a half miles of the Old Colony Road consist of a double track, and the residue, together with the other roads of this line, of single track.

2d. PROVIDENCE, OR SOUTHERN LINE.

This line takes its departure from the station on Pleasant street, near the bottom of the Common, and proceeds in a southerly direction to Providence, where it connects with the Stonington road, and proceeds diagonally through the State of Rhode Island, to Stonington in Connecticut. It there connects with a second daily steamboat line to New York, it being the Southern *Steamboat Mail* Line. An express train runs between Boston and Stonington in connexion with the steamboat line, without exchange of carriages. The line diverges on the left, half way between Boston and Providence, to New Bedford, from which latter point there is a line of steam communication with Nantucket. It connects near Providence with the Providence and Worcester road, and enters the city of Providence on a track by the side of that road. Near Boston, a branch of the Boston and Providence road diverges from the main line on the right to Dedham, and at that point it connects with the Norfolk County road, which terminates at Blackstone, in Worcester County. The several parts of this line are as follows:

Boston and Providence, - - -	41	$3,370,270	$370,727
Dedham and other Branches, - -	12		
Stoughton Branch, - - - - -	4	93,433	6,423
Taunton Branch, - - - - -	11	307,136	57,606
New Bedford and Taunton, - -	20	498,752	93,043
Norfolk County, - - - - -	26	1,060,990	57,840
Providence and Worcester, in Mass.,	25½	923,288	101,375
Total in Mass., - -	139½	$6,253,869	$687,014
PARTS OUT OF THE STATE.			
Providence and Worcester, in R. I.,	18	901,508	101,376

Sixteen miles of the Boston and Providence, and five of the Providence and Worcester roads, have a double track. The residue of this line consists of single track roads, the trains thereon being so arranged and running with such regularity that they meet at the stations, so as rarely to occasion the delay of either train.

3D. WORCESTER, OR WESTERN LINE.

This line begins at the passenger station at the corner of Lincoln and Beach streets, opposite to the United States Hotel, and at the freight station, bordering on the harbor, and by means of a depression of eight feet in the grade of the road, it crosses the city, passing under three of the principal avenues, and thus reaches the back bay, and the basin of the Mill Dam Corporation, which it crosses, and reaches the country without interrupting any street.

The main line, consisting of the Boston & Worcester and Western roads, passes westerly through Worcester, Springfield and Pittsfield, traversing the whole length of the State, to the city of Albany, 200 miles. In this distance it follows the course of several of the head waters of the State to their sources, and crosses the summits which divide all the principal rivers in the State, with but one tunnel, and with no grade so steep as materially to retard the travel of the most rapid trains. Two daily passenger trains run between Boston and Albany, and large quantities of merchandise are transported over the whole line.

At Worcester the Norwich and Worcester road diverges from this line in a southerly direction, and proceeds to Norwich and Allyn's

Point, where it connects with the third daily steamboat line running to New York. Express trains from Boston without change of cars connect with this line. The distance from Boston to Allyn's Point, 110 miles, is usually travelled in four hours. The passage between Boston and New York is usually made, in each direction, between 5 o'clock, P. M., and 7 o'clock, A. M. At Worcester the line connects, also, on the right, with the Worcester & Nashua road, which comes in from the north, and forms a connexion with all the northern, northeastern, and northwestern routes.

At Springfield this line connects with the New Haven and Hartford railroad, which there diverges on the left, and by means of this and the New York and New Haven road, it forms a continuous line to the city of New York. On this line two daily express trains run between Boston and New York, the distance being 240 miles, and the journey is performed in about 9 hours. The morning train on this line conveys the great Southern *land mail.* From this line, also, at Springfield, the Connecticut River road diverges on the right, and runs chiefly on the western bank of the Connecticut River, to Northampton and Greenfield, and to the border of Vermont. It there connects with other railroads which follow the western bank of the Connecticut, to within 50 miles of the Canada border, and at different points it forms a connexion with all the lines of railroad in Vermont and New Hampshire,

This line of railroad is also united, at Palmer, with the New London and Willimantic road, which passes through Connecticut; at Pittsfield with the North Adams road, and also with the Stockbridge, Berkshire, and Housatonic, which latter traverses the State of Connecticut; and at the State line it connects with the Berkshire, and the Hudson and Berkshire roads. The following are the several parts of the line:

Boston & Worcester, - - - -	$44\frac{5}{8}$	$4,882,148	$757,947
Six Branches, - - - - -	24		
Western, - - - - - -	117 4-5	8,032,814 }	1,369,514
Providence & North Adams, -	$18\frac{1}{3}$	443,678 }	
Norwich & Worcester, in Mass., -	20	772,106	87,086
Worcester & Nashua, - - -	40	1,282,691	123,479
Fitchburg & Worcester, - -	14	259,074	19,159
New London & Palmer, in Mass.,	10	180,000	10,000
Connecticut River, - - -	50	1,798,825	191,587
Hartford & New Haven, - -	6	215,808	36,000
Stockbridge and Pittsfield, - -	$22\frac{3}{4}$	448,700	31,409
West Stockbridge, - - -	$2\frac{3}{4}$	41,516	1,823
Berkshire, - - - - - -	21	600,000	42,000
Total, - - - - -	$391\frac{1}{4}$	$18,959,367	$2,670,004

OUT OF THE STATE.

Albany and West Stockbridge, -	38 1-5	1,930,895	
Norwich & Worcester in Conn., -	46	1,826,408	174,173
Har. & N. H. in Conn., - -	56	2,534,000	414,757
N. London and P. in Conn., -	$55\frac{2}{3}$	1,155,000	69,400
Wor. & Nash. in N. H., - -	$5\frac{3}{3}$	127,506	29,959
Total, - - - - -	$201\frac{1}{2}$	$7,577,809	$688,289

The Albany and West Stockbridge was built by the Western Railroad Company of this State, at their exclusive cost, and it is managed by them as a part of the Western road, as is also the Pittsfield and North Adams. The stock of the Worcester and Nashua road is owned chiefly in Massachusetts; that of the roads which terminate in Connecticut is held but partially in this State.

4TH. FITCHBURG, OR WEST-NORTH-WESTERN LINE.

	Miles.	Cost.	Income. 1850.
Fitchburg, - - - - - - - -	51 }	$3,552,283	$551,607
Branches, - - - - - - - -	15 }		
Lexington and W. C., - - - -	6½	212,161	
Peterborough and S., - - - - -	14	272,647	
Harvard Branch, - - - - -	⅔	26,223	
Vermont and Mass., - - - - -	67	3,192,051	177,695
Cheshire, in Mass., - - - - -	11⅓	2,739,318	208,414
	165½	$10,024,643	$937,716

OUT OF THE STATE.

	Miles.
Vt. and Mass., in N. H., - - - -	10
Cheshire, - - - - - - - -	52⅓
	42½

The branch railroads connected with this line, are worked by the Fitchburg company, and their income is included in the statement of revenue of that road. The stock of the Vermont and Massachusetts, and the Cheshire Roads is in a great proportion owned in this State; and, as we have no means of distributing either the cost or the income of the parts between the portions in and out of the State, the whole of these items is given above with the Massachusetts portion.

This line takes its departure from the Fitchburg station, near the Warren Bridge, and runs first in a westerly, and then in a north-westerly course, approaching near to the Boston and Worcester Road at Waltham, and thence passing through Concord to Fitchburg; it proceeds thence by the Vermont and Massachusetts Road, to Greenfield, and to Brattleborough, in Vermont. From the latter place, the line is continued by the Vermont Valley Railroad, which extends to Bellows Falls, and there connects with the Rutland and Burlington Road.

A branch of this line is formed by the Cheshire Railroad, which diverges from the Vermont and Massachusetts, at a point eleven miles above Fitchburg, and proceeds by way of Keene to Bellows Falls, whence the line is continued by the Rutland and Burlington, by way of Chester, Rutland, Brandon and Middlebury, to Burlington—the distance from Boston being 233 miles. Here the line of travel connects with the steamboat line on Lake Champlain. At Bellows Falls, a diverging line on the right, consisting of the Sullivan Railroad, proceeds to Windsor, the lower terminus of the Vermont Central Railroad. There is also a diverging line on the left, from Rutland to Castleton, and thence to Whitehall, at the upper extremity of Lake Champlain. It there connects with the Saratoga and Washington Road, which at its southern extremity unites with the lines leading from Troy and Schenectady. This line forms an eligible and expeditious route from Boston to Saratoga Springs, by which the journey is made in ten hours to Saratoga, and in twelve to Schenectady.

5TH. LOWELL, OR NORTH-WESTERN LINE.

Boston and Lowell, - - - - -	$25\frac{3}{4}$	$1,945,647	$406,421
Woburn Branch, - - - - -	$1\frac{3}{4}$		
Nashua and Lowell, in Mass., - -	$9\frac{1}{2}$	651,215	129,617
Stony Brook, - - - - - -	13	265,526	16,189
Total, - - - - -	50	$2,862,388	$552,227

OUT OF THE STATE.

Nashua and Lowell, 5 miles, cost and income included above.

This is the shortest line in the State, of the Railroads proceeding from Boston; but it has a large extension beyond the limits of the State, by Railroads built in great part by proprietors residing within the State, and which sustain important lines of travel terminating in Boston. This line begins at the Lowell Railroad station, in the north-eastern part of the city, and proceeds through East Cambridge and Medford to the city of Lowell. It has a short branch at Woburn, and it formerly composed a part of the Boston and Maine line, which united with it at a distance of 14 miles from the city. That connexion has been dissolved, and the Maine Road enters the city by an independent line. From Lowell, the line is continued by the Nashua and Lowell Road to Nashville. To this point, the line consists of a double track. The line is thence extended by the Concord Railroad along the valley of the Merrimack river, 35 miles, to Concord, the Capital of New Hampshire, and thence by the northern, 82 miles, to the Connecticut river in Lebanon. It there crosses the Connecticut, and unites with the Vermont Central Railroad at the mouth of White river. This Road, which begins at Windsor, on the Connecticut river, 14 miles below this point of junction, and at the terminus of the Sullivan Railroad above mentioned, continues the line along the valley of the White river, by way of Royalton to the summit of the Green Mountain, and thence by Northfield to Montpelier, the Capital of Vermont. Thence it pursues the valley of Onion, or Winoosky river, to Burlington, 245 miles from Boston. From Burlington, or rather from Essex, six and a half miles east from Burlington, the Vermont Central Road is met by the Vermont and Canada Railroad, by which the line is extended to Rouse's Point, where it crosses Lake Champlain, near its outlet. It is thence extended by the Champlain and Montreal Railroad to the St. Lawrence, near Montreal, which city it reaches in a distance of 326 miles from Boston. It is continued also from Rouse's Point, over the Northern Railroad of New York, to the town of Ogdensburgh, at the foot of navigation on Lake Ontario, a distance of 403 miles from Boston.

In addition to these extensive lines of Railroad, all connected with the Boston and Lowell as the main trunk, there are several other diverging lines of some importance. Among these are the Boston, Concord, and Montreal. This Road, destined as its name imports, to reach the city of Montreal, but by a very different route from either of those already described, proceeds from Concord along the eastern branch of the Merrimack river, and by the outlet of Winnipiseogee Lake, to Meredith, and thence by Plymouth to Warren, a distance of 71 miles. It will be in a short time further extended, and probably united with the Atlantic and St. Lawrence, now in progress from Portland to Montreal. Another branch of this general route diverges from the main line at the mouth of White river, and passes over the Connecticut and Passumpsic River Railroad, which follows the course, first of the Connecticut, and then of the Passumpsic to St. Johnsbury, a distance of 61 miles. It is intended to extend it thence to the Canada line, near Lake Memphremagog, and thence to some point of junction with the St. Lawrence and Atlantic Railroad in Canada.

There are two other Railroads connected with this general line, leading westwardly from Concord, which are yet unfinished, viz: the Concord and Claremont, which is opened for a distance of 25 miles to Bradford, and the Contoocook Valley Railroad, which is opened about an equal distance through Henniker to Hillsborough Bridge. These several Railroads, together with the Nashville and Milford, already opened, form an aggregate length connected with this line, of 632 miles.

6TH. BOSTON AND MAINE, OR NORTHERN LINE.

Name of Company.	*Miles.*	*Cost.*	*Inc.* 1850.
Boston and Maine, - - - - -	37	$4,021,606	$594,263
South Reading Branch, - - - -	8	231,601	
Manchester and Lawrence, - -	5	717,543	
Lowell and Lawrence, - - - -	12	333,254	
Grand Junction, - - - - -	6	678,116	
Total, - - - - -	68	$5,981,533	$594,263
OUT OF THE STATE.			
Boston and Maine, - - - - -	37¼		
Branches, - - - - - -	8¾		
Manchester and Lawrence, - -	28⅓		
	671		

About half the Boston and Maine Railroad, and the greater part of the Manchester and Lawrence are without the limits of the State. As we have no rule for the division of the cost and income, it is all placed in the above table with the Massachusetts portion, a great part of the stock being owned here.

This line of Railroads begins at the Boston and Maine station, in Haymarket square, in the northerly part of the city, and proceeds by way of Andover, Lawrence, Haverhill, Exeter, and Dover, to Great Falls, and to the junction with the Eastern Road in Berwick. It connects at Dover with the Cocheco Railroad, leading to Winnipiseogee Lake, and at Great Falls with the Great Falls and Conway Railroad. It forms one of the great lines of travel between Boston and Portland, and receives a great number of passengers from the large manufacturing towns through which it passes. By means of the Manchester and Lawrence Road, it furnishes a second Railroad route to Concord, in New Hampshire, and thereby forms a connexion with the great north-western lines above described. Besides the union of this line with the Portsmouth, Saco and Portland Railroad at Berwick, it will, on the completion of the York and Cumberland Road, form another route to Portland.

7TH. NORTH-EASTERN LINE.

Eastern, in Mass.,	38 1-5	$3,120,392	$589,076
Gloucester Branch,	13 1-2		
Marblehead Branch,	3		
Salisbury Branch,	3 1-2		
Salem and Lowell,	17	316,943	15,505
Essex,	20	537,869	47,383
Total,	95 1-5	$3,975,204	$651,964
OUT OF THE STATE.			
Eastern, in N. H.,	16	493,883	

This line takes its departure from the station on the Eastern Railroad wharf, whence the passengers are transported by a steam ferry specially appropriated to the railroad, to a similar wharf at East Boston, from which place the railroad trains take their departure. The main line passes through Lynn, Salem, Ipswich and Newburyport, to Portsmouth, and proceeds thence by the Portsmouth, Saco and Portland Railroad, to Portland, thence by the Kennebeck Railroad to Brunswick, Bath and Richmond. This railroad will shortly be completed through Gardiner and Hallowell, to Augusta, the Capital of Maine, a distance of 166 miles from Boston. The line diverges by branches to Marblehead, Gloucester, and Amesbury, in Massachusetts; and by an independent line to Georgetown. At Portsmouth, it connects with the Portsmouth and Concord Railroad, which is yet opened but little more than half its length.

At Portland commences the Atlantic and St. Lawrence Railroad, which is stretching its course towards Montreal, in the expectation that it will shortly be united with the St. Lawrence and Atlantic, which is advancing by a vigorous effort of the people of Canada, to meet it at the Canada frontier. This road is already open 91 miles to Gorham, N. H., at the base of Mount Washington. The Atlantic portion of the same line has been for some time open from Montreal to St. Hyacinthe. In connection with this line, the Androscoggin and Kennebeck Railroad is already open, from its junction at Danville, 27 miles from Portland, to Waterville, on the Kennebeck River, 20 miles above Augusta, and 82 miles from Portland. The line will doubtless be further extended to the Penobscot River, at Bangor, and ultimately to the adjoining provinces of New Brunswick and Nova Scotia, should the enterprise already strongly encouraged, of the European and St. Lawrence Railroad, be carried into execution. There is also in operation another branch of this line, 13 miles in length, running from Mechanic Falls to Buckfield.

This enumeration will serve to show, to what extent the people of the Commonwealth are accommodated with the means of internal communication, and of intercourse with the neighboring States, and with the more distant parts of the country. For the purpose of showing the aggregate extent of railroad, and also the amount of cost, as well as that of their annual income, which is the best test of their utility, we present the following recapitulation. The statement of income is that of 1850. There has been an increase on most of the lines, perhaps all, the present year.

	Miles of Road.	Cost to Jan. 1, 1851.	Income.
Old Colony Line, - - - - - - -	127 3-4	4,540.270	563,108
Providence do - - - - - - -	139 1-2	6,253.869	687,014
Worcester do - - - - - - -	391 1-4	18,959.367	2,670.004
Fitchburg do - - - - - - -	165 1-2	10,024.643	937,716
Lowell do - - - - - - -	50	2,862.388	552.227
Bost.& Maine do - - - - - - -	68	5,981.533	594,263
Eastern do - - - - - - -	105 1-5	4,082.029	651,964
	1,047 1-5	$52,704.099	$6,656,296

In this statement are not included the length and cost of the Albany and West Stockbridge road, built exclusively by the Western Company of this State, and portions out of the State, of certain others which begin in the State, some of which belong almost exclusively to proprietors residing within the State. If we increase the above aggregate by the addition of these items, it gives for the entire length of railroads situated in whole or in part in Massachusetts, an extent of railroads of 1411 1-5 miles, at an aggregate cost of $60,992,183, affording a gross income, in 1850, of $7,445,961. The stock of such of these roads as extend into Connecticut and Rhode Island, is owned in great measure by proprietors residing in those States, and in New York.

This statement embraces no part of the works, or of their cost and income, included in the foregoing statement, which are situated wholly without the limits of Massachusetts. Several of these are owned by companies of large capital, the proprietors of which are residents of this State, and some of them are in great part owned elsewhere. It would extend this article to too great a length to attempt a description of the whole. We present, however, a table of some of the principal companies, with the length and cost of their respective roads, including only such as are in actual operation, and are connected with the lines of railroad above enumerated, which terminate in Boston.

	Miles.	Cost.
Rutland & Burlington, - - - - - - - -	120	$3,854.253
Rutland & Washington, - - - - - - - -	10	250.000
Sullivan, - - - - - - - - - - -	25	673.500
Nashua & Concord, - - - - - - - - -	35	1,385.788
N. H. Northern, - - - - - - - - - -	82	3,016.634
Vermont Central, - - - - - - - - -	115	5,084.470
Vermont & Canada, - - - - - - - - -	38	1,200.000
New York Northern, - - - - - - - - -	118	3,641.426
Conn. & Passumpsic, - - - - - - - - -	61	1,500.000
Concord & Claremont, - - - - - - - -	25	560.624
Contoocook, - - - - - - - - - -	20	219.450
Concord & Montreal, - - - - - - - - -	71	1,567.073
Portsmouth & Concord, - - - - - - - -	23	850.000
Cocheco, - - - - - - - - - - -	18	500.000
Portsmouth, Saco and Portland, - - - - - -	52	1,293.640

	Miles.	Cost.
Kennebeck & Portland, - - - - - - - -	54	1,000,000
Atlantic & St. Lawrence, - - - - - - - -	70	1,500.000
Androscoggin & Kennebeck, - - - - - -	55	1,621,878
York & Cumberland, - - - - - - - - -	11	360,000
Total, - - - - - - - - -	1003	$30,078,736
Add Roads in Massachusetts, - - - - - -	1047	52,704,099
Partly in Massachusetts, - - - - - - -	370	8,966,200
Total, - - - - - - - - -	2420	$91,749,035

In this enumeration are not included several minor works in the State, on our northern border, nor the Stonington and New York and New Haven roads, which form part of the lines of daily communication between this city and New York. Were we to include the entire cost of the railroads in the New England States now in operation, connected with lines leading to Boston, it would doubtless exceed $100,000,000.

It should have been stated, in our description of some of the roads leading from Boston, in yesterday's paper, that the main trunk of the Boston & Worcester road, the Western road from Worcester to Springfield, the Fitchburg and Boston and Lowell roads, consist of a double track, as do also 27 miles of the Maine road, and 16 miles of the Eastern. The rest consist chiefly of a single track.

For the purpose of showing to what extent the whole people of the State participate in the benefit of the lines of railroad, which traverse the State as above described, it may be pertinent to state that there are in Massachusetts 32 cities and towns which have each 5000 inhabitants and upwards, and that one or more of these railroads passes through, or terminates in each of these towns, with the exception of Nantucket only, which is an island, 20 miles removed from the main land; and that on each railroad, two or more passenger trains run to and from Boston daily, (Sundays always excepted, when daily travelling on railroads is spoken of.) There are in the State *ninety-eight* towns of a population varying from 2000 to 5000, of which *seventy-three* are situated on some one of the said lines of railroad, and have the same facilities of communication as the larger class of towns. Of the 25 towns of from 2000 to 5000 inhabitants, in which there is no railroad station, 13 are seaport towns, mostly in the Old Colony, and a large proportion are situated near a railroad station in an adjoining town. The population of the smaller class of towns have the opportunities of railroad accommodation, in nearly the same proportion as those of the class above mentioned.

GRAND JUNCTION RAILROAD.

The Grand Junction Railroad Company was chartered in 1847, with a capital of $1,200,000, for the purpose of constructing a line of Road to connect the Eastern, Boston and Maine, Fitchburg, and Boston and Lowell Railroads, with the depot grounds of the Company upon tide water at East Boston, where they have ample wharf and storage-room for the accommodation of the extensive business which it is expected their enterprise will command. The objects of this Company, though somewhat various, are all eminently designed to promote the trade and commerce of this city; to facilitate the operations of commerce with the interior trade of the country; to aid in distributing the productions of other countries, and in the export trade of our own. By it, the cars for the interior are brought into immediate connection with vessels from every port, and the freight of the ship may be exchanged for that of the cars, without any other agency than that afforded by the accommodations of this Company. A ship from England may unload her cargo of merchandise, to go to Canada, on one train of cars, and receive her cargo of flour for the return voyage from the next. Or, by its warehouses, the same cargo of merchandise, or the same freight of flour, may be placed in store or bond until required, and it will be seen that whatever the commodity, wherever it came from, or wherever designed to be sent, the saving of expense in the facilities afforded by this Company would equal a large part of the cost of conveying it to the interior from the ship, or to the ship from the interior.

The grounds of the Company consist of some thirty acres, the greater portion of which is *made land*, enclosed by a substantial sea-wall, 2395 feet in length. These grounds front on Marginal street, east of the Cunard Steamers' Wharf, and their piers extend to the Commissioners' line. These piers are eight in number; four of them 350 feet in length and 75 in width, and the others of somewhat less length. They have been constructed of oak, and are built in the most substantial manner. From the main track of the Road, a branch runs along the edges of each of these piers, so that merchandise can be transferred from the cars to the ships. Each pier is to be roofed over, so that they will be in effect ample and commodious depots. At the head of these piers or wharves is abundant land for the construction of warehouses, four of which, to be built of substantial granite, are to be immediately erected by the Company. The charter of the Company permits it to lease or sell to other Railroad Corporations such portions of its grounds as may be desirable, for the erection of freight depots; and the whole thirty acres of its grounds are expected to be occupied in that manner. The Company's grounds are accessible from the open sea on the south to the largest class of ships, and the docks are protected from easterly storms. They contain 1,465,920 square feet of land, piers and docks, divided as follows, viz:—1,058,251 square feet of land, 183,195 do. oak piers,

244,474 do. docks; and have a frontage on Marginal street of 1650 feet in length. Besides the above, the Company owns about 456,721 square feet of land, with a water front of 1000 feet, near the bridge over Chelsea creek. The real estate owned by the Company comprised in these two lots amounts to 1,922,641 square feet, including 9351 feet in length of wharf accommodations, in the deepest and best part of the harbor for commercial purposes. The Railway will extend from the Company's depots and the warehouses at East Boston, through Chelsea and North Malden, to the Boston and Maine Railroad in Somerville, north of the Middlesex Canal, and will intersect the Boston and Lowell, and Fitchburg Roads, in Somerville, near the present crossing of these Roads. The depots on the grounds of the Company are thus connected with four of the principal Railroads entering the city, (and through them with the interior roads reaching to the Canadas and great lakes.) viz:—the Eastern, Boston and Maine, Fitchburg, and Boston and Lowell Railroads,—thus affording a chain of Railroad communication from deep water at our wharves, through the great manufacturing districts of New England, to the Canadas, the Lakes, and the great Western country; and probably, at no very distant day, uniting by one continuous Railroad line the Atlantic and Pacific Oceans. The length of the Grand Junction Railroad itself is 6 and 6-10ths miles, and, as was remarked by many of the guests who rode over it on the second day of the Jubilee, when it was first opened, the Road is finished in a very superior manner.

The officers of the Company are:—President—Samuel S. Lewis; Directors—David Henshaw, Charles Paine, of Northfield, Vt., Ichabod Goodwin, of Portsmouth, N. H., and John W. Fenno, of Boston; Chief Engineer—William L. Dearborn; Treasurer—Dexter Brigham, Jr.; Clerk—J. P. Robinson.

RUTLAND AND BURLINGTON RAILROAD.

The Rutland and Burlington Railroad, extending from Bellows Falls on the Connecticut River, to Burlington on Lake Champlain, a distance of 120 miles, commenced running throughout its entire length January 1, 1850, and opened to Boston enterprise an entirely new field of operations.

The Green Mountains had hitherto interposed a barrier which effectually shut out a country so fertile, that it has been aptly termed the Garden of New England,—abounding in agricultural productions —its hills grazed by countless flocks—and the bowels of the earth yielding inexhaustible quantities of iron ore and marble. Lake Champlain and the Hudson River had heretofore furnished the natural and only channels by which these riches found their way to the distant markets of New York. The Rutland and Burlington Railroad would, it was thought, form a highway which might divert a share at least to the city of Boston; and that it has successfully done so, the statistics of the Road abundantly prove. According to the printed Report, submitted to the Stockholders June 18, 1851, we learn that—

The income for the year 1850 was - - -	$197,774 50
While the income for the year 1851 will reach -	350,000 00
Exhibiting the extraordinary increase of - -	152,225 50

or over 75 per cent. This surprising gain has been caused by no fortuitous circumstances, but has been steady, gradual, and healthful; the result, unquestionably, on the one hand, of the superior facilities for communication throughout the year which a Railroad furnishes,—and on the other, of the stimulus which a work of this nature invariably exerts upon the resources of the region through which it passes.

Fresh capital is continually being called out for the purpose of developing the still hidden wealth of this part of Vermont; and, among other enterprises, we may mention that of our respected fellow-citizen, Col. Thomas H. Perkins, who, with others, have invested largely in the purchase of Belden's Falls—a place yet fresh from the hands of its Maker, and whose rocky sides furnish marble that rivals the finest Carrara can produce.

Besides the local traffic of the Road, its connection with the Ogdensburg Railroad, with the St. Lawrence River, and, by means of the Rutland and Washington Railroad, with the great chain of Railroads leading from Schenectady to Buffalo, greatly enhances the prospects of the Road for an immense increase in its freight and travel, in consequence of so ready a communication with the Great West.

The tourist, as well as the merchant, has been greatly benefitted by the construction of this Road, which not only passes through scenery unrivalled for beauty, and yet new to pleasure-seekers, but is the most direct route to many of the old standard places of interest. It is shorter, by some ten miles, from Boston to Saratoga, by this route, than by any other—a fact which cannot but largely increase the amount of the pleasure-travel of the Road: while northward, Montreal, Quebec, the Saguenay, and the Thousand Islands of the St. Lawrence cannot fail to draw their quota of visitors, who will of course avail themselves of the most direct avenue to those places.

NORTHERN, OR OGDENSBURG RAILROAD.

The Northern, or, as it is popularly called, the Ogdensburg Railroad, commences in the town of that name, on the St. Lawrence River, at the foot of the navigation of the Great Lakes, and extending entirely across northern New York, terminates at Rouse's Point on Lake Champlain. Its whole length is about one hundred and eighteen miles. The charter of this Company was obtained from the Legislature of New York on the fourteenth of May, 1845, and the road was opened in its entire length on the first day of October, 1850. The whole cost of the work, when fully equipped, will be over $4,000,000. It is in all respects a railroad of the first class, having been built in the most substantial and thorough manner. The depot grounds at Ogdensburg and Rouse's Point are most ample. At the former place they consist of more than 60 acres of land, having a water front, where vessels can be discharged, of nearly a mile in length. At Rouse's Point there are nearly 3,000 feet of wharf, from which freight can be discharged into vessels on Lake Champlain. The road here also connects with the lines on the East side of the Lake by means of a floating bridge, or boat, over which trains pass without difficulty, and at a rapid rate of speed.

The great objects in view in constructing this road were, to aid in developing the varied resources of Northern New York—a most fertile, healthful and productive country; to connect the navigable waters of the Great Lakes with Lake Champlain, and with the railroads in the New England States; to open a new, cheap, and expeditious route between the East and the West, and an avenue between the upper and Lower Provinces of Canada. In all these things the road bids fair fully to answer the expectations of its projectors. Already it has produced a most enlivening effect in the country through which it runs, where trade, the arts, and agriculture are assuming a new aspect. Large quantities of freight are passing from the city of New York, up the Hudson and through Lake Champlain, to Rouse's Point, and thence by this line to Canada and the West; while equally large quantities take the same direction from Boston over the New England roads. The products of Canada and the Great West are shipped to Ogdensburg, and there take the cars of this road, and are delivered in Boston without breaking bulk, or are reshipped at Rouse's Point, and pass Southward to the city of New York.

The Montreal Railroad enters upon this road a short distance West of Rouse's Point, and its cars are allowed to pass Eastward over the bridge of this Company, on to the Vermont Road, and thus a complete connexion exists between Boston and Montreal, and between Boston, Montreal and Ogdensburg.

There are some important and interesting points on this railroad. One of them is the viaduct at Chatauque River. This stream is turned through a tunnel cut in solid rock, and the ravine through which it ran is filled with earth, making an embankment one hundred and sixty feet high.

VERMONT CENTRAL RAILROAD.

The Vermont Central Railroad Company was chartered on the 31st of October, 1843, with authority to construct a railroad from the eastern shore of Lake Champlain to a point on the Connecticut River, convenient for its connection with railroads from Boston, either by the way of Concord, N. H., or Fitchburg, Mass.

On the 23d of July, 1845, the Company was organized with a capital of two millions of dollars; on the 15th of December of that year, the first ground was broken at Windsor, and on the 1st of January, 1850, the whole of the Central Road was open for running trains, from Windsor to Burlington, a distance of 117 miles—costing, for track and equipments, up to July 1st, 1851, exclusive of interest, $5,773,964.37.

Regarded in a local view, only, this railroad possesses great advantages in its grades, the maximum of which, on the main line, is 4 feet to the mile—in its curves, three-fourths of the line being straight—in its scenery, which is among the most attractive to be found in New England—and in a country to furnish local business, abounding in resources for agriculture and manufactures, and inhabited by an energetic and thrifty péople. The originators and promoters of the Central road were men of enlarged views, and happily, also, of great sagacity and unflinching energy.

From the outset, they designed the establishment, not merely of an important railroad for Vermont, but of *a great northern line of railroads*, extending from the Atlantic to the St. Lawrence and the Western Lakes—a line of the highest importance to the commerce of New England and the Western States, of Canada and Great Britain.

The Central road was regarded as an indispensable link in this great chain. Its construction was begun, and has been prosecuted with a conviction that its success would insure the construction of the whole. In every stage of its progress, it has been kept strictly subordinate to the grand design. When the Central Railroad Company was organized in July, 1845, there was no railroad constructed within 69 miles of the Central line on the East, and no road constructed, and no Company organized West or North of the Central line, except 18 miles of Summer railway from Laprairie to St. Johns.

The Central suspended its calls upon capitalists for stock, and commenced work with less than one-half of its own capital subscribed, in order, as the directors remarked, in their first annual report, to leave the field in Boston for a time open to the friends of the Ogdensburg road, which was the last link in the chain to connect the Atlantic with the Great Lakes.

Aided by this forbearance, as well as by support on the part of promoters of the Central road, the Ogdensburg was organized in June, 1846. At the same time the Northern (N. H.) and Sullivan railroads were also put in progress. The promoters of the Central road had also succeeded in enlisting, to some extent, the favor of leading men in Montreal, and had procured a charter for the "Vermont & Canada Railroad Co.," to construct the remaining part of the great line between the Central and Ogdensburg roads—so that in July, 1846, nearly the whole line was in progress, and the directors of the Central road, in their first report, used the following language:

"Upon the completion of those railroads in New England with which the Central road will connect, and which are now in progress of completion, direct communication will be furnished for Vermont and Northern New York, through various parts of New Hampshire; Massachusetts, Rhode Island, and Connecticut, and into Maine; while, for a large portion of Vermont, the Central will also form a link in the chain of direct communication with the Middle and Southern States. On the North, via Lake Champlain and the St. Johns Railroad, the Central road will be connected, as soon as finished, by steam with Montreal; and at no distant day, we trust, in a constant and speedier manner, by cars and engines running upon the Vermont and Canada Railroad. Means will thus be furnished for transportation direct from Boston to Montreal; indeed, we should rather say, for regular, certain, direct steam communication between Great Britain and the capital of her North American Colonies. Under a liberal policy, between the governments of England and the United States, such as would seem to prevail, the amount of transportation will not be inconsiderable, and the number of passengers must be large.

We dare not attempt to estimate the amount of business which is to pour into the capital of New England, through the Central road, when it shall, as it undoubtedly will, be connected with Montreal on the North, and Ogdensburg on the West. A new outlet will thus be afforded, on the seaboard, for those productions which are now being gathered into the Northern Lakes from the vast and fertile lands which surround them.

Boston, as is well known, has the reputation of affording one of the best markets in the Union, for the manufactures and the agricultural products of our own country, and the productions of foreign countries. When once a road of such easy gradients and curves, as those of the Vermont Central road, shall have been opened to Lake Champlain, who can properly estimate the reciprocal benefits which must result therefrom to the merchant of Boston, and to the trader of Vermont? and, when a connection shall have been established with Ogdensburg and thus with all those great Lakes which wash the shores of seven States of this Union, and Canada West, who can calculate the effect to be produced upon the trade of Boston? Verily, what the Western Railroad would be to Boston, were there no Hudson river, and if the New York roads carried freight all the year and paid no tolls,—such, we believe, will the line of railroad, from Boston to the St. Lawrence, be to the capital of Massachusetts,—bringing flour from Cleveland to Boston at less rate via Ogdensburg than it can be brought by the present arrangements to any point on the seaboard. It will thus be found, that while this line of roads is to benefit both the producer and the consumer, directly, another, and no less important effect, which will result from the completion of the line, will be the vast increase that must ensue to the shipping business of Boston. By uniting the St. Lawrence at Ogdensburg, and the same river at Montreal, with the capital of New England, by a common iron tie, and there connecting with the Royal Mail Steamships, the Vermont Central Railroad, with its connections, is to become the grand highway for freight, and for business and pleasure travel, between the mother country and our own, and the principal English Colonies of the Western world."

To carry out the great scheme thus indicated, the Vermont and Canada road was leased by the Vermont Central, with a guarantee of 8 per cent. upon its cost. And thus means were procured to open that road on the 1st of January 1851, and the whole scheme was completed, by the opening of the Champlain and St. Lawrence road, on the 1st of September last.

This Vermont Central Railroad commences at Windsor, Vermont, connecting there with the Sullivan Railroad, and through it with railroad lines extending both to Boston and New York city, and to all the most important towns in Connecticut and Rhode Island and that part of Massachusetts lying west and south of Boston. Running from Windsor, fourteen miles, to White River Junction, the road there connects with the Northern line to Concord, N. H., Lowell, Lawrence, and Boston, also to Salem, Portsmouth and Portland, and also with the Passumpsic and Connecticut River Railroad, which extends, up the valley of the Connecticut river, to Northern Vermont and New Hampshire.

From White River Junction the Central road extends through Vermont, via Royalton, Bethel, Randolph, Northfield, Montpelier, Waterbury, Richmond and Essex, to Burlington on Lake Champlain, 103 miles. At Essex Junction, 7 miles east of Burlington, the Central connects with the Vermont and Canada railroad, which is leased by the Central and run by it as a part of the great Northern line from Boston and New York to Canada and the West, extending 47 miles from Essex, to Rouse's Point; the line then connects with railroads running west to Ogdensburg, and north to Montreal, thus forming together with the lower roads an unbroken line, and the *only* unbroken line of railway from the Atlantic, at New York and Boston, to the St. Lawrence at Montreal and Ogdensburg.

The Central is one of the best constructed roads in New England, and well equipped, and is the first railroad in this country which has provided a speedy passage, across navigable waters, for entire trains of locomotives and cars without the aid of a bridge. This is done at Rouse's Point by a boat fitted with proper tracks, and extending across the entire channel, a novel and highly successful expedient enforced by the unyielding opposition of other interests to the construction of a railway bridge by the Vermont and Canada and Ogdensburg roads.

The design of this floating bridge is due to Gov. Paine, the President, and it was constructed by H. R. Campbell, Esq., the Chief Engineer of the Central Railroad Company.

The Vermont Central Railroad Company has striven strongly, and suffered severely, in carrying out the original design with which its founders started, but it is beginning to reap the reward to which it is entitled; its business now requires two passenger, and four freight trains daily each way, and its superior facilities for transportation will it is hoped, in due time give it rank among the greatest, and most successful roads in the country. This line has been selected for the transportation both of the United States, and British mails between Boston and New York and Canada.

STATISTICS OF THE PUBLIC SCHOOLS.

The following tables relating to the schools of Boston, were prepared by N. Bishop, Esq., the able Superintendent of Public Schools, to show the expenditures of the City, for purposes connected with education, during the last ten years. They are exceedingly valuable, not only for present reference, but as affording the means for future comparison:—

Estimated cost of all the Public School Estates to May 1st, 1851.

1. Cost of the Latin and English High School Estate, and of the improvements on the same, - -		$81,151.51
2. Cost of all the Grammar School Estates, and of the improvements on the same, - - - - -		762,744.22
3. Cost of all the Primary School Estates, and of the improvements on the same, -	366,214.81	
Since May 1st, 1851, the amount expended for Primary School Estates, is - -	61,163.03	
Making the entire cost of the Primary School Estates,		*427,377.84
Total cost of all the Public School Estates, -		$1,271,273.57

* This sum is much smaller than it would be, if a large number of Primary Schools did not occupy rooms in the Grammar School Houses, and many others, rooms *hired* for their use.

ANNUAL AMOUNT *paid for Tuition and for incidental expenses, and rate per scholar, for the last ten years.*

I. IN HIGH AND GRAMMAR SCHOOLS.

Years.	Number of Scholars.	Amount paid for salaries.	Rate per Scholar.	Incidental Expenses.	Rate per Scholar.	Total Expense.
1841–'42	6,433	$73,258 83	$ 11 39	$14,305 10	$ 2 22	$ 13 91
1842–'43	6,823	75,734 68	11 10	16,761 22	2 46	13 56
1843–'44	7,533	80,957 68	10 75	15,879 46	2 11	12 86
1844–'45	7,935	89,005 11	11 22	21,134 00	2 66	13 89
1845–'46	8,511	98,876 40	11 62	21,940 39	2 58	14 20
1846–'47	8,513	104,675 34	12 30	25,589 93	3 01	15 40
1847–'48	8,836	114,011 86	12 90	34,878 12	3 95	16 85
1848–'49	9,114	118,060 84	12 95	36,935 67	4 05	17 00
1849–'50	9,332	120,895 83	12 95	34,314 26	3 67	16 62
1850–'51	9,694	125 464 60	12 94	39,820 82	4 11	17 05

Average number of Scholars for the last ten years, 8,272.
" tuition of each scholar per annum, $12.10.
" increase of scholars " " 5 per cent.
" " " tuition " " 7 " "
Entire " " scholars for ten years, 50 " "
" " " tuition " " " 71 " "
Average annual *incidental expenses* per scholar, $3.16.
" rate of increase of incidental expenses per annum, 17 4-5 per cent.
Entire increase of incidental expenses for ten years, 178 " "

II. IN PRIMARY SCHOOLS.

Years.	Number of Scholars.	Amount paid for salaries.	Rate per Scholar.	Incidental Expenses.	Rate per Scholar.	Total Expense.
1841–'42	5,968	$23,934 84	$ 4 01	$ 8,889 71	$ 1 48	$ 5 49
1842–'43	6,355	25,324 79	3 98	10,876 14	1 71	5 69
1843–'44	7,540	27,884 14	3 70	11,075 34	1 47	5 17
1844–'45	8,173	29,239 84	3 57	10,968 12	1 34	4 91
1845–'46	8,599	31,070 35	3 61	13,346 36	1 55	5 16
1846–'47	9,003	44,675 69	4 96	17,425 39	1 93	6 89
1847–'48	10,060	47,910 64	4 76	22.530 18	2 24	7 00
1848–'49	10,657	53,671 99	5 04	23.993 98	2 25	7 29
1849–'50	11,257	56,461 31	5 02	23,685 61	2 10	7 12
1850–'51	11,949	58,434 08	4 89	21,214 39	1 77	6 66

Average number of scholars for the last ten years, 8,956.
" tuition per scholar " " " " " $4.45.
" increase of scholars per annum, 10 per cent.
" " " tuition per annum, 14 2-5 " "
Entire " " scholars for ten years, 100 " "
" " " tuition " " " 144 1-10 " "
Average annual *incidental expenses* per scholar, $1.83.
" rate of increase of incidental expenses per scholar, 17 per cent.
Entire increase of incidental expenses for ten years, 170 " "

From this Table it appears that, for the last ten years, the average cost of instruction for each scholar in the High and the Grammar Schools, has been $15.26 per annum; and that for each scholar in the Primary Schools it has been $6.28 per annum. The whole average cost of instruction is $10.59 per annum for each scholar in the Boston Public Schools.

AMOUNT *annually expended for the Erection and Alteration of School Houses for the last ten years.*

	HIGH AND GRAMMAR SCHOOLS.			PRIMARY SCHOOLS.		
Years.	Number of Scholars.	Amount expended.	Rate per Scholar.	Number of Scholars.	Amount expended.	Rate per Scholar.
1841–'42	6,433	$21,314 80	$ 3,31	5,968	$12,457 25	$2 09
1842–'43	6,823	7,442 33	1,09	6,355	10,210 18	1 61
1843–'44	7,533	53,551 56	7,11	7,540	9,926 14	1 32
1844–'45	7,935	48,414 45	6,10	8,173	12,502 27	1 53
1845-'46	8,511	46,338 80	5,44	8,599	16,570 86	1 93
1846–'47	8,513	62,451 61	7,34	9,003	34,592 02	3 84
1847–'48	8,836	90,153 02	10,20	10,060	39,290 46	3 90
1848–'49	9,114	35,567 24	3,90	10,657	35,923 72	3 37
1849–'50	9,332	63,964 46	6,85	11,257	17,756 86	1 58
1850–'51	9,694	29,969 14	3,09	11,949	51,010 69	4 27

Average amount expended annually for the last ten years on the High and the Grammar School estates, - - - - - -	$ 45,916 74
Average amount expended annually for the last ten years on the Primary School estates, - - - - - - - - - -	24,024 04
Whole amount expended during the last ten years on the High and the Grammar School estates, - - - - - - -	459,167 41
Whole amount expended during the last ten years on the Primary School Estates, - - - - - - - - - - - -	240,240 45
Total amount expended during the last ten years on the Public School estates, - - - - - - - - - - -	699,407 86

AMOUNT *annually expended for all Public School purposes, except the building and the alteration of School Houses, for the last ten years.*

Years.	Number of Scholars.	Tuition and Incidental Expenses.	Rate per Scholar.
1841–'42	12,401	$ 120,388 48	$ 9,71
1842–'43	13,178	128,696 83	9,77
1843–'44	15,073	135,796 62	9,01
1844–'45	16,108	150,347 07	9,33
1845–'46	17,110	165,233 50	9,66
1846–'47	17,516	192,366 35	10,98
1847–'48	18,896	219,330 80	11,61
1848–'49	19,771	232,662 48	11,77
1849–'50	20,589	235,357 01	11,43
1850–'51	21,643	244,933 89	11,32

Average number of scholars in all the Schools during the last ten years,	17,228
The whole amount expended for all School purposes exclusive of School Houses, for the last ten years, is - - - - -	$1,825,113 03
The average amount of these expenses per scholar, - -	10 59
" " rate of increase of scholars per annum, - -	7 1-2 per cent.
" " " " " in the above expenses, is - -	10 2-5 " "
The entire increase of scholars for the last ten years, - -	75 " "
" " " in the above expenses for the last ten years,	103 " "

The amount of Taxes assessed on Real and Personal Estates in the City of Boston, for the past ten years, and the proportion of the same expended for Public Schools have been as follows :—

1841–2.

Valuation of Real Estate, - - - - - -	$61,963,000.00
Valuation of Personal Estates, - - - - -	36,043,600.00
Total valuation, - - - - - - -	98,006,600.00
Tax at 60 cents per $100, - - - - - -	588,039.60
Number of Polls 18,950 at $1.50, - - -	28,372.50
Total Tax 1841–2, - - - - - - -	616,41,210
Whole amount expended for Schools, - - -	154,260.53
Proportion of Tax expended for Schools, - -	25 per cent.

1842–3.

Valuation of Real Estate, - - - - - -	65,499,900.00
Valuation of Personal Estates, - - - - -	41,223,700.00
Total Valuation, - - - - - - -	106,723,700.00
Tax at 57 cents per $100, - - - - - -	608,325.09
Number of Polls 19,636 at $1.50, - - -	29,454.00
Total Tax for 1842–3, - - - - - -	637,779.09
Whole amount expended for Schools, - - -	138,771.93
Proportion of Tax expended for Schools, - -	21.7 per cent.

1843–4.

Valuation of Real Estate, - - - - - -	$67,673,400.00
Valuation of Personal Estates, - - - - -	42,372,600.00
Total Valuation, - - - - - - -	110,046,000.00
Tax at 62 cents per $100, - - - - - -	682,285,20
Number of Polls 20,063, at $1.50, - - -	30,094.50
Total Tax for 1843–4, - - - - - -	712,379.70
Whole amount expended for Schools, - - -	201,256 26
Proportion of Tax expended for Schools, - -	28.2 per cent.

1844–5.

Valuation of Real Estate, - - - - - -	$72,048,000.00
Valuation of Personal Estates, - - - - -	46,402,300.00
Total Valuation, - - - - - - -	118,450,300.00
Tax at 60 cents per $100, - - - - - -	710,701.80
Number of Polls 22,339 at $1.50, - - -	33,508.00
Total Tax for 1844–5, - - - - - -	744,210.30
Whole amount expended for Schools, - - -	205,277.68
Proportion of Tax expended for Schools, - -	27.6 per cent.

1845-6.

Valuation of Real Estate, - - - - - -	$81,991,400.00
Valuation of Personal Estate, - - - - -	53,957,300.00
Total Valuation, - - - - - - -	135,948,700.00
At 57 cents per $100, - - - - - -	774,907.59
Number of Polls 24,287 at $1.50, - - -	36,430.00
Total Tax for 1845-6, - - - - - -	811,337.59
Whole amount expended for Schools, - - -	226,019.09
Proportion of Tax expended for Schools, - -	27.8 per cent.

1846-7.

Valuation of Real Estate, - - - - - -	$90,119,600.00
Valuation of Personal Estate, - - - - -	58,720,000.00
Total Valuation, - - - - - - -	148,839,600,00
At 60 cents per $100, - - - - - -	893,037.60
Number of Polls 25,974 at $1.50, - - -	38,961.00
Total Tax for 1846-7, - - - - - -	931,998.60
Whole amount expended for Schools, - - -	298,619.49
Proportion of Tax expended for Schools, - -	32 per cent.

1847-8.

Valuation of Real Estate, - - - - - -	$97,764,500.00
Valuation of Personal Estate, - - - - -	64,595,900.00
Total Valuation, - - - - - - -	162,360,400.00
At 60 cents per $100, - - - - - -	974,162.40
Number of Polls 27,008 at $1.50, - - -	40,512.00
Total Tax for 1847-8, - - - - - -	1,014,674.40
Whole amount expended for Schools, - - -	348,887.40
Proportion of Tax expended for Schools, - -	34.3 per cent.

1848-9.

Valuation of Real Estate, - - - - - -	$100,403,200.00
Valuation of Personal Estate, - - - - -	67,324,800.00
Total Valuation, - - - - - - -	167,728,000.00
At 65 cents per $100, - - - - - -	1,090,232.00
Number of Polls 27,726 at $1.50, - - -	41,589.00
Total Tax for 1848-9, - - - - - -	1,131,821.00
Whole amount expended for Schools, - - -	303,581.67
Proportion of Tax expended for Schools, - -	26.8 per cent.

1849–50.

Valuation of Real Estate, - - - - - -	$102,827,500.00
Valuation of Personal Estate, - - - - -	71,352,700.00
Total Valuation, - - - - - - - -	174,180,200.00
At 65 cents per $100, - - - - - -	1,132,171.30
Number of Polls 28,363 at $1.50, - - -	42,544.50
Total Tax for 1849–50, - - - - - - -	1,174,715.80
Whole amount expended for Schools, - - -	311,494.95
Proportion of Tax expended for Schools, - -	26.5 per cent.

1850–1.

Valuation of Real Estate, - - - - - -	$105,093,400.00
Valuation of Personal Estate, - - - - -	74,907,100.00
Total Valuation, - - - - - - - -	180,000,500.00
At 68 cents per $100, - - - - - -	1,224,003.40
Number of Polls 28,018 at $1.50, - - -	42,027.00
Total Tax for 1850–51, - - - - - - -	1,266,030.40
Whole amount expended for Schools, - - -	325,126.60
Proportion of Tax expended for Schools, - -	25.7 per cent.

A TABULAR REPRESENTATION

OF THE

PRESENT CONDITION OF BOSTON,

IN RELATION TO

Railroad Facilities, Foreign Commerce, Population, Wealth, Manufactures, etc.; with a few Statements relative to the

COMMERCE OF THE CANADAS.

Prepared from the most reliable sources, under the direction of a Sub-Committee of the Joint Special Committee on the Railroad Celebration.

The following statistics have been compiled with as much care and accuracy as the limited time allowed would admit. Even when not obtained from *official sources*, they are believed to be nearly, if not perfectly, correct.

As, in some instances, it is designed to show the advantages possessed by Boston, as compared with other cities, great pains has been taken to make the collection as impartial as possible, and to give to those cities the benefit of prospective improvements in their communications with the Canadas and the West.

Much labor has been bestowed upon the accompanying map, to make it as accurate as the best available sources of information would permit. No doubt errors and omissions may be found in it; but it is believed they are not of a character to affect its general correctness.

Free use has been made of an article on "Boston, as a Commercial Metropolis, in 1850," by E. H. Derby, Esq., originally published in Hunt's Merchants Magazine, for November, 1850.

At the close of the pamphlet, important conclusions are drawn from the facts it contains, and to these conclusions, with accompanying summary statements, it is hoped by the Committee, that special attention will be directed.

E. S. CHESBROUGH, *City Engineer*.

Boston, September 17th, 1851.

RAILWAYS AND STEAMERS.

"The growth of Boston and her environs, has been more rapid during the past ten years, than in any previous decade. The South has ascribed her progress principally to cotton mills. In common with commerce, the fisheries, and other manufactures, these have doubtless contributed to her increase; but the cotton business grew more rapidly in the preceding ten years, and is now less important than the manufactures of leather."

"The principal cause has undoubtedly been the construction of railways. These have given great facilities to her commerce, enlarged her market, attracted merchants, stimulated every branch of manufacture, created a demand for houses and stores, and advanced the value of real estate. September 30th, 1839, there were but one hundred and sixty-seven miles of railway radiating from Boston." In 1851, Boston is wedded to more than one thousand miles of railway in Massachusetts, more than eighteen hundred in the five other States of New England, and six hundred and fifty more in New York. "In all, three thousand miles. In September, 1839, her railway horizon was bounded by Salem, Bradford, Nashua, and Providence. It now encircles a web spreading over Massachusetts, and extending to the Kennebec, the St. Lawrence and the Lakes. This great system of railways has been principally planned and directed by her sagacity. Boston invested largely in lines to the North, and in distant railways, —the Michigan Central, Mad River, Reading and Wilmington; and she also expended five millions in an aqueduct, and as much more on factory cities. The aqueduct has been in operation three years. Her last investments promise to be remunerative, and will bring with them a strong current of trade from newly acquired territory. Railroads have become the great interest of Boston, and her investment in them exceeds fifty millions of dollars.

From the American Railway Times, of July, 1851.

NAMES, LENGTH, AND COST, OF NEW ENGLAND RAILROADS.

Names of Railways.	No of miles in operation, including branches.	No. of miles in course of construction.	Cost.
Maine.			
Androscoggin.		36	
Androscoggin and Kennebec,	55		$1,621,878
Atlantic and St. Lawrence,	70	86	1,500,000
Bangor and Piscataquis,	12		350,000
Buckfield Branch,	13		370,000
Calais and Baring,	6		100,000
Kennebec and Portland,	54	15	1,000,000
Machias Port,	8		100,000
Portland, Saco and Portsmouth,	52		1,293,640
York and Cumberland,	11	42	360,000
New Hampshire.			
Ashuelot,	24		510,000
Boston, Concord and Montreal,	76	17	1,567,073
Cheshire,	54		2,584,143
Cocheco,	18		500,000
Concord,	35		1,385,788
Concord and Claremont,	26	24	560,624
Contocook Valley,	14		219,450
Eastern, (included in Eastern (Mass.) Railway Company, operated by the latter Company.)			
Great Falls,	3		60,000
Great Falls and Conway,	12		300,000
Manchester and Lawrence,	26		717,543
New Hampshire Central,	26		600,000
Northern,	82		3,016,634
Portsmouth and Concord,	23	17	850,000
Sullivan,	25		673,500
Wilton,	11		600,000
Vermont.			
Bennington Branch,		6	100,000
Connecticut and Passumpsic,	60	54	1,500,000
Rutland and Burlington,	119		3,455,256
Rutland and Washington,	10		250,000

Troy and Rutland,		55	$ 550,000
Vermont Central,	115		5,081,767
Vermont and Canada,	38		1,200,000
Vermont Valley,	24		500,000
Western Vermont,		53	530,000
Massachusetts.			
Berkshire,	21		600,000
Boston and Lowell,	28		1,945,647
Boston and Maine,	83		4,021,607
Boston and Providence,	53		3,416,233
Boston and Worcester,	69		4,882,648
Cape Cod Branch,	29		626,543
Connecticut River,	52		1,798,825
Dorchester and Milton,	3		128,172
Eastern, (including Eastern (N. H.) which is operated by the former.)	75		3,624,152
Essex,	21		537,869
Fall River,	42		1,068,167
Fitchburg,	66		3,552,283
Fitchburg and Worcester,	14		259,074
Grand Junction,	6		763,844
Harvard Branch,	1		26,213
Lexington and West Cambridge,	7		242,161
Lowell and Lawrence,	12		333,254
Nashua and Lowell,	15		621,215
New Bedford and Taunton,	21		498,752
Newburyport,	9		106,825
Norfolk County,	26		1,060,990
Old Colony,	45		2,293,535
Peterboro' and Shirley,	14		272,647
Pittsfield and North Adams,	18		443,678
Providence and Worcester,	43		1,824,797
Salem and Lowell,	17		316,943
South Reading Branch,	8		231,601
South Shore,	11		420,434
Stockbridge and Pittsfield,	22		448,700
Stoney Brook,	13		265,527
Stoughton Branch,	4		93,433
Taunton Branch,	12		307,136
Troy and Greenfield,		67	
Vermont and Massachusetts,	77		3,406,244
Western,	156		9,963,709
West Stockbridge,	3		41,516
Worcester and Nashua,	46		1,410,198
Rhode Island.			
Plainfield and Providence,		30	
Providence and Stonington,	50		2,614,484

Connecticut.

Collingsville Branch,	11		$ 275,000
Hartford and New Haven,	62		1,650,000
Hartford, Providence and Fishkill,	32		1,500,000
Housatonic,	110		2,500,000
Housatonic Branch,	11		275,000
Middletown Branch,	10		250,000
Naugatuc,	62		2,000,000
New Haven and Northampton,	45		1,500,000
New London, Williamantic and Palmer,	66		1,250,000
New London and New Haven,		55	
New York and New Haven,	76		3,700,085
Norwich and Worcester,	66		2,598,514
Stonington and New London,		10	
Total in Connecticut,	551	65	$17,498,599

RECAPITULATION.

States.	No. Roads including Branches.	No. of miles in operation.	No. of miles in course of construction.	Cost.
Maine,	10	281	179	$6,695,518
New Hampshire,	15	455	58	16,145,755
Vermont,	9	366	168	13,467,013
Massachusetts,	37	1142	67	51,884,572
Rhode Island,	2	50	30	2,614,484
Connecticut,	13	551	65	17,498,599
	87	2845	567	$106,305,941

[From the Boston Daily Evening Transcript.]

TABLE, *showing the* GROSS RECEIPTS *and the* NUMBER OF PASSENGERS *on the Massachusetts Railroads, for the years* 1848, 1849 *and* 1850.

Names of Roads.	Gross Receipts.			Number of Passengers.		
	1848.	1849.	1850.	1848.	1849.	1850.
Western,	$ 1,332,068	$ 1,343,810	$ 1,369,514	405,610	435,800	467,068
Boston and Worcester,	716,284	703,361	759,947	807,140	959,560	1,001,989
Boston and Maine,	511,628	522,336	594,963	1,057,570	1,205,000	1,221,071
Eastern,	479,158	517,929	539,076	1,021,170	1,049,110	1,006,552
Fitchburg,	486,266	493,060	551,607	745,830	875,410	1,080,286
Boston and Providence,	354,375	354,332	370,727	569,130	573,360	591,949
Cheshire,	80,034	172,107	208,414	40,090	94,990	118,952
Norwich and Worcester,	218,073	236,198	261,259	151,100	172,000	177,603
Old Colony,	227,350	275,067	296,171	552,200	773,120	684,263
Boston and Lowell,	461,339	416,488	406,421	525,760	593,830	558,993
Providence and Worcester,	193,844	217,254	202,751	305,480	306,740	305,938
Connecticut River,	165,242	192,072	191,587	299,870	325,520	305,900
Fall River,	184,344	174,043	210,081	241,110	252,770	273,957
Nashua and Lowell,	169,187	156,435	129,617	254,970	258,860	261,459
Cape Cod,	35,635	51,282	56,856	58,800	66,820	69,311
New Bedford and Taunton,	136,152	134,390	144,473	94,550	97,740	104,591
Pittsfield and North Adams,	28,320	31,358	32,605	33,370	34,010	28,485
Lowell and Lawrence,	20,744	42,533	38,758	68,660	131,600	99,202
Taunton Branch,	108,101	108,398	114,466	101,460	100,290	106,886
Vermont and Massachusetts,	-	145,118	177,695	-	146,300	168,054
Worcester and Nashua,	-	108,126	144,439	-	145,400	186,723
Norfolk County,	-	26,250	57,841	-	35,000	64,592
Salem and Lowell,	-	-	15,505	-	-	11,687
Fitchburg and Worcester,	-	-	21,431	-	-	41,528
South Reading Branch,	-	-	9,124	-	-	36,624
Total,	$ 5,908,144	$ 6,421,947	$ 6,903,328	7,333,870	8,633,230	8,973,681

[From the Daily Evening Traveller.]

STEAMERS.

"The following tables, carefully prepared from official documents, will show the amount of freight business, which has been done by the British Cunard line of Steamships, from the time when the line commenced running to Boston, in 1840, to the first of January last.

"The original design contemplated little beyond the transportation of the mails and passengers. Hence, the freights were very small during the first year, and the duties trifling. From the small amount paid in 1840, namely, 2,928 dollars, the duties have swelled to 1,322,383 dollars,—the amount paid last year. The smallest amount ever paid by any one steamer, was 29 dollars and 38 cents only, by the Acadia, on her first trip in 1840. The largest amount was paid by the America, in February, 1850, namely, 217,483 dollars. There have been eight arrivals which paid over 100,000 dollars, and three which have paid over 200,000 dollars each. The Hibernia, the Cambria, and the Caledonia, have each paid over a million of dollars revenue to the government. It is probable that during the whole time, the steamers have brought to Boston, 12,000 passengers."

TABLE,

Showing the number of trips made by each steamer annually, from 1840, to 1851, and the amount of duties paid by each, during the year.

Duties Paid.	Year.	No. of Trips.	Amount.
By the Acadia,	1840,	3	$1,473.06
Britannia,		3	864.17
Caledonia,		2	591.76
Acadia,	1841,	5	21,312.94
Britannia,		5	14,592.32
Caledonia,	1841,	5	16,925.37
Columbia,		6	20,978.60
Acadia,	1842,	4	21,417.48
Britannia,		6	46,415.32
Caledonia,		4	23,492.65
Columbia,		4	29,649.22
Acadia,	1843,	5	133,617.53
Britannia,		3	103.817.84
Caledonia,		5	132,845.24
Columbia,		2	33,932.11
Hibernia,		5	236,359.33
Acadia,	1844,	5	198,511.04
Britannia,		5	186,289.29
Caledonia,		5	172,900.68
Hibernia,		5	358,497.29

Duties Paid.	Year.	No. of Trips.	Amount.
By the Acadia,	1845,	2	$93,510.05
Britannia,		4	152,262.38
Caledonia,		4	127,547,78
Cambria,		6	361,598.42
Hibernia,		4	288,074.12
Acadia,	1846,	1	26,860.36
Britannia,		4	149,351.23
Caledonia,		5	171,701.50
Cambria,		5	351,679.23
Hibernia,		5	348,139.34
Acadia,	1847,	1	37,546.12
Britannia,		4	161,910.70
Caledonia,		4	146,164.07
Cambria,		5	382,946.35
Hibernia,		6	471,404.54
Acadia,	1848,	5	134,963.59
Britannia,		4	105,627.12
Caledonia,		3	79,312.83
Cambria,		2	70,473.14
Hibernia,		2	71,954.31
Niagara,		4	142,930.06
America,		1	15,200.60
Europa,		1	28,716.85
America,	1849,	4	252,791.93
Caledonia,		5	138,180.56
Cambria,		4	199,789.97
Canada,		1	40,426.91
Hibernia,		2	62,522.08
Niagara,		2	172,034.27
Europa,		4	95,962.79
America,	1850,	4	380,980.95
Asia,		2	131,827.20
Cambria,		3	81,275.75
Canada,		4	93,492.15
Hibernia,		3	83,432.10
Niagara,		3	444,795.65
Europa,		2	106,579.50
Asia,	1851,	1	27,758.75
America,		5	383,158.95
Cambria,		2	50,667.55
Canada,		7	588,147.15
Europa,		5	472,102.45
Niagara,		3	283,224.45

SUMMARY OF THE FOREGOING TABLE.

Year.	Trips Made.	Duties Paid.
In 1840,	8	$ 2,928.99
In 1841,	21	73,809.23
In 1842,	18	120,974.67
In 1843,	20	640,572.05
In 1844,	20	916,198.30
In 1845,	20	1,022,992.75
In 1846,	20	1,047,731.75
In 1847,	20	1,199,971.78
In 1848,	22	649,178.50
In 1849,	22	961,708.51
In 1850,	21	1,322,383.30
In 1851,	23	1,805,059.30
	235	$9,763,509.13

TABLE OF DISTANCES.

From Liverpool, via Halifax.

To Halifax by Steamer, - - - - - -	2,500 miles.
Quebec (via proposed railroad from Halifax) -	3,135 "
Melbourne, - - - - - - - -	3,225 "
Montreal, - - - - - - - -	3,300 "
Toronto, - - - - - - - -	3,620 "
Detroit, - - - - - - - -	3,870 "
Chicago, - - - - - - - -	4,150 "
Galena, - - - - - - - -	4,333 "

From Liverpool, via Boston.

To Boston by Steamer, - - - - - - - -	2,900 miles.
Montreal, by Railroad from Boston, - - - -	3,226 "
Albany " " " - - -	3,100 "
Buffalo, by Railroad from Albany, - - -	3,421 "
Detroit, through Rochester, Niagara and London, (C. W.) - - - - - - - -	3,671 "
Cleveland, by Railroad through Albany, and Buffalo,	3,596 "
Chicago, via Cleveland, - - - - - -	3,947 "
Galena, - - - - - - - - - -	4,130 "
Cincinnati, via Buffalo, Cleveland and Columbus,	3,852 "
St. Louis, via Cleveland, Bellefontaine and Indianapolis, - - - - - - -	4,097 "

From Liverpool, via New York.

To New York by Steamer, - - - - - -	3,100 miles.
Albany, (by Hudson River Railroad) - -	3,244 "
Montreal, by shortest proposed route, - -	3,475 "
Buffalo, via Albany, - - - - - -	3,565 "
Detroit, via Albany, Niagara and New London (C. W.) - - - - - - - - -	3,815 "
To Cleveland, via Philadelphia and Pittsburg (shortest route,) - - - - - - - -	3,683 "
Chicago, via Cleveland, - - - - -	4,034 "
Galena, - - - - - - - - -	4,217 "
Cincinnati, via Philadelphia, and proposed Railroad through Wheeling, between Pittsburg and Columbus, - - - - - - - -	3,854 "
St. Louis, via Pittsburg and Bellefontaine, - -	4,139 "

NOTE. In the Report to the Stockholders of the East Boston Company, received after the above table was prepared, the Agent of the Cunard line of Steamships, gives the distances from Liverpool, by Steamer, as follows, viz:

To Halifax, - - - - - - - - -	2,508 miles.
To Boston, direct, - - - - - - -	2,856 "
To New York, direct, - - - - - - -	3,073 "

Were these distances adopted, instead of those in the table, the comparison would be still more favorable to Boston.

The following statistics were taken by the Day and Night Police force, on Saturday, September 6th, 1851, under the direction of the City Marshal. The force, consisting of 55 men, was stationed at 6½ o'clock, A. M., and continued without intermission to keep regular count, until 7½ P. M.

The vehicles which entered the City by the various routes, not including those that came from East or South Boston, numbered 6,626. The number that went out, 7,063.

The number of Railway Passenger Trains, which entered the City, was 116. The number that went out, 120. The number of Freight Trains, which entered, was 39. The number that went out, 38. Total Passenger and Freight Trains, 313.

41,729 persons came into the City, and 42,313 persons went out, as follows:

	CAME IN.	WENT OUT.
By Passenger Trains, - -	11,963	12,952
Freight Trains, - -	308	307
Vehicles, - - -	14,942	15,964
On Foot, - - - -	14,310	12,887
On Horseback, - - -	127	124
With Handcarts, - - -	79	79
Total,	41,729 persons.	42,313 persons.

FOREIGN COMMERCE.

Year.	Foreign Arrivals.	Imports.	Exports.	Duties.
1842	1,738	$12,633,713	$7,226,104	$2,780,186
1843	1,716	20,662,567	7,265,712	3,491,019
1844	2,174	22,141,788	8,294,726	5,934,945
1845	2,305	21,591,877	9,370,851	5,249,634
1846	2,090	21,284,800	8,245,524	4,872,570
1847	2,739	28,279,651	12,118,587	5,448,362
1848	3,009	23,388,475	10,001,819	4,908.872
1849	3,111	24,117,175	8,843,974	5,031,995
1850	2,885	29,909,376	9,332,306	6,127,817
1851	2,872	31,850,558	9,342,336	6,496,527

SHIPPING OF BOSTON.—TONNAGE.

Year.	Registered.	Enrolled.	Total.
1842	157,116	36,385	193,502
1843	165,482	37,116	202,599
1844	175,330	35,554	210,885
1845	187,812	37,290	228,103
1846	192,879	42,185	235,064
1847	210,775	44,038	254,812
1848	232,769	45,100	277,869
1849	247,336	45,123	292,459
1850	270,710	42,482	313,192
1851	298,776	44,532	343,308

FISHERIES.

In 1849, 204,000 barrels of Whale and Sperm Oil, three fifths of the entire Fishery of the Union, were brought into Massachusetts; also, 231,856 barrels of Mackerel. A large portion of these imports find their way to Boston.

For more than a century, Boston has been the chief mart for the sale of dried Fish, and a large proportion of the Fishermen engaged in both the Cod and Mackerel fishery, resort to Boston, for outfits and sales.

CATTLE TRADE.

Large sales of Live Stock are made weekly at Brighton, near Boston, brought principally from other States, by Railway. Many Horses are also brought by the same conveyance. Cattle are killed in the environs.

SALES AT BRIGHTON.

[Compiled from the Daily Advertiser.]

Year.	Beef Cattle.	Store Cattle.	Sheep.	Swine.	Total estimated amount of sales.
1845	48,910	13,275	107,960	56,890	$1,893,648
1846	38,670	15,164	105,350	44,940	1,871,113
1847	43,425	20,738	133,550	62,015	2,719,462
1848	40,784	20,550	146,755	87,690	2,830,302
1849	46,465	20,085	148,955	80,120	2,976,265
1850	42,830	27,820	164,170	78,330	2,989,902
1851	53,020	23,810	183,880	80,830	3,502,320

Another large Market for Cattle and other Live Stock, is now held weekly at Cambridge. Large quantities of Pork in bulk are in the winter conveyed by railway to Boston, from the interior of New York.

EXPANSION OF BOSTON.

"A peninsula less than one square mile in extent, was soon found insufficient for Boston; and the State, in 1804, annexed to her Dorchester Point, a peninsula containing about six hundred acres. To this she is wedded by two travelled, besides railroad, bridges. At a latter period, ferries were established to Noddle's Island, an area of six hundred acres, and this island now forms a ward of the city, and is named East Boston. Some hundred acres have also been reclaimed from the sea; but these narrow limits, less than two miles square, proved entirely inadequate, and have been long exceeded."

"The population of Boston, outside of her chartered limits, already equals the population within. We should do injustice to Boston, were we to confine her to such narrow bounds, or within such arbitrary lines. Her true limits as a commercial metropolis, are those marked out by her business men for their stores, piers, shops and dwellings—the space occupied by those who resort daily to her banks and warehouses, or meet at her exchange. How is it with her sister cities? Philadelphia, by the last census, embraced within her chartered limits less than half her inhabitants; the residue were diffused through the extensive districts of Spring Garden, Moyamensing, and

Northern Liberties. She virtually extends, under different charters, from Richmond, six miles down the Delaware."

"New York reaches fourteen miles from King's Bridge to the Battery."

"New Orleans embraces three distinct municipalities, on the crescent of the Mississippi."

"London, the queen of commerce, contains but six hundred acres, and less than one hundred and thirty thousand people in her chartered limits; but her streets stretch eight miles on the Thames. Within her metropolitan districts are eighteen square miles of buildings, and three millions of people."

"Boston, with less scope than New York, has, like New Orleans, Philadelphia and London, overstept her 'sea girt isles.' She has attached herself to the main by one wide natural avenue, the Neck, paved and planted with trees; by one granite structure, the Western Avenue, a mile and a half in length; by six bridges, seven railways, and three ferries, one terminating in a railway. Seven railways branch into sixteen, and ten avenues divide into thirty, within the first nine miles from her Exchange. These diverge like a fan, and on the streets thus made, is found a large population under separate municipalities. As land rises in value, hotels, offices, and blocks of stores usurp the place of dwellings. The old residents, leaving the low and reclaimed land to foreign laborers, plant themselves in the suburbs. There they build tasteful houses, with flower plats and gardens, availing of the frequent omnibuses, or of special trains, run almost hourly, and commuting for passage at $20 to $40 a year, they reach their stores and offices in the morning, and at night sleep with their wives and children in the suburbs. No time is lost, for they read the morning and evening journals as they go and return. Some of the wards appropriate for stores, thus rise in value, but diminish in population. The suburbs extend, and the commercial community grows in a widening semicircle."

Dr. Lardner well remarks, in his late treatise on railways, "The population of a great capital is condensed into a small compass, by the difficulty and inconvenience of passing over long distances; hence has arisen the densely populated state of great cities like London and Paris. If the speed, by which persons can be transported from place to place, be doubled, the same population can, without inconvenience, be spread over four times the area; if the speed be tripled, it may occupy nine times the area."

"Boston, the first of our American cities to adopt improved modes of locomotion—instance her early Stages, her Middlesex Canal, and Quincy Railway,—is entitled to avail of these laws of science, and in computing her population and wealth, should embrace the surrounding districts within nine miles, or half an hour's distance, equivalent to a two miles' walk from her exchange."

TABLE OF INCREASE OF POPULATION AND WEALTH OF BOSTON AND VICINITY.

The following table exhibits the population and wealth of the metropolitian district of Boston, by the census and valuation of 1850 and 1840, with the growth of each.

This district is sixteen miles in length, by nine and a half average width; about one fourth of it is occupied by water, marsh, or rocky hills, too steep for building.

Name of District.	Distance from Exchange.	Population by State Census, 1840.	Population by U. States Census, 1840.	Population by State Census, 1850.	Assessed Valuation, 1840.	Assessed Valuation, 1850.
Boston,		83,979	93,383	138,788	$ 94,581,600	$ 179,525,000
Roxbury,	2	8,310	9,087	18,316	3,257,503	13,712,800
Charlestown,	2	10,872	11,484	15,933	4,033,176	8,862,250
Cambridge,	3	8,127	8,409	14,825	4,479,501	11,434,458
Brookline,	3	1,123	1,365	2,353	743,963	5,382,000
Chelsea,	3	2,182	2,390	6,151	696,781	3,472,650
Dorchester,	4	4,458	4,875	7,578	1,691,245	7,199,750
Malden,	4	3,027	3,351	5,017	586,136	1,461,436
Medford,	4	2,275	2,478	3,581	1,095,195	2,128,470
Brighton,	5	1,405	1,425	2,253	458,485	1,146,212
Somerville,	5	new	new	3,110	new	2,778,125
West Cambridge,	5	1,338	1,363	2,120	472,423	2,330,281
North Chelsea,	5	new	new	819	new	772,000
Melrose,	5	new	new	1,190	new	483,419
Watertown,	6	1,896	1,810	2,592	973,835	2,614,100
Winchester,	6	new	new	1,320	new	866,432
Stoneham,	6	1,007	1,017	2,043	217,960	539,000
Milton,	7	1,684	1,822	2,222	663,247	1,200,800
Woburn,	7	2,931	2,993	3,788	987,388	2,241,144
Quincy,	8	3,309	3,486	4,958	912,105	2,200,000
Saugus,	8	1,212	1,098	1,505	208,856	359,305
Dedham,	9	3,157	3,290	4,379	1,218,548	3,509,180
Newton,	9	3,027	3,351	5,017	897,255	3,793,083
Waltham,	9	2,593	2,504	4,483	1,069,171	2,973,750
Lexington,	9	1,559	1,642	1,920	561,549	1,469,551
Lynn,	9	9,075	9,367	13,613	1,319,656	4,191,648
		158,546	171,992	269,874	$ 120.114,574	$ 266,646,844

CITY TAXES.

The Amount Assessed for Taxes has been as follows:—

Years.	Amount of tax assessed.*	Rate on $1,000.	Property assessed.
1840	$ 546,742	$ 5.50	$ 94,581,600
1841	616,412	6.00	98,006,600
1842	637,779	5.70	105,723,700
1843	712,379	6.20	110,056,000
1844	744,210	6.00	118,450,300
1845	811,338	5 70	135,948,700
1846	931,998	6.90	141,839,600
1847	1,014,674	6.00	162,360,400
1848	1,131,821	6.50	167,728,000
1849	1,174,715	6.50	174,180,200
1850	1,236,030	6.80	179,525,000
1851	1,358,296	7.00	187,947,000

* The amount of tax assessed includes the Poll Tax.

Number of Polls, and State Valuation of Personal and Real Estate in Massachusetts, for the years 1840 and 1850.

Counties.	Valuation of 1840.		Valuation of 1850.	
	Polls.	Property.	Polls.	Property.
Suffolk,	19,078	$110,000,000.00	33,705	$217,587,172.00
Essex,	24,006	31,110,204.00	30,816	56,556,466.89
Middlesex,	28,045	37,592,082.00	39,819	83,264,719.50
Worcester,	25,859	29,804,316.00	34,671	55,497,794.00
Hampshire,	7,934	7,298,351.00	8,855	13,331,240.00
Hampden,	9,935	10,188,423.71	13,439	22,621,220.77
Franklin,	7,500	6,548,694.00	7,866	11,211,309.00
Berkshire,	10,911	9,546,926.76	12,264	17,197,607.00
Norfolk,	14,041	15,522,527.00	19,630	47,034,521.56
Bristol,	14,821	19,493,685.84	18,382	39,243,560.00
Plymouth,	12,140	10,694,719.00	14,410	19,200,668.00
Barnstable,	8,002	4,896,683.00	8,104	8,897,349.74
Dukes,	1,104	1,107,343.00	1,162	1,698,005.00
Nantucket,	2,532	6,074,374.00	2,019	4,595,362.00
Total,	185,908	$299,878,329.31	245,142	$597,936,995.46

MANUFACTURES OF MASSACHUSETTS.

The products of the principal branches in 1845 were,—

Miscellaneous, - - - - - - -	$ 19,357,000
Boots, Shoes and Leather, - - - - - -	18,635,000
Cotton Goods, (817,473 spindles) - - - -	12,193,000
Woollen and Worsted Goods, - - - - - -	10,366,000
Manufactures of Wood, including ships and carriages,	11,596,000
Manufactures of Metals, Tools, &c., - - -	8,024,000
Oil, Candles and Soap, - - - - - - -	4,931,000
Hats, Caps and Bonnets, - - - - -	2,384,000
Paper, - - - - - - - - - -	1,750,000
Cordage, - - - - - - - - -	906,000
Glass, - - - - - - - - - -	758,000
Total, - - - - - - - - - -	$91,000,000

No valuation of the same products has been taken since 1845, but it is believed their increase since that time, is not less than 30 per cent.

STATEMENT, *showing the Progress of Agricultural Imports into the United States from Canada, by Inland Ports, for the years* 1840, 1845, 1849, *and up to September* 30*th*, 1850, *distinguishing the articles.*

ARTICLES.		1840.		1845.		1849.		Three Quarters of 1850.	
Products of Agriculture.		Quantities.	Value.	Quantities.	Value.	Quantities.	Value.	Quantities.	Value.
Pork, salted and fresh,	pounds,	553	$ 27		$	5,940	$ 658	4,656	$ 802
do do do do	barrels,					44		87	
Beef, do do do	pounds,	829	29			1,620	7,115	5,230	2,649
do do do do	barrels,					4,465		806	
Butter,	pounds,	260	21	819	92	550,856	43,554	272,610	29,408
Wool,	do	254	30	60,843	5,437	497,539	46,431	365,151	51,459
Hides and Skins,	number,		3,850	1,482	2,409	98,615	14,671	86,993	10,253
Hams, shoulders, and bacon,	pounds,							77,071	2,361
Eggs,	dozens,			5,240	234	90,768	4,487	176,086	9,391
Poultry,	number,							54	
Horses,	do	8	575	445	12,806	4,935	135,577	4,754	156,804
Horned Cattle,	do			110	1,526	16,285	53,978	5,391	51,512
Flour of Wheat,	barrels,	1	4	5	14	221,422	812,141	192,039	716,590
do do	pounds,					1,000		4,268	
Wheat,	bushels,	286	268	135	125	830,419	573,172	647,934	647,934
Rye,	barrels,					217	8,696	746	1,617
do	bushels,			7	3	22,105		49	
Barley, pearl and malt,	do	30	26	4,301	1,342	6,822	3,366	58,898	23,266
Oats and Oatmeal,	do	73	57	69	52	327,863	83,883	445,822	85,048
do do	barrels,	19		11		1,246		269	
Peas and Beans,	bushels,			33	16	74,785	36,650	30,308	18,379
Potatoes,	do	10	10	1,564	219	9,665	2,886	12,927	3,079
Clover and Grass Seed,	do	307	307	6,814	3,511	22,664	18,167	19,505	47,835
Flax Seed,	do			2,244	1,150	5,017	3,365	1,631	2,251
Total value in the years,		1840	$ 5,204	1845	$ 28,936	1849	$ 1,848,797	1850	$ 1,860,633

Statement of the aggregate value of Imports into the United States, from Canada, as entered in the Custom House Books, at the following ports of entry, for the year ending December 31st, 1850.

District and Port of Chicago, - - - - - -	$ 4,345
District and Port of Detroit, - - - - - -	103,556
District of Miami and Port of Toledo, - - -	16,771
District and Port of Sandusky, - - - - - -	31,452
District of Cuyahoga and Port of Cleveland, - -	237,177
District of Presque Isle and Port of Erie, - - -	2,831
District and Port of Buffalo Creek, - - - - -	446,900
District of Niagara and Port of Lewiston, - - -	61,807
District of Genesee and Port of Rochester, - - -	100,189
District and Port of Oswego, - - - - - -	2,087,622
District and Port of Sackett's Harbor, - - - -	26,137
District and Port of Cape Vincent, - - - - -	53,079
District of Oswegatchie and Port of Ogdensburg, - -	211,925
District of Champlain and Port of Plattsburg, - -	314,555
District of Vermont and Port of Burlington, - -	821,094
District of Bath, in Maine, including line of Canada Railroad, - - - - - - - - -	4,866
Total, - - - - - - - - -	$4,524,306

COMMERCE OF CANADA, 1850.

	EXPORTS.	IMPORTS.
Great Britain, ...	$ 6,085,119.05	$ 9,631,920.80
North American Colonies, ...	808,776.25	385,619.90
British West Indies, ...	8,376.00	4,451.85
United States of America, . . .	4,951,159.58	6,594,860.48
Other Foreign Countries, ...	108,281.27	365,215.67
Total, ...	$11,961,712.15	$ 16,982,068.70

CONCLUSIONS AND SUMMARY STATEMENTS.

An inspection of the foregoing tables and statements, will show that Massachusetts has, up to this time, constructed 1,150 miles of Railroad, at a cost of $52,000,000 ; and that the other New England States have constructed over 1,700 miles more, at a cost of $55,000,000. To these might be added the Northern N. Y. (or Ogdensburg) Railroad, which is virtually a New England road, making a total of about 3,000 miles of Railroad, constructed at a cost of upwards of 110,000,000.

The gross earnings in 1850, of all the Railroads in Massachusetts, and of those that are partly in Massachusetts and partly in adjoining

States, were $6,903,328. The next earnings during the same time, were $3,480,347. The cost of these Roads was $53,264,000. The net income was therefore more than 6 per cent. on the total cost.

The number of passengers transported over these Roads during the same time, was 8,973,681, which gives an average of 28,761 a day, for 312 days.

The annual amount of duties, paid on freight brought by the Cunard Steamers to Boston, shows a constant yearly increase from $73,809, in 1841, to $1,322,383, in 1850, except for the year 1848, when the New York freight by the Steamers ceased to pass through Boston, and the amount of duties declined from $1,199,972 to $649,178.

Assuming Liverpool as the starting point from Europe, for the trade of the Canadas and the Great West, the "Table of Distances" shows that Boston is on the shortest route, for a very extensive territory, including the cities of Montreal, Albany, Buffalo, Cleveland, Kingston, Toronto, Detroit, Chicago, St. Louis and Galena. If the exact distances across the Atlantic, given by the Agent of the Cunard Line, and the improvements they are making between Albany and Buffalo, by which it is said the present travelled route will be shortened 30 miles, be taken into account, even Cincinnati will be 50 miles nearer Liverpool, through Boston, than through any other important seaport. If Cincinnati be nearer, it follows that every other point below on the Ohio River must be. These are natural advantages, which an accurate knowledge of the geographical position of Boston, and of the topographical features of the territory embraced in this comparison, will show, can never be taken from this City.

As Steamers on the Ocean, and Railways on Land, are now the modes which must be adopted by all who would compete successfully for the commerce of Great Britain and this Country, nothing but a failure of that enterprise which has ever characterized this City can prevent Boston from securing her full share.

The Foreign Commerce of Boston, including exports and imports, has increased from $19,859,817 in 1842, to $39,241,682 in 1850. Its Shipping has increased during the same time, from 193,502 tons, to 312,192 tons. The expansion and growth of population and wealth of Boston and the neighboring towns, in which the families of so many of her business men reside, has been very remarkable during the last ten years. In 1840, the population of this district was, by the State Census, 158,546; by the same Census in 1850, it was 269,874. The assessed valuation in 1840, was $120,114,574, in 1850 it was $266,646,844. This population and wealth must preserve to Boston her station among the three first cities of the Union.

The rapid growth of Boston and vicinity, has not been at the expense of the rest of the State; for the population of Massachusetts has increased from 737,700 in 1840, to 948,665 in 1850, by the U. S. Census; and her property valuation, from $229,828,399, to $597,936,995, or about double the former amount.

The imports from Canada, by Inland Ports into this Country, have increased in value, from $5,204, in 1840, to $1,860,636, for three quarters of 1850, or to about $2,500,000 per annum. If this remarkable increase took place before our Railway system reached the Canadas, what may not be expected, now that it is completed and in operation both to Montreal and to Ogdensburg?

On the accompanying map will be found a plan of "Boston Harbor and Railroad Termini." An inspection of it will show how all the Railroads entering the City have been, or may be, connected, by means of the Grand Junction Railroad, and the proposed Horse Track along the heads of the wharves in the City Proper. As the increasing commerce of the City will require enlarged wharf facilities, this plan will show the extent of water front, partially or wholly unoccupied, in South and East Boston, in both of which it is proposed to extend greatly the lines of wharves and docks, so that the accommodations for shipping may be kept equal to the greatest probable demand. The Harbor of Boston has sufficient water front, susceptible of improvement, to accommodate all the shipping of the Union.

GOVERNMENT
OF THE
CITY OF BOSTON,
1851.

MAYOR,
JOHN PRESCOTT BIGELOW.

ALDERMEN,
HENRY BROMFIELD ROGERS,
BILLINGS BRIGGS,
MOSES GRANT,
HENRY MANNING HOLBROOK,
ABEL B. MUNROE,
CALVIN WHITING CLARK,
MOSES KIMBALL,
BENJAMIN SMITH.

COMMON COUNCIL,
FRANCIS BRINLEY, PRESIDENT.

Ward No. 1.

John Cushing,
James G. Hovey,
Joel M. Holden,
Charles H. Stearns.

Ward No. 2.

Cyrus Washburn,
James B. Allen,
William H. Calrow,
Richard Shackford.

Ward No. 3.

Solomon Carter,
Hiram Bosworth,
Thomas Sprague,
Andrew Abbott.

Ward No. 4.

Asa Swallow,	James Lawrence,
Henry J. Gardner,	Harvey Jewell.

Ward No. 5.

Benjamin Beal,	Abraham G. Wyman,
Avery Plumer, Jr.,	Ezekiel Kendall.

Ward No. 6.

Henry Lincoln,	Charles Brown,
John P. Putnam,	Ebenezer Dale.

Ward No. 7.

Francis Brinley,	David Chapin,
James W. Sever,	John B. Dexter, Jr.

Ward No. 8.

John M. Wright,	Oliver B. Dorrance,
Daniel N. Haskell,	Francis C. Manning.

Ward No. 9.

Newell A. Thompson,	Francis Richards,
Edward S. Erving,	Peter C. Jones.

Ward No. 10.

Ezra Lincoln,	Otis Kimball,
Aaron H. Bean,	Edward Reed.

Ward No. 11.

Bradley N. Cumings,	Andrew J. Loud,
Albert T. Minot,	Theodore P. Hale.

Ward No. 12.

Josiah Dunham, Jr.,	Samuel D. Crane,
Joseph Smith,	Zibeon Southard.

SCHOOL COMMITTEE.

John P. Bigelow, Mayor, *Chairman*, } *Ex officiis.*
Francis Brinley, *Pres. Common Council*, }

Ward No. 1....Rev. Edward Beecher,
Benson Leavitt.

2....Dr. William H. Thorndike,
Silas B. Hahn.

3....Dr. Edward D. G. Palmer,
Rev. Pharcellus Church.

4....Rev. Samuel K. Lothrop,
Rev. Hubbard Winslow.

5....Frederick Emerson,
Loring Norcross.

6....Sampson Reed,
Frederick U. Tracy.

7....Hamilton Willis,
Dr. Zabdiel B. Adams.

8....Rev. J. I. T. Coolidge,
Samuel W. Bates.

9....Joseph M. Wightman,
Samuel E. Guild.

10....Rev. Joseph B. Felt,
Rev. George M. Randall.

11....William H. Foster,
George Eaton.

12....Alvan Simonds,
Francis Alger.

Samuel F. McCleary, Jr., *Secretary*.

INDEX.

www.ingramcontent.com/pod-product-compliance
Lightning Source LLC
LaVergne TN
LVHW010224110826
845151LV00004B/1178